# The Social Self and Everyday Life

# The Social Self and Everyday Life

Understanding the World Through
Symbolic Interactionism

*Kathy Charmaz*
*Scott R. Harris*
*Leslie Irvine*

# WILEY Blackwell

*Registered Office*
John Wiley & Sons, Inc., 111 River Street, Hoboken, NJ 07030, USA

*Editorial Office*
9600 Garsington Road, Oxford, OX4 2DQ, UK

For details of our global editorial offices, customer services, and more information about Wiley products visit us at www.wiley.com.

Wiley also publishes its books in a variety of electronic formats and by print-on-demand. Some content that appears in standard print versions of this book may not be available in other formats.

*Library of Congress Cataloging-in-Publication data applied for*

Paperback ISBN: 9781118645338

Cover Design: Wiley
Cover Images: © Magnia/Shutterstock; © VolodymyrSanych/Shutterstock

Set in 10/12pt Warnock by SPi Global, Pondicherry, India
Printed in Singapore by C.O.S. Printers Pte Ltd

10  9  8  7  6  5  4  3  2  1

# Contents

# Preface

Symbolic Interactionism is a major theoretical and research tradition within sociology. This book provides a student-friendly introduction to that perspective, appropriate for courses on sociological social psychology (a.k.a. Self and Society, Microsociology, Social Interaction). It could also be used as a supplement in courses on Introduction to Sociology or on Social Theory. Symbolic interactionism is gaining attention in other disciplines across the globe. Colleagues from varied places and disciplines may also find that this volume provides a useful introduction to symbolic interactionism for their students. We hope our book not only extends the reach of the perspective but, moreover, sparks ideas about developing it beyond disciplinary and national borders.

We welcomed Wiley-Blackwell's invitation to write a social psychology text using the symbolic interactionist perspective with detailed excerpts from rich qualitative studies. We kept this approach in mind before and as we wrote this book. We asked ourselves: What would interest students in studying social psychology? How can teachers make concepts come alive for their students?

*The Social Self and Everyday Life* provides a means of teaching symbolic interactionist social psychology that starts where students are. Sociology students are interested in themselves and their situations, as well as in social issues. Our text involves students in familiar experiences and issues that they care about, and then shows how a symbolic interactionist perspective illuminates them. We begin each chapter with an intriguing and readable excerpt from a personal account or qualitative study. We then analyze these excerpts from an interactionist perspective, and forge connections to concepts and findings from classic and current research.

We thus offer a "gentle" introduction to symbolic interactionism. Our book focuses on those ideas we have found to be the most interesting and useful to our students. We occasionally sacrifice some breadth or depth to prioritize students' understanding and connection with the material.

*The Social Self and Everyday Life* can be seen as a kind of hybrid – combining the best features of a conventional textbook (e.g. authoritative summaries, clear definitions of key terms) with that of a reader (e.g. enticing empirical excerpts and selective attention to popular ideas).

Instructors should note that Chapters 2–11 each conclude with at least one unanalyzed excerpt for students to analyze on their own (i.e. individually or in class discussions). These concluding excerpts could provide the basis for assignments and/or class discussions.

## Respecting the Classics while Embracing Recent Research

Many significant works in symbolic interactionism – such as those by Howard Becker, Charles Cooley, Erving Goffman, Arlie Hochschild, George Herbert Mead, and many others – were written in the last century. Such work is valuable for instructors who want to expose students to important theoretical insights, methodological strategies, and empirical findings.

Sometimes, however, students challenge professors who assign or even discuss books and articles that were published in the last century. Understandably, students wonder if instructors have chosen the most "up to date" or "cutting edge" material to cover in class. When pressed with such questions, we raise one or more of the following points.

Students need to keep in mind that many factors shape an instructor's decision to focus on a particular author, idea, or reading. While timeliness is one criterion to consider, it is not the only one. Instructors and textbook authors may consider several other factors. Is the research interesting enough to hold the attention of a large percentage of the students in the class? Is the research understandable? Will most of the students be able to comprehend an author's theory, methods, and findings? Is the research representative of a general field of scholarship? Is the research influential and important? Are an author's findings or concepts relevant across decades if not centuries or millennia?

Thus, it is almost certainly an error to focus on "new vs. old" as the sole or even primary standard for assessing an idea or a piece of research. Newer is not necessarily better. A relatively recent publication date is not a sufficient measure of quality or utility. In this textbook, as in our classrooms, we try to satisfy as many of the above criteria as possible (among other considerations), when selecting concepts and pieces of research to discuss. In short, we try to respect the classics while also embracing compelling new research.

# Acknowledgments

Kathy thanks Julia Teweles, formerly with Wiley, for the conception of this book and invitation to write it, and Julia Kirk for her interest in the project and earlier help with it. Kathy also appreciates discussing the book with Jennifer Dunn and Kerry Ferris during the early phases of the work. We all thank Manish Luthra of Wiley for bringing the project to completion and handling the permissions.

# 1

# An Invitation to Learn about Self, Situation, and Society

"This past winter, Sara Fader, a 37-year-old social media consultant in Brooklyn who has generalized anxiety disorder, texted a friend in Oregon about an imprending visit, and when a quick response failed to materialize, she posted on Twitter to her 16,000-plus followers, 'I don't hear from my friend for a day – my thought, they don't want to be my friend anymore,' she wrote, appending the hashtag #ThisIsWhatAnxietyFeelsLike." (Williams 2017:1)

"One student, who has A.D.H.D, anxiety, and depression, said the pressure began building in middle school when she realized she had to be at the top of her class to get into high school honors classes, which she needed to get into Advanced Placement classes, which she needed to get into college. 'In sixth grade,' she said, 'kids were freaking out.'" (Williams 2017:2)

"In most ways, Kim looks like a well-adjusted college student. She dates her high school sweetheart and is studying psychology at a university in the Midwest. For the past five years, however, Kim has struggled with severe depression. When it was at its worst, she could not force herself to get out of bed to go to class. After hours of therapy and courses of antidepressant drugs, Kim was stable and ready to graduate; then she had a relapse. Now it will take her another year to finish college as she tries to manage her depression." (Twenge 2014:117)

"Jill, 23, describes her overachieving family as 'a recipe for quiet terror.' Although she's done well in school, 'always, always before those grades come out, I struggle under the weight of a cloud of fear and depression,' she says. 'Every year I'm silently convinced that this will be the one – this time I'll actually screw it all up. It's a scary way to live.'" (Twenge 2014:131)

*The Social Self and Everyday Life: Understanding the World Through Symbolic Interactionism*, First Edition. Kathy Charmaz, Scott R. Harris, and Leslie Irvine. © 2019 John Wiley & Sons, Inc. Published 2019 by John Wiley & Sons, Inc.

Each fall, two professors at Beloit College in Wisconsin amass approximately 50 facts, events, and figures into a list describing the experiences and assumptions of students entering college for the first time.[1] This "Mindset List" began as an email circulating among faculty members, providing an amusing reminder of how students change over time and how quickly cultural references become outdated. This point is especially relevant for professors because they grow older each year but the students they teach remain (more or less) within the same age bracket. References to "Seinfeld," the popular 1990s TV sitcom, would bring on blank looks rather than the intended laughter. For professors who recall life before the invention of microwave ovens, it can be helpful to recognize that, for students, popcorn has always been made in the microwave.

Beginning with the Class of 2007, students did not know a time when computers would not fit in their backpacks. Students in the Class of 2020 grew up "connected." As "digital natives," they have "spent their entire lives surrounded by and using computers, videogames, digital music players, video cams, cell phones, and all the other toys and tools of the digital age" (Prensky 2001:1). They take a networked world for granted.

By creating composite portraits of generations of students, the Beloit College Mindset List shows how deeply the social context influences people's perspectives and experiences. Along with the social class into which we are born, and along with our race, ethnicity, gender, religion, and other social categories, the events and inventions of an era also shape our perspectives (Elder 1994). Cultural developments, such as information technology, economic trends, such as the Great Recession of 2008, and historical events, such as 9/11 influence people's thoughts, feelings, and actions.

## #ThisIsWhatAnxietyFeelsLike

The excerpts that begin this chapter describe a set of experiences not included on the Mindset List. Among young people in the United States (US) today, anxiety has become the new normal. The college years and the transition to early adulthood have long been a time when young people face many uncertainties, often without the familiar social support of families. However, research documents a dramatic change. One 2016 survey of American college students found that 62% reported experiencing "overwhelming anxiety," a 12% increase in five years (American College Health Association 2017). Another survey asks incoming college students whether they feel overwhelmed by all they had to do (Eagan et al. 2017). When the survey first included this question in 1985, 18% of students reported feeling overwhelmed. By 2016, the figure had risen to 41%.

Living with anxiety, "freaking out," and feeling constantly overwhelmed will have a profound impact on how one thinks about oneself and interacts with others. The increase in the numbers of young people reporting anxiety and stress did not occur in a vacuum. As sociologists, we look to the larger social context for insight into this change. We also ask how this change will affect the social context.

Social psychology is a branch or subfield of sociology that focuses on the interplay between what's "out there" and what's "in here." Social psychologists address two important questions: How are people created by social order? And, in turn, how do people create the social orders that shape and mold their behavior? (Lindesmith, Strauss, and Denzin 1988:2).

As you'll see, social psychologists approach these questions about the relationship between society and individuals from different perspectives. The symbolic interactionist perspective used in this book provides a particularly useful set of tools for investigating these questions.

## Sociology, Psychology, and Social Psychology

You will find social psychology courses, and social psychologists, in departments of sociology *and* psychology. However, symbolic interactionism has its home in sociology. Of course, scholars in both fields have long been interested in studying the relationship between the mind and social behavior. In 1908, sociologist Edward Alsworth Ross wrote *Social Psychology,* and psychologist William McDougall published *Introduction to Social Psychology.* The texts differed in how much they emphasized the mind or society. McDougall grounded mental activity in biological processes and in what he referred to as "instincts." Ross, in contrast, emphasized the effects of the social world on the individual.

Psychology and sociology co-existed well at first but went their separate ways after World War II. This resulted in two social psychologies. *Psychological social psychology* examines how *intra*personal psychological processes, or those thought to exist "within" individuals, such as traits and dispositions, influence people's behavior within their social surroundings. Social psychologists working in psychology departments typically use experiments to conduct their research. *Sociological social psychology* examines *inter*personal processes, or relations between people. It emphasizes both the influence of society on individuals and how individuals influence society. Sociological social psychologists use a variety of methods in their research.

*Psychological social psychology tends to examine how intrapersonal psychological processes, or those thought to exist "within" individuals, such as traits and dispositions, influence people's behavior within their social surroundings.*

*Sociological social psychology tends to examine interpersonal processes, or relations between people. It emphasizes the influence of social structures such as institutions, groups, and organizations on the individual.*

## Symbolic Interactionism and Other Perspectives

Sociological social psychology has several perspectives, branches, or "faces" within it (House 1977; Smith-Lovin and Molm 2000).

One of social psychology's "faces" is the "social structure and personality" perspective, or SSP. Although SSP originates in sociology, it has much in common with psychological social psychology. Its very name reveals its hybrid nature. Its ties to psychology give it an emphasis on the importance of personality. Through its ties to sociology, SSP also recognizes the importance of the "macro" level processes that exist on a large, society-wide scale. Researchers using the SSP perspective investigate "relationships between macro-social systems or processes and individual feelings, attitudes, and behaviors" (House 1992; McLeod and Lively 2003:77).

Classic research in the SSP perspective comes from studies of the reproduction of social inequality (Kohn 1969; Kohn and Schooler 1973, 1978; Lareau 2011). This refers to how class differences are transmitted to new generations. SSP research finds that social class, as measured by occupation, influences the values people hold and pass on to their children. When children grow up and begin working, they usually seek jobs that are, for the most part, consistent with the values they learned from their parents.

For example, middle-class occupations typically require employees to make decisions, collaborate with others, ask questions of those in authority, solve problems, and innovate new ways of doing things. People who hold these jobs tend to value autonomy, or self-direction, and creativity. In contrast, the expectations of working-class jobs often include obeying orders, getting the work done, and not questioning, but respecting, those in authority. People in these jobs tend to value conformity and obedience. These class-based values influence parenting practices, or what parents teach their children, and how they teach them – a topic we revisit in Chapter 3. Working-class parents' understanding of appropriate behavior differs considerably from the understanding of parents in the middle class. In general, children of working-class parents learn that they should do what they are told, and that asking questions or seeking help from others might have negative consequences. Middle-class children develop the confidence to be self-directed, but also to reach out to others for support in reaching goals.

The values children learn prepare them for the kinds of jobs they will hold as adults. Of course, one's job prospects also depend on educational opportunities, geographic location, the state of the economy, and other factors. Nevertheless, people who have learned to value self-direction will generally seek out jobs that allow them to be self-directed at work. As values are transmitted across generations, so are class cultures. In shaping how people view the world and their place in it, social class has psychological effects (Schnittker 2007).

Although this summary simplifies a sophisticated body of research, these studies established how social structure influences individuals by "flowing through" the day-to-day experiences of work (Spenner 1988) and parenting. These studies, like many in the SSP tradition, often rely on statistical analysis of large-scale survey data that is collected longitudinally (over years or decades).

*The social structure and personality perspective examines the relationship between large-scale or macro-level social patterns and individual attitudes and behaviors.*

Another perspective in sociological social psychology focuses on group processes. As the name suggests, research in this perspective focuses on "how various social processes operate in groups" (Lucas 2007). The processes of interest here include power and status, among others.

To illustrate using the example of power, it might be tempting to think of power as an individual characteristic, as in "a powerful person." A person with power, such as your boss at work, can hire you, fire you, or promote you. But the boss's power doesn't come from individual traits. It comes from his or her position in the structure of the workplace. If the boss is demoted, she or he no longer has the power to hire and fire. If a new person becomes the boss, that person then acquires that power. The conditions of groups, rather than of people, generate power differences.

The same applies to status, or the respect or esteem one receives from others. A person only attains a position of status relative to others. The status one holds depends on the group context. A person who has a position of low status at work might have a high-status position on a sports team outside of work.

Researchers who use this perspective often collect data through laboratory experiments designed to simulate processes that occur among groups in every-day life. Participants are often college students recruited from classes; some volunteer, some receive payment, and others receive course credits for participating.

*The group processes perspective focuses on how social forces, such as power and status, affect the structure of and interactions within groups.*

The third "face" of sociological social psychology – and the one we use in this book – belongs to symbolic interactionism. In the next chapter, we describe this as a perspective that assumes that people construct selves, social worlds, and societies through interaction. The chapters that follow use symbolic inter-actionism to examine how people's interpretations and definitions of one another's actions guide various aspects of social life (Blumer 1969).

Sociologists have long emphasized the value of using a "sociological imagination" to reveal the ways individual biography intersects with history and social structure (Mills 1959). The sociological imagination allows people to see the relationship between personal experiences, choices, and actions and the larger society. In other words, it allows us to understand how conditions that exist "out there," such as economic changes or the development of digital technology, get "in here," shaping how we lead our lives.

Symbolic interactionists use the sociological imagination to examine the influence of the social context on people's feelings, thoughts, and actions. The perspective provides tools to explore the relationship between real, living people who think, feel, and act and the social forces that shape their thoughts, emotions, and behavior. In conducting their research, many symbolic interactionists use qualitative methods, including (but certainly not limited to) interviews and participant observation, which involves having an active membership in the group one is studying.

Look back at the excerpts that opened this chapter. Symbolic interactionism will equip you to investigate the causes and consequences of the new reality experienced by contemporary young adults. We don't mean that you will be able to understand the physiological and biological workings of anxiety and stress. We leave those explanations to mental health professionals. Rather, symbolic interactionism sheds light on the relationship of emotions of anxiety and stress to the sense of self and identity. You can use interactionism to investigate how individuals subjectively define their experiences as "anxious," "freaking out," or "quiet terror" (Harris 2015, ch. 6). You can also explore the interactional contexts that produce anxiety and stress and learn how individuals cope with or avoid these emotions (Thoits 2013).

*Symbolic interactionism assumes that people construct selves, social worlds, and societies through interaction.*

Our task in this book is to introduce you to symbolic interactionist social psychology through examining rich ethnographic and qualitative studies. Before we proceed, we must point out that two vibrant quantitative traditions also use symbolic interactionism: identity theory and affect control theory. Identity theorists conduct quantitative studies to explain why individuals choose one course of action when alternatives are available. Sheldon Stryker (1980, 2000) and his colleagues (Serpe 1987; Stets and Burke 2014; Stets and Serpe 2016; Stryker and Serpe 1982) developed identity theory to address how social structure constrains choices across a wide range of situations and to correct an earlier view of society as unitary yet somewhat unstable. Richard T. Serpe (1987) offers a cogent clarification and extension of how identity theory links self and social structure. Stryker's initial statement of identity theory assumed that other symbolic interactionists neglected the diverse social structures in which people act and interact. We disagree with Stryker's criticism because some symbolic interactionists have always addressed social structure and now many do.

Identity theory emphasizes how people choose the roles they adopt. This theory assumes the self consists of multi-faceted but hierarchically organized identities. People become committed to the identities they most value, which inform their actions and aspirations (Burke 1991). Thus, identities holding greater salience to a person are likely reflected by the role he or she chooses.

> *Identity theory emphasizes how people choose the roles they adopt and assumes the self consists of multi-faceted but hierarchically organized identities. People become committed to the identities they most value and these commitments are likely reflected in their role choices.*

Identity theorists have studied identity salience, commitment, and role choice in an impressive range of varied roles and contexts such as convicts rejecting a criminal identity (Asencio and Burke 2011), students who complete science training programs (Merolla et al. 2012) and relationships between students' moral identity and cheating (Stets and Carter 2011). For example, Jan E. Stets and Michael J. Carter (2011:198) created a test in which a person could be tempted to cheat. The authors hypothesized that student research participants with high moral identity standards would be less likely to cheat when they lacked the ability to do well on the test than those with lower identity standards. In addition to studying participants' views of their moral of identity standard, Stets and Carter also investigated participants' emotions about their test responses, including when they believed other people would see a moral discrepancy between their actual behavior and their moral identity standard. In short, the authors demonstrated that identity theory generates useful explanations and sophisticated predictions about individuals' moral identity, commitments, and actions.

A year before Stryker (1980) made his groundbreaking statement of identity theory, David R. Heise (1979) published his major explication of affect control theory. This theory addresses how people's emotions are embedded in their identities and assumptions about their situations and arise in social interaction (MacKinnon and Robinson 2014). Like identity theory, affect control theory explicitly takes social structure into account. Affect control theory assumes that people try to maintain social order. They achieve it when their interactions with others and interpretations of these interactions fit cultural expectations (shuster and Campos 2017).

> *Affect control theory assumes that people try to maintain social order. They aim to confirm their feelings about themselves and others during their interactions and act in ways to produce appropriate emotions for the situations they are in.*

People aim to confirm their feelings about themselves and others during their interactions. Hence, they act in ways to produce appropriate emotions for the situations they are in. When their actions cannot maintain the feelings, they had earlier viewed as appropriate, they change how they define the situation. Thus, as Heise (2002) contends, these individuals' emotions indicate the relationship between their experiences and their definitions of situations.

Affect control theory unites mathematical sociology and computer applications with a symbolic interactionist perspective. In a creative application of affect control theory and its companion computer program, *Interact,* stef m. shuster and Celeste Campos-Castillo (2017) studied archival data covering the pivotal but failed 1980 Iowa Equal Rights Amendment (ERA) to the U.S. constitution. This amendment would give women equal rights as men. Shuster and Campos-Castillo's analysis found that pro-ERA groups used "frame resonance," a concept from the social movements literature, to depict social activists' strategy of aligning issues with ideologies. But the authors also discovered that anti-ERA groups used a contrasting strategy, what shuster and Campos call "frame dissonance." This concept reveals how anti-ERA groups invoked a new strategy to show how passing the ERA would clash with their ideologies. Through their innovative study, shuster and Compos-Castillo (i) demonstrate the explanatory power of affect control theory, (ii) show how *Interact* can be used with archival data, and (iii) contribute a compelling new concept to the social psychology of social movements.

This chapter has situated symbolic interactionism within its disciplinary and theoretical context. In doing so, we have included perspectives that are not the focus of this book. Let's turn now to a preview of the topics and concepts that we will cover in the chapters to come.

## Overview of the Book

In our classes, we have found that students learn more when we minimize our lecturing and make our illustrations as interesting and current as possible. Consequently, each chapter in this book opens with a vivid excerpt depicting ordinary experiences and concerns that you have had or may encounter.

We start with these excerpts to bridge the gap between readers' experiences and concerns and a theoretical understanding of them. We introduce symbolic interactionist concepts and show how they illuminate these "real life" experiences and concerns. Then, we let you apply symbolic interactionist concepts and use the perspective to develop your ideas through "Learn by Using" sections that conclude each chapter. We encourage you to analyze the excerpts by asking questions such as:

- What is happening here?
- How do we *know* what is happening?

- What knowledge can we gain from the excerpt about individuals and their social worlds?
- How does the excerpt reveal people's situations and social locations?
- How does the excerpt illuminate major concepts?

Throughout the book, we point out how symbolic interactionism offers the tools for *developing* concepts in addition to *applying* them. We want you to understand how social, cultural, economic, and temporal contexts shape your individual interactions and, conversely, how individual and collective actions may shape the social world. The "Learn by Using" sections allow you to practice the skills involved in using symbolic interactionism to examine your own experiences and concerns.

## Chapter Previews

Chapter 2 introduces you to the symbolic interactionist perspective and its essential concepts. It opens with an interview excerpt from Sheila Katz (Charmaz and Katz 2017) depicting one young woman's path from gang member to responsible parent and college student. The woman, who chose to be identified by the initials, "MMM," dropped out of school in seventh grade and joined a gang. She had her first child at age 15 and her second a year later. Her life consisted of partying, getting high, and hanging out. Social workers placed her children in foster care.

MMM eventually served a two-year prison sentence, during which she earned a General Education Diploma, or high school equivalency. After her release, she enrolled in a program to get off drugs, which was necessary to get her children back. She had two more babies and struggled to support her family on welfare benefits.

MMM managed to turn her life around. She completed community college and enrolled in an elite university. The interview reveals choices and actions, collective influences, self and identity, and the significance of interaction. Throughout the chapter, we emphasize how symbolic interactionist concepts account for MMM's choices and actions and the changes in self, identity, and situation that occurred. By using these concepts you may not only look at this young woman's life differently, but also begin to see your own life, and the lives of those around you, differently too.

Chapter 3 examines socialization as a lifelong process. The chapter explores the implications of varied childhood experiences for shaping selves and establishing social identities. Research on socialization used to depict children as passively soaking up the adult world in preparation for "real" life, otherwise known as "adulthood." But current symbolic interactionist research recognizes that children's lives do not consist simply of imitating adults. They also create social worlds that revolve around other children. In Chapter 3, for example, you'll see how homeless children strive to make themselves acceptable to their peers.

Building on George Herbert Mead's analysis of the development of the self, this chapter establishes the major perspectives on socialization and situates symbolic interactionism as an alternative to theories that depict stages through which every "normal" person must purportedly progress. The chapter also explores the influence of race and class and introduces essential concepts such as primary and secondary groups. Consistent with the interactionist view of socialization as a lifelong process, the chapter also discusses how socialization occurs in adulthood and in settings outside of the family.

Chapter 4 examines the social dimensions of bodies. At first glance, this seems an unlikely topic for sociological study. After all, aren't bodies simply biological? In this chapter, we show how culture, inequality, and other social factors shape how our bodies are perceived, experienced, used, and modified – by ourselves and by those around us. Our physical selves are rooted in the eras and communities in which we live. Our perspectives on our bodies shape our identities and self-esteem. Our physical appearance even shapes the kinds of relationships we develop and the career paths we may take. Everyone experiences some form of bodily stigma – though to significantly different degrees – due to deviations from cultural ideals. We may be judged too fat or thin, too dark or light skinned, too tall or short, too hairy in some places (eyebrows, backs, legs) or insufficiently hairy in others (scalps), or inappropriately smelly in our breath, body odor, or flatulence. People develop and learn interactional strategies for hiding, disguising, and transforming their physical attributes. Sometimes individuals and groups defy or challenge bodily norms, such as when activists promote "fat acceptance" or "size acceptance" (Saguy and Riley 2005). Upon completing this chapter, you'll be convinced that our bodies are as much social as they are biological.

In Chapter 5, you will investigate how health, illness, and disability affect people's lives and their understanding of their experiences. Meanings of health, illness, and disability are varied, complex, and often contradictory. Have you thought about what health means to you and whether those you care about share your meanings? People may agree on what health means, but not agree about what being healthy entails or how much priority to give it. Like New Year's resolutions, our actions may not coincide with our beliefs and good intentions. To what extent do you believe in individual responsibility for health? What do you think society should do to protect your health and that of the community? Questions about health and responsibility evoke considerable thought when a person or family member has a serious chronic illness or disability. Illness and disability can change our views of ourselves and our relationships with others. Managing daily life can become difficult, as self-care, household tasks, family obligations, and work may all require more time and effort than ever before. Simultaneously, when people struggle with the logistics of managing everyday life, they likely become increasingly affected by the claims and consequences of institutionalized medicine and biomedicine. Symbolic interactionism can help you understand your experience with health and illness as well as with health services and practitioners.

In Chapter 6, you'll learn about the symbolic interactionist perspective on emotion. Emotions feel like "natural" responses to certain situations, and they involve physiological processes such as heart rate, trembling hands, and dry mouth. Without denying the corporeal aspects of emotion, symbolic interactionism shows how emotions are also shaped by culture, interpretation, and social interaction. Norms, or rules, shape what we feel and how we express our feelings, and there are even sanctions for emotional deviance. Norms vary between groups and over time. In our private lives and in our jobs, we learn to manage or control emotions via theatrical strategies of "surface acting" and "deep acting." Those of you who must greet and serve customers enthusiastically – no matter how rude or disinterested they may be – should be especially drawn to this chapter's discussion of emotional labor.

Here we will summarize interactionist research on the strategies employers and employees use to create "appropriate" emotions in the workplace.

Chapter 7 examines the diverse forms and meaning of "family." It introduces the idea of the Standard North American Family, or SNAF, also known as the "nuclear" family (Smith 1993). Although SNAF is the standard by which many of us judge families, it is by no means a universal or eternal model. Polygyny (multiple wives), polyandry (multiple husbands), and other kinship practices can be found cross-culturally. Single-parent, step, foster, same-sex, childfree, and other forms of family are abundant in the United States. What meanings do people give to their own and others' family practices and interactions? Symbolic interactionism recognizes that people have the freedom to define what they mean by "family." They might, in some cases, include pets as beloved kin while excluding certain blood relatives as "strangers." However, interactionism also recognizes that freedom has limits. Upon completing this chapter, you'll have the interactionist skills to analyze familial interpretations and practices that are promoted or disparaged by pundits, politicians, parents, and others in your social world.

Chapter 8 examines how communication technologies and social media construct our social worlds and individual identities. Think for a moment about the amount of information and ideas that enters your life through your phone. Music streaming services offer an endlessly varying soundtrack for your activities. Social media transforms the meaning of "friendship." Facebook friends might also follow you on Instagram, Twitter, or other social networking sites. Wearable technologies such as Fitbit and other smart devices have created a "quantified" version of you, represented by the measurement of miles run, steps walked, or calories consumed. You can share your goals and milestones with millions of other people. These new forms of interaction come with new obligations and opportunities that pull your attention in many different directions. This chapter invites you to consider the symbolic interactionist model of the self in light of what digital technologies make possible.

In Chapter 9, you'll see how symbolic interactionism approaches the study of issues considered social problems. The discussion emphasizes the role of interpretation when considering social problems. After all, many situations could potentially rise to the level of problems. Yet, we ignore some potentially troublesome situations entirely. We regard some as normal and acceptable. Often our attention and resources are mobilized when claimsmakers adopt frightening rhetoric – perhaps by declaring we are at "war" with crime, drugs, poverty, or even Christmas. Symbolic interactionism offers a systematic and consistent way to understand how some issues become social problems, requiring significant responses from government, the medical profession, educators, law enforcement, or other entities. After reading this chapter, you should be equipped to identify and critically examine potentially inflated claims about dire threats.

Chapter 10 considers the relationship between individuals and social institutions. Because sociologists use the word "institutions" frequently, the chapter first helps you understand how we use it. Briefly, it refers to patterned ways of doing things, which people collectively recognize as "how things are done." We use the example of work to illustrate how institutions shape people's actions and beliefs, but school is another good example of an institution with this influence. Think about some of the lessons you learned in school that had nothing whatsoever to do with reading, writing, math, history, and so on. Along with subject matter, schools also teach children the importance of following directions, arriving on time, sitting still, paying attention, and taking turns. By the end of the chapter, you'll have the tools to analyze how school, work, and other institutions influence individuals. You'll also be able to consider what happens when people challenge institutions. And, in keeping with emerging developments in social psychology, we introduce you to new ideas about how space and time shape the opportunities and obstacles people face in institutions.

Chapter 11 examines inequality, a topic that receives a lot of attention from sociologists. When you hear "inequality," you might think first of difference. On its own, however, difference does not mean that a situation is unequal. Suppose you have two friends who live in the same apartment building. One friend pays a higher rent than the other pays. Would you interpret the differing rents as a form of inequality? If you learned that one apartment had "extras" that the other lacked, you probably would not. But if you learned that people of color paid higher rent for apartments that cost their white neighbors less money, you would think otherwise. By understanding the patterns of interaction that produce and maintain inequality, symbolic interactionism can enrich your understanding of this important sociological topic (Schwalbe 2016; Schwalbe et al. 2000).

Chapter 12 concludes the book by summarizing the benefits of taking the symbolic interactionist perspective. We hope this will not be just one more thing you learned for a class and then forgot once the semester ended. Instead, symbolic interactionism can be useful and relevant for your life beyond the classroom.

## Note

1 Retrieved November 2, 2017 (https://www.beloit.edu/mindset).

## References

American College Health Association. 2017. *American College Health Association-National College Health Assessment II: Undergraduate Student Reference Group Executive Summary Fall 2016*. Hanover, MD: American College Health Association.

Asencio, E. and Burke, P. 2011. "Does Incarceration Change the Criminal Identity? A Synthesis of Labeling and Identity Theory Perspectives on Identity Change." *Sociological Perspectives* 54:163–182.

Blumer, H. 1969. *Symbolic Interaction: Perspective and Method*. Berkeley: University of California Press.

Burke, P. 1991. "An Identity Theory Approach to Commitment." *Social Psychology Quarterly* 54:239–251.

Charmaz, K. and S. Katz. 2017. "Subjective Stories and Social Issues: Strategies for Making Connections." *Qualitative Methods in Psychology Bulletin* 23(Spring):8–14.

Eagan, K., E. Stolzenberg, H. Zimmerman, M. Aragon, H. Sayson, and C. Rios-Aguilar. 2017. *The American Freshman: National Norms, Fall 2016*. Los Angeles, CA: Higher Education Research Institute, UCLA.

Elder Jr., G. 1994. "Time, Human Agency, and Social Change: Perspectives on the Life Course." *Social Psychology Quarterly* 57:4–15.

Harris, S. R. 2015. *An Invitation to the Sociology of Emotions*. New York: Routledge.

Heise, D. R. 1979. *Understanding Events: Affect and the Construction of Social Action*. Cambridge: Cambridge University Press.

Heise, D. R. 2002. "Understanding Social Interaction with Affect Control Theory." Pp. 17–40 in *New Directions in Sociological Theory*, edited by J. Berger and M. Zelditch. Boulder, CO: Rowman and Littlefield.

House, J. 1977. "The Three Faces of Social Psychology." *Sociometry* 40:161–177.

House, J. 1992. "Social Structure and Personality." Pp. 525–561 in *Social Psychology: Sociological Perspectives*, edited by M. Rosenberg and R. Turner. New Brunswick, NJ: Transaction.

Kohn, M. 1969. *Class and Conformity: A Study in Values.* Homewood, IL: Dorsey.

Kohn, M. and C. Schooler. 1973. "Occupational Experience and Psychological Functioning: An Assessment of Reciprocal Effects." *American Sociological Review* 38:97–118.

Kohn, M. and C. Schooler. 1978. "The Reciprocal Effects of the Substantive Complexity of Work and Intellectual Flexibility: A Longitudinal Assessment." *American Journal of Sociology* 84:24–52.

Lareau, A. 2011. *Unequal Childhoods: Class, Race, and Family Life,* 2nd ed. Berkeley, CA: University of California Press.

Lindesmith, A., A. Strauss, and N. Denzin. 1988. *Social Psychology,* 6th ed. New York: Prentice-Hall.

Lucas, J. 2007. "Group Processes." In *Blackwell Encyclopedia of Sociology,* edited by G. Ritzer. Blackwell Reference Online. Retrieved 22 November 2017. http://www.blackwellreference.com/subscriber/tocnode.html?id=g9781405124331_chunk_g978140512433113_ss1-73.

MacKinnon, N. and D. Robinson. 2014. "Back to the Future: 25 Years of Research in Affect Control Theory." *Advances in Group Processes* 31:139–173.

McLeod, J. and K. Lively. 2003. "Social Structure and Personality." Pp. 77–102 in *Handbook of Social Psychology,* edited by J. Delamater. New York: Kluwer Academic/Plenum Publishers.

Merolla, D., R. Serpe, S. Stryker, and P. Schultz. 2012. "Structural Precursors to Identity Processes: The Role of Proximate Social Structures." *Social Psychology Quarterly* 75(2):149–172.

Mills, C. W. 1959. *The Sociological Imagination.* New York: Oxford University Press.

Prensky, M. 2001. "Digital Natives, Digital Immigrants, Part 1." *On the Horizon* 9:1–6.

Saguy, A. and K. Riley. 2005. "Weighing Both Sides: Morality, Mortality, and Framing Contests over Obesity." *Journal of Health Politics, Policy, and Law* 30(5):869–923.

Schnittker, J. 2007. "Social Structure and Personality." Pp. 89–115 in *Handbook of Social Psychology,* edited by J. Delamater and A. Ward. New York: Kluwer Academic/Plenum Publishers.

Schwalbe, M. 2016. "Overcoming Aprocessual Bias in the Study of Inequality: Parsing the Capitalist Interaction Order." *Studies in Symbolic Interaction* 46:95–122.

Schwalbe, M., D. Holden, D. Schrock, S. Godwin, S. Thompson, and M. Wolkomir. 2000. "Generic Processes in the Reproduction of Inequality: An Interactionist Analysis." *Social Forces* 79:419–452.

Serpe, R. T. 1987. "Stability and Change in Self: A Structural Symbolic Interactionist Explanation." *Our Social Psychology Quarterly* 50(1):44–55.

Shuster, S. M. and C. Campos-Castillo. 2017. "Measuring Resonance and Dissonance in Social Movement Frames with Affect Control Theory." *Social Psychology Quarterly* 80(1):20–40.

Smith, D. E. 1993. "The Standard North American Family: SNAF as an Ideological Code." *Journal of Family Issues* 14:50–65.

Smith-Lovin, L. and L. Molm. 2000. "Introduction to the Millennium Special Issue on the State of Sociological Social Psychology." *Social Psychology Quarterly* 63:281–283.

Spenner, K. 1988. "Social Stratification, Work, and Personality." *Annual Review of Sociology* 14:69–97.

Stets, J. E. and P. Burke. 2014. "The Development of Identity Theory." *Advances in Group Processes* 31:57–97.

Stets, J. E. and M. J. Carter. 2011. "The Moral Self: Applying Identity Theory." *Social Psychology Quarterly* 74(2):192–215.

Stets, J. E. and R. Serpe, eds. 2016. *New Directions in Identity Theory and Research*. New York: Oxford University Press.

Stryker, S. 1980. *Symbolic Interactionism: A Social Structural View*. Menlo Park, CA: Benjamin/Cummings.

Stryker, S. 2000. "Identity Theory." Pp. 1253–1258 in *Encyclopedia of Sociology*, 2nd ed., Vol. 2, edited by E. F. Borgatta and R. J. V. Montgomery. New York: Macmillan Reference USA.

Stryker, S. and R. Serpe. 1982. "Commitment, Identity Salience, and Role Behavior: A Theory and Research Example." Pp. 199–218 in *Personality, Roles, and Social Behavior*, edited by W. K. Ickes and E. S. Knowles. New York: Springer-Verlag.

Thoits, P. 2013. "Self, Identity, Stress, and Mental Health." Pp. 357–377 in *Handbook of the Sociology of Mental Health*, edited by C. Aneshensel, J. Phelan, and A. Bierman. Dordrecht: Springer.

Twenge, J. 2014. *Generation Me: Why Today's Young Americans Are More Confident, Assertive, Entitled – And More Miserable than Ever Before*. New York: ATRIA/Simon and Schuster.

Williams, A. 2017. "Prozac Nation is now the United States of Xanax." *The New York Times* (10 June). Retrieved 17 August 2018. https://nyti.ms/2t5F0uJ.

## 2

# Looking at Life from the Symbolic Interactionist Perspective

"We had gang members who lived across the street, and I didn't look at them like, oh, you dirty gang members, like how could I, I mean I have the tattoos to prove that I… I understand that, but I also understood that look, I'm 30 years old, and that [gang life] gets old after a while, and they hadn't really realized that and were older too. And they would look at me, and say, 'Oh, you forgot where you came from' and I would say, 'How can I forget? I live here (laughs) I don't forget my way home (laughs), I have the tattoos, the scars, the emotional scars, the headaches, the whole thing, I didn't forget, but I just know that – when do you get beyond that? When do you get to move on from that? I mean you guys have children, do you want to see your kids out here drinking and partying and fighting and getting that,' and I just didn't want that for my kids, I just didn't want them to experience all that pain because I know what's out there." (Charmaz and Katz 2017:8–9)

During an interview with sociologist Sheila Katz,[1] MMM,[2] a former gang member who became a student at the University of California, Berkeley, recounted the exchange above that had transpired while she was attending junior college in Southern California. You might ask, how did she go from being a gang member to a college student at an elite university? How did this transformation occur?

To answer your questions, it helps to know something about MMM's life and the worlds in which she lived. MMM came to look at her life differently as she became a responsible parent and pursued getting an education. At the time of the interview, MMM was a 31-year-old Latina woman who had dropped out of school in seventh grade, joined a gang, and became pregnant at 15 with her first child and a year later had a second child. After leaving her abusive partner, MMM "went wild" with partying, drugs, and hanging out. Government social workers soon removed her children from her care. MMM turned to crime but

*The Social Self and Everyday Life: Understanding the World Through Symbolic Interactionism*, First Edition. Kathy Charmaz, Scott R. Harris, and Leslie Irvine.

was caught, convicted, and landed in prison for two years where she completed high school. On her release, she enrolled in a probation program to get off drugs and get her kids back. MMM had to see herself from the standpoint of officials who would decide whether to let her have the children. She had two more babies but only had meager welfare benefits to support her family. With the encouragement of a friend and the discouragement of social workers, she entered a community college and persevered.

MMM possessed an insider's knowledge of what gang life meant. She knew the danger and suffering reentering her former lifestyle could cause and the havoc it would wreak upon her children. During her junior college years, MMM had lived at the edge of the gang world but not in it. By then, she looked at the world from the standpoint of being 30 years old and having to care for her children.

The emotional scars of the past lived on in MMM's consciousness. The gang tattoos and scars on her body imposed constant reminders of who she was, not of the woman she was becoming. These mementos of the past were ever-present, ever-visible, at least to her. MMM's past identity remained with her along with its social locations marking who she was and where she came from. Moving away from a neighborhood filled with gangs to the unfamiliar world of the university brought her safety but uncertainty. To move forward into the future on her own terms could mean crossing a chasm for MMM.

At the junior college, MMM had received new and unfamiliar images of herself – as an exceptional student who could do well at a first-rate university. Yet her intermittent doubts still surfaced. Taking one step at a time became MMM's way of moving along her educational path. She recalled how she had viewed going on for her bachelor's degree when she was in junior college:

> "I started thinking well, I can do this, I like school, it's kind of cool, and to go on for my Bachelor's it was like a thought, but *I thought it was like somebody else's dream, not mine* (our emphasis). And now that I'm here doing it, it's like ok, it's real to me now, but my Master's, that's for somebody else right now, that's not for me, or my PhD. Everybody else says, 'Oh, you're going to go on and you're going to do just fine and you're going to get your PhD,' and I'm like, 'But I can barely do one class' (laughs)...." (Charmaz and Katz 2017:8)

What is MMM saying in this interview excerpt? How might we interpret her statement? In her own words, her life seems like "somebody else's dream." Earlier, being a promising community college student also hadn't seemed quite real to MMM either. Now undergraduate life at Berkeley was becoming real but beyond that? Possible next steps up the educational ladder also seemed unreal – somebody else's dream – although she conceded that moving in this direction might be possible. One step at a time.

How does MMM's experience influence her view of herself in the future? MMM's time horizons likely lie closer to the present than most students at Berkeley. She had moved away from yesterday and was concentrating on today. Time changed, space changed. She changed. School and parenting shaped the rhythms of her day and the spaces she traversed. But MMM hadn't forgotten, as she had told the gang members who lived across the street in her former neighborhood. The images of her earlier life and past self stayed with her.

When MMM talked of living somebody else's dream, she implied that it remained beyond her reach in an unreal world she cannot imagine sharing. For her, the dream reflected something she could not or, perhaps, should not have. At this time, MMM's self-concept lingered near her past. Yet others imparted positive images of her present and future self. These reflected images helped her choose the path to a new identity.

In part, MMM's new identity developed by default as well as by intent. The education and safety of her children were her most compelling reasons for attending University of California, Berkeley. Rather than taking one small step by moving to Berkeley, she made a large leap – for her children. They become the constant positive reference point for reconstructing her life and thus developing her new identity. Simultaneously, the gang members in her former neighborhood served as a negative reference point. These men had become visible symbols of what she no longer wanted to be and wished to spare her children from becoming.

Our lives are situated in specific structural conditions and thus who we are and who we become reflects our social, historical, and economic locations. These locations may be invisible to you, but they loomed large in MMM's life. Her story represented more than the choices she made; it also reflected the structural conditions of her life. The constraints of the U.S. welfare system called the Temporary Assistance for Needy Families (TANF) program restricted the lives of women in MMM's position.[3] Overall, the TANF program aimed to move families off welfare through marriage and/or work and rewarded states for reducing the number of welfare recipients. The TANF form of assistance weakened the limited safety net previously available to impoverished mothers because it imposed time limits on receiving assistance and forced workforce participation. The rationale supporting these moves claimed to support family values and employment that would get women off welfare. In effect, however, the program relegated its participants to the lowest paying jobs and reduced their possibilities for seeking education and job training that could lead to sufficient income to support their families. Some TANF recipients received financial assistance from their colleges and student loans. The funding never stretched far enough. They all continually struggled to make ends meet. They went hungry, considered illicit activities to get money, and sometimes even had to sell their much-needed food stamps (Katz 2013a).

How did we arrive at the analysis of MMM's situation? We looked at her life through the lens of symbolic interactionism, the guiding perspective for this book. MMM learned to see her life differently than she had during her gang years. Her images of the future foretold a better life for her kids.

This chapter introduces the symbolic interactionist perspective. Symbolic interactionism can give you new ways to see your life and other people's lives and situations. The concepts from this perspective will help you understand the dynamic relationship between how people make sense of their situations and act. We'll start with explaining symbolic interactionism as a theoretical perspective and discussing its assumptions, so you will learn what it involves. Throughout the chapter, we'll pick up threads in MMM's story and other stories and show how we can use symbolic interactionism to look at them. This perspective assumes that as human beings we interpret our situations but recognizes that our interpretations occur within a social context preceding us.

To help you better understand the perspective, we'll present the premises of symbolic interactionism, which illuminate how people confer meaning on objects and events in their lives. Next, we devote much of the chapter to the development of self and how images from others affect our sense of self and identity. Then, we move on to look at the significance of defining situations and the crucial role naming things has for what we do and know. Symbolic interactionists who have adopted the metaphor of the theater to analyze everyday life have made major contributions to theoretical understandings of it. Thus, we introduce you to its main concepts before concluding this chapter.

Now let's go deeper into this perspective.

## Symbolic Interactionism as a Theoretical Perspective

Symbolic interactionism consists of several major assumptions and a loosely connected set of concepts. Our rendering of MMM's story takes into account ideas about identity and self-concept, definitions of her situation, symbolic meanings, reference points, and people. Recall the definition of symbolic interactionism in Chapter 1. It is a theoretical perspective that assumes that people construct selves, social worlds, and societies through interaction (Charmaz 1980). This perspective consists of a "framework of premises and concepts for viewing social realities" (Charmaz 2014:262). As a perspective, it offers a lens for looking at ourselves, everyday life, and the world, not an explanatory theory that specifies variables and predicts outcomes.

*Symbolic Interactionism is a theoretical perspective that assumes that people construct selves, social worlds, and societies through interaction. As a perspective, it offers a lens for looking at ourselves, everyday life, and the world.*

To start, think of symbolic interactionism as giving you a way of understanding relationships between the individual and society. Because this perspective is fundamentally a sociological social psychology, we take collective life into account. To understand why individuals think, feel, and act the way they do, we need to understand their worlds from their standpoints. Essentially, the symbolic interactionist perspective focuses on how people construct and negotiate meanings and actions in their everyday lives. Thus, we will emphasize meaning-construction throughout this book.

> *Essentially, the symbolic interactionist perspective focuses on how people construct and negotiate meanings and actions in their everyday lives.*

Interaction is pivotal in the symbolic interactionist perspective. To interact, we rely on **shared symbols**, including spoken and unspoken shared language. We can define a symbol as something people create, such as an abstract category to represent something else, which may be a tangible object or another abstract idea. We use symbols to communicate with others. A symbol does not have intrinsic meaning. Meanings of symbols are conferred by people. Shared symbols are those to which members of a group confer the same meaning. **Language** is a system of shared symbols with other members of our groups and communities that we use for representation and communication.

> *A symbol is something people create, such as an abstract category to represent something else, which may be a tangible object or another abstract idea, and to communicate with others. Shared symbols are those to which members of a group confer the same meaning.*

Consider the messages that MMM's tattoos impart. To what extent are her tattoos shared symbols? You might see their size, location on her body, and relative artistry and make some assessment of the tattoos – and of her – without knowing the message she had once intended to display. Members of MMM's former gang, however, would know exactly what her tattoos mean in their world. Such symbols, like other meanings, gestures, and words (think of special gang terms), precede us; they are part of collective life.

> *Symbols, meanings, gestures, and languages precede us; they are part of collective life.*

We learn about ourselves, other people, everyday life, and society through interaction. And we may change our lives and our worlds because of our interactions. Hence, symbolic interactionists see human existence as fluid and in process.

Like any theoretical perspective, symbolic interactionism shapes what you look at and how you see it. The perspective gives you concepts for looking at people's lives and their worlds. Certain kinds of questions flow from this perspective such as: In what kinds of interactions are people involved? How might these interactions affect how other people identify them and they identify themselves? How do people define their situations? In which ways do people explain their actions? How do their actions influence the meanings that they attribute to their endeavors? These are just a few of the kinds of questions we will raise throughout this book as we study the social psychology of everyday life through symbolic interactionism.

Now we present some fundamental assumptions so that you can better understand this perspective.

## Assumptions about Human Nature and Social Life

Symbolic interactionism rests on several crucial assumptions about human nature. First, this perspective assumes that as human beings, we have some choice about the actions we take. Thus, we are active agents in our lives; choice gives us **agency** (we return to this concept in Chapter 10). When we think about MMM's situation, we can identify choices she made such as trying to reestablish herself to get her children back, deciding to go to junior college, and rejecting gang life. By being an active agent in her life, MMM tried to control who she became. Her choices and actions along the way influenced who she was and could become. MMM's responses to her situation exemplify the symbolic interactionist assumption that human beings make choices and exert some control over their lives.

> *The symbolic interactionist perspective assumes that as human beings we make choices and exert some control over our lives.*

As human beings, we do not act like robots mechanically replicating our various cultures and significant affiliations. Rather, we can think. Thus, another major symbolic interactionist assumption about human nature is that human beings are interpretive creatures. We can interpret what occurs in our situations and subsequently can alter our actions. We may not be able to alter the structure of situations we find ourselves in, but we may rethink and alter how we act in those situations. We are reflective beings.

> *Human beings are interpretive creatures. We can interpret what occurs in our situations and subsequently alter our actions.*

This point means that symbolic interactionist perspective holds a dynamic, but not deterministic, view of individual existence and social life. Individuals affect the world through their choices and actions and are affected by the world.

Our ability to think, to choose makes us creative. We can create new ways to act. With the encouragement of her junior college counselors, MMM took a new path in life. She acted on the opportunity before her. Life consists of **action**, whether we pursue opportunities or remain on the same path. From a symbolic interactionist perspective, possibilities arise for a creating a novel interpretation or a new twist in how we live. In short – and this point is significant – symbolic interactionists view human beings as social, creative, reflective, and active creatures. We see life as fundamentally social and active.

> *Symbolic interactionists view human beings as social, creative, reflective, and active creatures. We see life as fundamentally social and active.*

MMM's story tells us about how she made choices and took actions that changed the direction of her life and the structure of her children's lives. MMM is involved in practical activities to manage everyday life. Symbolic interactionism emphasizes how people accomplish such activities. Yet MMM does not have complete autonomy, and although she shows remarkable initiative, MMM does not act solely as an individual who commands her own fate. The social structure in which she lives precedes her, shapes her choices, and constrains her actions.

Here are two key points: First, symbolic interactionists assume that society and collective life precede the individual. Second, individuals are a part of collective life, not separate from it – and experience its constraints.

> *Society and collective life precede the individual. We are a part of collective life, not separate from it – and we experience its constraints.*

Such constraints are part of human existence and hence extend across the globe. Elaine Keane's (2009, 2011a, 2011b, 2012, 2013) studies of higher education in Ireland demonstrate differences between the worlds of middle-class students and students from disadvantaged backgrounds. Like MMM, many of Keane's (2013) research participants such as Jamie grew up in a world far removed from university life. Jamie is a young man whose entry into the university came by way of participating in a special access program aimed to increase opportunities for disadvantaged youth (Keane 2011a, 2011b, 2012). Keane reports what Jamie told her:

> A huge proportion of the college are from a different background to myself ... You can sense the kind of surroundings ... you're in a different, em, set-up ... Different societal kind of backgrounds, different ways of

thinking, different attitudes … A lot of insecurities and stuff … lower income kind of backgrounds … You feel uncomfortable … out of your depth. You're in with people that … are a lot more comfortable in their surroundings. (Keane, personal communication, 2009)

Jamie also mentioned:

You'd have a lot of traditional students coming in … family backgrounds that are you know, academically minded … they can go home in the evening and their parents would ask them how did they got on, what did they do and the kids could turn around and say "oh we done this or we done that" and the parents can maybe acknowledge what they've done and talk about it for half an hour whereas maybe those from lower dis-advantaged background that didn't go to college there isn't, "oh how is university, what did you do today?" Or there isn't any current affairs talk, or talk of anything on that kind of level like.

Jamie's comments reveal his discomfort in the university setting and the dis-tance he defines between his family and those of other students. MMM acknowledged sometimes being "really hard on myself or really critical, but I guess I can do it" (Katz, personal communication, 2009). Their remarks sug-gest that they question their ability to handle the challenges they face in the university. Perhaps then, they internalized the social constraints that they experienced earlier, which add to the hardships they face in constructing their college lives.

How do such situations pertain to symbolic interactionism? What can this perspective teach us about ourselves and our situations? Through symbolic interactionism we not only can learn relationships between social identity and social inequality but also how social identities and social locations influence what we think about ourselves. Symbolic interactionists believe that our lives are interwoven with the social worlds in which we live and interact. Interaction occurs within social, cultural, and historical contexts that shape but do not mechanistically determine life. This view echoes Karl Marx's (1852/2016:4) famous proclamation, "Men make their own history, but they do not make it just as they please; they do not make it under circumstances chosen by them-selves, but under circumstances directly encountered, given and transmitted from the past."

We agree with Marx's statement and add one further comment here. Our actions shape who we are and what our lives become but take form in social structures and worlds not of our making – *and of which we may be unaware.*

Although sometimes constraints may be evident, symbolic interactionists see reality as fluid, open-ended, and **emergent** and thus, somewhat **indeterminate**. This indeterminacy suggests the fourth assumption of symbolic interactionism: Society and social life fundamentally consist of processes and change, rather than structures and stability.

> *Symbolic interactionists assume that society and social life fundamentally consist of processes and change, rather than structures and stability.*

Think about how your everyday life unfolds. Don't your daily choices and actions, including your many interactions, create changes – both large and small – in your life?

This emphasis on process and change distinguishes symbolic interactionism from most other social scientific perspectives. Instead of viewing social structures as unquestioned fixed and stable entities, symbolic interactionists contend that people construct and reproduce structures through their everyday choices and actions. Actions and interpretations certainly can solidify into persistent, rigid structures and thus become inflexible, albeit still formed through the reproduction of individual and collective actions. Thus, symbolic interactionists study processes that taken together constitute social structures.

By looking at how processes create social structures, symbolic interactionists begin analysis at a different starting point than most sociological perspectives which treat social life as structured and given in social institutions. In contrast, symbolic interactionists ask how structures are created. This approach does not deny the existence of social structures. Instead symbolic interactionists argue that people construct and reproduce them through their routine actions. For example, surveys show that most people in the United States condemn sexual harassment in the workplace (Tinker 2012). Nonetheless sexual harassment persists. Why? Justine E. Tinker (2012) found that micro-level mechanisms supported individuals' ambivalence about enforcing regulations and, moreover, sustained their resistance against enforcement. Both men and women engaged in actions, albeit different ones, that negated enforcement. To resist enforcement, these workers invoked humor, trivialization of harassment complaints and training, gender stereotypes (e.g. women as duplicitous and equivocal), and concern about threatening workplace interaction norms. The process of resisting enforcement was imbedded in workers' everyday beliefs and actions (see Chapter 11 for a detailed discussion of such processes). The point here is that symbolic interactionists assume life consists of processes and we explain how everyday processes create stability (Charmaz 2014).

## Premises of the Symbolic Interactionist Perspective

You may find that these symbolic interactionist ideas come together as you think about the premises on which the perspective rests. Herbert Blumer (1969:3), who devised the name, "symbolic interactionism," set forth three premises forming the basis of the perspective:

- Human beings act toward things on the basis of the meanings that things have for them.
- The meaning of such things is derived from, or arises out of, the social interaction that one has with one's fellows.
- These meanings are handled in, and modified through, an interpretative process used by the person in dealing with the things he encounters.

Blumer's premises highlight the significance of meaning in the symbolic interactionist perspective. Ordinarily, people attribute meanings as being inherent in an object, whether the object is a thing, person, or event.

Such meanings tend to be taken for granted and shared. In the United States, for example, many people assumed for decades that going to college meant a ticket to a good job, as though this definition represented its intrinsic meaning. Blumer, however, argues that the meaning of an object derives from what people do with it. Hence, going to college may mean more about partying and socializing than future jobs or broadening one's knowledge. One affluent student in Keane's (2012) study, attributed several meanings to going to college. He said, "I'd see it … as doing my degree course and going into college and learning but I also saw it as an opportunity … for meeting new people and as a social outlet … I see university as I suppose just kind of a lifestyle" (Keane 2012:154–155).

Blumer argues that meanings are social, rather than individualistic. His first premise implies that meanings precede action, although defining new meanings or reconfirming past meanings occurs through acting. We develop our meanings in interaction. Quite clearly, meanings have consequences. Meanings influence how people define each other and the decisions they make as a result.

> *Meanings have consequences. Meanings influence how people define each other and the decisions they make as a result.*

Let's take another look at how people confer meanings on objects and actions. How about something ordinary like a sweatshirt with your college logo? The meaning of a sweatshirt may seem obvious – something warm to wear around the house and campus. A sweatshirt is a sweatshirt, right? Yet Matilda, a 52-year-old undergraduate in Dawn R. Norris's (2011) study saw it differently. Her daughter who attended the same school had already told her that other students referred to Matilda as "that old lady" and had instructed her to "BE-HAVE" (2011:188). A logo sweatshirt no longer held a simple mundane meaning for Matilda. She said:

> You just have to be age-appropriate…. I would never wear a [university] logo sweatshirt here…. That's *their* [traditional-age students] right, but I don't really feel like it's my right…. I *have* them, and I wear that at home, but not here…. It's probably in my head, probably because I have my daughters at home telling me to behave. (Norris 2011:188)

As Matilda shows us, even things that seem to have straight-forward meanings may take a different cast, depending on the situation. Meanings change as experience changes and people interact. Holmstrom, Karp, and Gray (2012) interviewed upper-middle class parents about preparing their children for college and paying for their education. These authors write:

> Willingness to pay plummeted when the child was not focused on education. For example, a father who himself had gone through private college via scholarship, work, and loans was painfully upset about the prospect of spending large amounts of money for his son because – as both parents reported – the son talked "about wanting a party school." The father's thinking shifted toward finding a relatively inexpensive public college. The wife added: "I don't see [him] as the type of student who … would be intellectually stimulated enough so that [private college] would be worth the money." (Holmstrom et al. 2012:277)

Holmstrom et al. (2012) stress that such decisions by these privileged parents arose from the interactions they had with their children, *not* from a prior commitment to cut college costs. They preferred to send their kids to selective private schools but their hopes of doing so dwindled, as they witnessed their children's actions during high school. For example, one family decided to forgo sending their less studious son to a selective private school but had supported their studious older daughter's desire to attend Bates College.

> The father said, "We just *went* for it." Both father and stepmother emphasized the financial strain, with the stepmother summarizing, "We struggled through it." Advice given to the son to do well in school "went in one ear and went out the other." The parents' willingness to pay sank ever lower. The father focused on a less expensive school for the less studious child. (Holmstrom et al. 2012:277)

These parents' decisions illustrate Blumer's point that social interaction *forms* conduct rather than merely expressing it. Their decisions arose through their interactions with their children and with each other.

Thus, a major contribution of the symbolic interactionist perspective is recognizing our meanings can change and our actions and interpretations can spur these changes.

> *A major contribution of the symbolic interactionist perspective is recognizing our meanings can change and our actions and interpretations can spur these changes.*

Our meanings may change slowly, and we may not be aware of how much they have changed. In contrast, students like Jamie who come from disadvantaged backgrounds may suddenly get caught between conflicting meanings and worlds as they interact with other students and attempt to deal with feeling out of place.

Blumer recognizes the significance of social experience but also emphasizes individual interpretations. People interpret what is happening to them and around them. Hence, we can reassess and change prior meanings. We can extend Blumer's position with three additional premises:

- Meanings are interpreted through shared language and communication
- Handling and negotiating meanings is a continual process
- The interpretive process becomes explicit when people's meanings and/or actions become problematic or their situations change (Charmaz 1980; Snow 2002).

The first two premises simply clarify two distinctive features of symbolic interactionism. To make meanings understandable, people need to share language and communication. The language may be nonverbal when people speak different languages and, of course, the possibilities of misunderstandings multiply. We impart, act on, and may alter our meanings during social interaction or as our experience changes.

The last premise alters the common view of symbolic interactionism as a perspective asserting that people constantly engage in making explicit interpretations. Blumer consistently argued that people engage in an interpretive process with themselves as well as others, as they go about accomplishing their daily lives. Both Charmaz (1980) and Snow (2002), however, contend that much of life is routine and taken for granted. People do not actively interpret many of the actions and events in their lives when routine activities proceed smoothly. Students like Jamie viewed their more affluent peers as making a seamless transition into university life that stood in sharp contrast to their own.

Experiencing either problematic situations or new possibilities prompts people to think about what's happening. That's when they engage in the interpretive process. Sheila Katz interviewed Michelle, a 29-year-old white junior college student who was a single parent of one child and pregnant with another. Think about how Michelle must be on constant alert in her neighborhood and apartment building as she goes about her everyday tasks with her daughter. Michelle said:

> I hate my neighborhood, I hate my neighbors, I come home and it's like music blaring, gun shots popping, helicopters overhead, I can't even barely hear the TV because of all the other environmental noises (laughs). I can't walk down to the corner store without people thinking I'm a prostitute, and it is literally at the corner (laughs).... I went to go

and do my laundry because they have a laundry thing downstairs, and there was this guy literally crouched in the corner, and I was like oh my gosh, there goes my laundry day, you know? So now that means I have to, I live on the 3$^{rd}$ floor, there's no elevator, so now I have to carry my laundry from the 3$^{rd}$ floor down, take it out to a Laundromat, fight for washers, fight for dryers, turn around and carry it up 3 flights of stairs. ... So it's lots of trips, I have a 5 year old that I'm carting along complaining all the time. (Katz 2013b:6–7)

Michelle must constantly attend to what is happening around her. Her daughter's safety depends on it. Note how she calculates the added work involved just to get the laundry done. Compare Michelle's situation with those of students living in a safe dormitory on a peaceful college campus.

## The Development of Self

Symbolic interactionism is perhaps most known for its theoretical analyses of the development of self. In particular, the perspectives of George Herbert Mead and Charles Horton Cooley have shaped sociological social psychology and may reshape how you think about the development of self.

### Society, Self, and Mind: The Social Psychology of George Herbert Mead

As discussed, symbolic interactionism assumes that society precedes the individual. Our heading for this section turns inside out the title of George Herbert Mead's classic treatise, *Mind, Self, and Society* ([1934] 1962). We think starting with society represents a more apt logic of Mead's position than his title infers. Mead's notion of social behaviorism means that behavior occurred within social life rather than separate from it. We are born into groups with a culture, language, and traditions that precede us and in which we interact. Interaction makes us human. Mead viewed children as developing their minds and selves simultaneously. To develop and possess a mind assumes social existence – society, self, and mind intertwine and reflect social processes.

In turn, social processes are founded in action. Actions are social. We act, but we act within a social context – in social worlds and spaces, institutions, and societies. In the U.S., many of us think of individuals as unique, separate beings. Mead ([1934] 1962) makes an important counterargument for you to consider. He argued that we must understand the behavior of a person's social group to understand his or her behavior. Thus, Mead reverses ordinary individualistic thinking that separates the person from his/her social context.

> *Mead argued that we must understand the behavior of a person's social group to understand his or her behavior. Thus, Mead reverses ordinary individualistic thinking that separates the person from his/her social context.*

Mead ([1934] 1962) proposes that the unity and structure of the selves reflects the unity and structure of the social process as a whole. From Mead's perspective, you cannot explain the individual's conduct without first understanding his or her collective affiliations. To understand MMM's actions, for example, we need to know about the groups of which she was once a part and those of which she later became a part. Mead's position also assumes that you can't understand the collective by merely looking at the behavior of each individual who is a part of it. Instead, the whole group is greater and different from the sum of its parts.

In addition, Mead challenges the belief that our minds exist first and propel us into social actions. He argues that the social act is prerequisite for the mind to emerge. Rather than being an entity inside us, the mind is a type of activity in which the individual engages. Then what Mead calls "minded activity" is entirely consistent with teachers you may know who implore their students to "Exercise your minds!" Having a mind means using it; it means attending to what is happening. Our minds develop as we grapple with problems – whether they are academic puzzles or everyday tasks and obstacles. To figure out how to solve the puzzles, do the tasks, and overcome the obstacles, we need to use and understand language and symbols.

The role of language is crucial. With language we can have conversations with others – and with ourselves. Consciousness is imbedded in possessing a self. Having a self means that we can act toward ourselves as we act toward others. What does this statement mean? Mead emphasized that we can take ourselves as an object to scrutinize as we can any other object in our world.

> *Having a self means that we can act toward ourselves as we act toward others. Mead emphasized that we can take ourselves as an object to scrutinize as we can any other object in our world.*

Think of the words we use to describe ourselves and what we do. Through using language, we can evaluate ourselves and our actions. Because we can take ourselves as objects, we can evaluate ourselves and our actions from different criteria than those reflected in other people's judgments of us.

The human capacity to hold inner conversations distinguishes symbolic interactionism from numerous other theoretical perspectives. Having a mind means that we can reflect on our situations and make choices. We are not socially, culturally, or economically determined beings. Nor are we stimulus-response creatures who automatically react to changes in our environments.

Rather, we can *respond* to our situations through thinking rather than *react* to them without thought.

In Mead's ([1934] 1962) view, the self is inherently social in its genesis and development. The social development of self begins and continues in social interaction. Mead analyzed the social development of self by beginning with the social act. Initially, action lacks organization, and focus in response to something until the person becomes conscious of this response. Mead then proceeds with an analysis of the subjective and objective components of the self, the "**I**" and the "**me**." As the subjective part of the self, the "I" initiates action. It is the initial, impulsive, spontaneous part of the self, the acting subject. The "I" responds in the immediate present.

The "me" is the reflective, evaluative part of the self. It exists in a dynamic relationship with the "I." Here, people respond to themselves as objects. Recall MMM's response to friends at junior college, "But I can barely do one class." In this comment, she was not only explaining herself but, moreover, was looking at herself as an object of evaluation, the "me." MMM was making a statement about her identity.

Moving between the I and the me can occur quickly. One's initial response as an "I" can soon become an object of reflection. The "me" becomes aware of the response of the "I" and, thus, the "me" responds to the moment just past. The "me" imagines how the self appears to the other and may subsequently alter the action. The "me" takes into account the social context. The reflective, evaluative character of the "me" depends on having internalized the norms and values of the group. The "me" allows you to exert control over your conduct.

**The Generalized Other** represents the internalized norms and values of the group or society. The generalized other is abstract in the sense of subsuming specific acts under general principles. These are principles members of the group invoke as they construct their actions. Quite clearly, we may be influenced by different "generalized others" at different times. By the time MMM entered junior college, she was neither influenced by nor drawn to gang actions and the principles to which they subscribed. Mead ([1934] 1962) proposes that you possess a generalized other when you can take the perspective of other people and view action and interpretation from this perspective. MMM could take gang members' perspective but she had gained another generalized other from school and work. As a result, she evaluated gang members' worlds and actions and rejected them.

Mead explains the generalized other by using the baseball game as an example of learning varied perspectives. Baseball has standardized set of rules with the players taking different roles. To play the game, you must be able to adopt the perspective of every other player. As you learn to take all the perspectives and are able to act on them, you also learn to look at yourself from the standpoint of the team.

The "I," the "me," and the generalized other are dynamic concepts that treat the social development of self as constructed through action.

> *The "I," the "me," and the generalized other are dynamic concepts that treat the social development of self as constructed through action.*

The generalized other depends on *role-taking* or the ability to take the role of the other. When you engage in role-taking, you understand the perspective and the actions of the other person from his or her standpoint. Role-taking involves empathetic understanding of the other person's situation. It leads you to adjust your actions to fit the situation. Our *interpretation* of the other person's role and perspective shapes our response; we do not automatically react. Role-taking introduces a dynamic dimension into the concept of social role. Through role-taking people improvise on their roles rather than executing them in lockstep fashion.

Role-taking is a mutual process, as people take into account the other person's perspective and role. Jill Tucker (2013:A1) tells the story of how Imani Evans and her mother, Quanikki Van Hook, took each other's views into account. Imani grew up in the projects [low-income housing for those receiving state assistance] with Quanikki, who at 42 years old had already lost her eyesight and a leg, and suffered from renal and heart disease due to diabetes. Imani had long served as Quanikki's caregiver and her mother was her major source of support. Yet Imani wanted to go to college. Although torn by her loyalty to her mother, Imani entered Humboldt State University. Quanikki was hospitalized during her first week of school and then had a heart attack at the beginning of the next term. Nonetheless, Quanikki avowed that she did not want Imani to forsake her dream of earning her degree. Family assistance in caring for Quanikki, encouragement from her advisor, and support from a campus service to help students cope all mattered. But most of all, Imani credits Quanikki for deciding to stay in school. She said, "If my mom wasn't understanding or basically didn't love me so much or prepare me so much, it probably wouldn't have gone so well. She's done so much to get me where I am now" (Tucker 2013:A1).

This anecdote suggests that Quanikki was able to take Imani's role and see the dilemmas it placed on her. Even in such difficult situations, potential problems may be quelled through role-taking and subsequent role-making when those involved are so close.

As George Herbert Mead's most prominent interpreter, Blumer (1969) integrated Mead's ideas into symbolic interactionism. In his study of action, Blumer emphasizes "joint action" – how group members fit lines of action to those of other members. We take into account the actions of others. Blumer contends that joint action has a distinctive character of its own that may be identified without breaking it down to component parts. Being married or being a student means more than the daily actions on which these joint actions are formed. Blumer reminds us that joint action is a part of group life and group life takes place on different levels of which we are often unaware.

## Charles Horton Cooley's "Looking Glass Self"

How we see ourselves takes into account how others see us. Charles Horton Cooley's ([1902] 1964, 2003) concept of the looking glass self brings subjectivity and feeling into the concept of self. Cooley's self is social and interpretive. For him, the social self is "any idea or system of ideas drawn from the communicative life, that the mind cherishes as its own" (2003:124). But what the mind cherishes as its own is always in relation to social life.

From Cooley's perspective, we can only reflect and form images of ourselves from *imagining* the views that others hold of us. The other holds a looking glass through which we see reflections of ourselves. Cooley (2003:123–124) identifies three principal elements of the looking glass self:

- We imagine how we appear to the other person
- We *interpret* what he/she must think and imagine his/her judgment of us
- Our imagined response to his/her judgment calls forth some sort of self-feeling, such as pride or shame

For these reasons, Cooley ([1902] 1964:26–27) stated, "the imaginations which people have of one another are the solid facts of society" – and of self. When we look at or interact with others we interpret what we observe. Similarly, others imagine what we may be seeing and feeling, thus completing the reflections of the looking-glass.

This looking-glass self is not a direct reflection of other's judgments – it is an *imagined* reflection built from cues gleaned from others.

> **This looking-glass self is not a direct reflection of other's judgments – it is an _imagined_ reflection built from cues gleaned from others.**

This point is crucial to Cooley's logic and is often overlooked. Cooley does not assert that we know how other people view us and simply accept these views. Instead, his analysis is considerably more nuanced. We do not mechanically adopt the images that we believe others hold of us. Instead, we *interpret* these images. Granted, if we believe that we are receiving the same images over and over, we are likely to accept them, even when they are negative.

In Mead's ([1934] 1962) terms, the unity of the social process has much to do with the unity of the self. If so, people who experienced upheavals in their lives might also believe that the images they receive of themselves undermine developing an integrated self. In the example below, Shaun Harper (2006) interviewed African American male students at six universities and asked about what it is like to be a high-achieving African American male college student at a large, predominantly white university. Harper was interested in whether the men had internalized racism and carried the burden of "acting white." The men described holding high educational and career goals and receiving encouragement from African American students that supported their growing success. These campuses had few African American male student leaders. Harper (2006:347) proposed that their scarcity worked to the men's advantage in gathering peer recognition, as exemplified by Bryant's interview comment:

> They know how it is to be the only African American student in all of your classes and they know that most Black organizations on campus are led by African American women, not the brothas'. So, when they see a brotha' who is involved and stepping up to be a leader in class or outside of the classroom, they are especially proud and supportive. (Harper 2006:347)

Seeing positive images in the looking glass indicating that valued others are proud of one's performance fosters pride. In turn, pride spurs further commitment to the actions constituting this performance.

*Seeing images in the looking glass indicating that valued others are proud of one's performance fosters pride. In turn, pride spurs further commitment to the actions constituting this performance.*

Despite being at predominantly white universities, these men appear to experience a unified social process and seem to be developing a unified self.

But what if the process is fragmented, selves are already fragmented, and current reflections of self do not appear to be positive? Dongxiao Qin and M. Brinton Lykes (2006) interviewed Chinese women students in the United States (U.S.), many of whom had felt fragmented and constrained in China for reasons such as limited opportunities, gender discrimination, discontent with corruption, and feelings of powerlessness. Qin and Lykes found that the process of fragmenting the self continued in the U.S. and intensified for the single women. The women "described painful experiences of discrimination, disrespect, loneliness and self-doubt" (2006:188) and felt like misfits in both their home and host cultures (2006:189). Wei-Ping had been a college professor in China, but felt discriminated against in the U.S. She said:

> You are just perceived as a foreigner here. In many respects, you are.... Well, I am not a native speaker. In that respect, I mean I can never be. Sometimes people judge you.... They judge you like "Well, you have a kind of accent...." Well, accent, you can never improve it unless you came here under 12-years-old. This kind of prejudice really puts you down.... (Qin and Lykes 2006:188–189)

What happens when people adopt negative images that they perceive in the looking glass? What does it do to how they define themselves and view the world? Another woman Qin and Lykes (2006:190) interviewed, Xin-Xin, a former college professor and now a doctoral student, told how the reflected images affected her:

> So life here is both a tragedy and a comedy, as [Charlie] Chaplin once said. I mean, at the very beginning I had self-esteem and wanted to do something for my country and I wanted to criticize the Western society. But in the end the comedy is that I was influenced by the learned prejudice and even I looked down upon myself and other people of color.

Rather than the looking glass mirroring the views of others of self, here the looking glass turns outward and becomes a magnifying glass. It enlarges pejorative views and not only turns them against self but also focuses these views on similar others.

### Self, Self-Concept, and Identity

We talk about changing selves and possessing "a" self as though it remained fixed and stable. How can we reconcile these views? Viktor Gecas (1982) offers a solution. He proposes that we view the self as both process and structure. Life is a process, so the self is in a continual process of developing. Events unfold, and we change as events and our situations change. But people still reveal consistency and continuity of self over time.

One way to clarify this distinction is to think of the self as in process and the self-concept as a stable structure. As Ralph E. Turner (1976) pointed out a long time ago, self-concepts are enduring. Once established, a self-concept only changes slowly. A self-concept consists of the feelings, values, attributes, and characteristics that we define as our own. Some things are me, others are not me. Thus, a self-concept has boundaries.

In the United States, having a self involves making continual evaluations of oneself (Charmaz 1991). Consistent with Mead, we view ourselves as objects like any other object, and thus judge and evaluate ourselves. As Xin-Xin absorbed American values she came to see herself as less than white U.S. natives. MMM had hinted that an advanced degree reached beyond the borders of her self-concept and thus seemed unreal. MMM implied that her self-concept lagged behind what was happening to her as she moved on to attend the University of California, Berkeley. We can sense the changes affecting MMM's self at that time. She looked ahead to a new, unknown life that made who she was ambiguous. Likely, however, her self-concept simultaneously remained anchored in the past. When thrust into unanticipated, unfamiliar sudden life changes, one's experience changes more quickly than the self-concept changes (Charmaz 1991).

Yet we receive images of who we are. These images may be fleeting or sustained, but they can mark turning points in change of self. While at the junior college, MMM received positive images of who she was and could become. Many of the special access students that Keane interviewed held negative views of themselves as students. It takes many more positive self-images to undo a negative self-concept than it does to create one (Charmaz 1991). Consistent with this point, Keane (2011b) found that the special access students continued to feel intimidated and anxious about their performance for long after they had established solid academic records. It took considerable affirmation through getting good grades for these students to have confidence in their abilities.

Similar to Xin-Xin, Keane's research participants' **social identities** had dominated their self-concepts. Social identities include a person's various locations in society such as race, gender, age, and religion (Hewitt 2003). Although people may not always embrace their social identities as part of their self-concepts, they often do. And thus, social identities become defining aspects of self. Now we turn to the significance of defining and naming for what we "know" in greater detail.

## Defining the Situation, Naming, and Knowing

### W.I. Thomas and Dorothy Swaine Thomas's Theorem

How people define situations matters. How we view our situations and name things in our worlds shape the actions we take. The Thomas theorem of the definition of the situation holds a central place in symbolic interactionist social psychology:

> If men [sic] define situations as real, they are real in their consequences. The total situation will always contain more and less subjective factors, and the behavior reaction can be studied only in connection with the whole context, i.e. the situation as it exists in verifiable, objective terms, and as it has seemed to exist in terms of the interested persons. (Thomas and Thomas 1928:572)

Thus, our actions reflect how we define the situation. *Definitions have consequences.* We can take the Thomas theorem one step further. The person or group defining the situation may not always assume their definition is real but intend that other people accept it as real. The consequences of such definitions can wreak havoc on the lives of those who accepted the proffered definition as real. Think of chemical companies that claim substances in their products are harmless while suppressing research to the contrary, or a financial consultant who knowingly promises high returns on worthless stock. In any case, when individuals or groups can make their definitions of the situation stick, they affect other people's actions as well as their own.

The definition of a situation arises from experience, whether it represents a considered judgment, taken-for-granted "truth," or an expedient manipulation. In a study in Western Ireland on give-and-take between the generations, a taken-for-granted "truth" surfaced in Rosalind's interview (Carney et al. 2014). Rosalind was a bright student in her twenties and a single, impoverished mother of two. She had been homeless in the past but now lived in a simple but stark abode. When asked about her expectations of receiving future help from the state, Rosalind said:

> I would be gearing up for leaving Ireland, so I don't expect to be keeping my contract with the State and I don't expect to be paying any tax back to them either when I do eventually start working. I think they are realising that now as a lot of people are leaving. Most people are going to Australia, aren't they?" (Carney et al. 2014:323)

Rosalind treats emigration as a taken-for-granted survival strategy, an obvious alternative and unquestioned truth. She was not alone. Leaving Ireland arose as an unexpected, but recurring possibility in the interviews with young people. Their definition of the situation took into account Ireland's long history of emigration. Definitions of the situation reflect social circumstances and processes. To put it in Marx's terms above, these young people's definition of their situation arises from circumstances directly encountered, given, and transmitted from the past. Our definitions of the situation are grounded in realities we can imagine and take form as we understand these realities. Would MMM or Michelle so readily think of emigration to a distant country to escape poverty if the job market offered few opportunities when they finished their degrees? It's doubtful. Leaving the United States for distant shores has not been part of the U.S. tradition or consciousness. However, for Irish youth, the long history and tradition of the Irish diaspora brings this possibility into view.

### Anselm Strauss and Naming and Knowing

Names shape how we know the world. Through naming the things and events in our world, we have a way of knowing, categorizing, and evaluating them (Charmaz 2014). Anselm Strauss (1959) stressed the crucial role of naming in everyday life. Naming delineates boundaries and outlines one's relationship to what is named (Charmaz 2014). Naming a phenomenon evokes or ensures evaluating it. Naming something by an individual or group implies how they will act toward it to and thus involves a line of action.

> *Naming delineates boundaries and outlines one's relationship to what is named. Naming a phenomenon evokes or ensures evaluating it. Naming something by an individual or group implies how they will act toward it and thus involves a line of action.*

Names often serve as shorthand labels for fuller definitions of the situation. We know the world through the names we give to objects and events within it, including ourselves and other people. Names reflect and reify the bonds we share and the divisions we create. Names serve as containers for condensed meanings and evoke images and memories. In the United States, 9-11 – the date of the 2001 terrorist attacks – provides one example. Newtown – the Connecticut community where a gunman slaughtered 26 schoolchildren and staff – provides another.

At a colloquium in Strauss's honor, one of us gave a talk about the lessons to be gleaned from him and his symbolic interactionist tradition (Charmaz 2008). Kathy introduced several tacit and explicit lessons from Strauss:

- To name is to know
- The renaming of any object amounts to a reassessment of your relation to it
- Alternatives are greater than [the person's] awareness
- Involvements are evolvements (Strauss 1959; adapted from Charmaz 2008:128).

Through naming something, whether it might be a person, object, event, or experience, we place it in a category, make it understandable, and anticipate how it will affect our actions and those of others. For example, naming someone as "my girlfriend" or "my boyfriend" not only distinguishes this relationship from casual friendships but also infers exclusiveness, intimacy, and a host of expectations and obligations. In contrast, renaming the person as "my ex" indicates emotional distance, physical, and social separation, and is often accompanied by disparaging labels such as "jerk," "loser," and "airhead."

By stating that alternatives are greater than one's awareness, Strauss states that the range of possible actions exceed what the person considers. A possible choice or action remains elusive until an individual becomes aware of it and names it as possible. For MMM, first earning an undergraduate degree and then going to graduate school seemed beyond the realm of possibilities, despite her friends' forecasting her future success.

From Strauss's view, involvements mean more than immediate experience or neutral pastimes. Instead, our involvements shape who we become. How we spend our time matters. For example, a student's life changed after she learned about impoverished families in her college town and decided to do something. Although she had been a shy person, she took the initiative to create a campus community-service organization. She recruited student volunteers, collaborated with local service agencies, and planned student placements. This student not only gained new skills but also decided to pursue graduate training in social work, a career she had not previously considered.

The lessons from Strauss help us to understand everyday life. Kathy (Charmaz 2008:128–129) tells a story of how the above list of Strauss's insights affected a student who took a social psychology class from her:

> Several years ago, a student in my class devoured these abbreviated bits of wisdom. They spoke to him. These insights illuminated his past and present. As a teenager, he had created more than his share of trouble. As a young man, he had found himself in even more trouble but later as a college student he worked on straightening his life out – and he tried to help other troubled students to find another path. I saw him telling a student who was having a rough time, "Alternatives are greater than awareness." He also would go home and announce to his housemates, "Involvements are evolvements." Did you know that? Watch your involvements. You can change them." This student said that he went home from class every day with a new thought to savor and share. (Charmaz 2008:128–129)

This student saw possibilities for personal and situational change through how we define situations and name things in our world. For him, alternatives were greater than awareness because we have not yet thought of all possibilities. Moving to Australia could be an alternative were we to conceive of it – but for many of us in the U.S., moving to Australia isn't something that occurs to us. For MMM, each stage of the educational process only became an alternative as her awareness grew and she learned different ways to define her situation.

## Erving Goffman's Metaphor of the Theater: Dramaturgical Analysis

In the previous analysis, we emphasized the dynamic relationships between action and interpretation. Now we focus on action by using Erving Goffman's dramaturgical analysis. Goffman's approach adopts the **theater as a metaphor** to study social life and individual behavior. The metaphor of the theater focuses on actors and audiences, roles and scripts, frontstage and backstage, scenes and settings, players and stagehands, performances, and rehearsals. Looking at everyday life through the lens of this metaphor reveals how actors attempt to *control* their situations, interactions, self-presentations, and settings (Goffman 1959).

Goffman views the individual as a social actor[4] who pursues goals and performs roles in daily life. He studies the social actor in face-to-face interactions and sees this actor as socially situated. Instead of enacting a consistent self-concept in one situation to the next, Goffman (1959, 1967) argues that the self is manufactured during situations and moments. As Goffman (1967:3) succinctly states, his studies are on "Not then, men [sic] and their moments. Rather, moments and their men."

The metaphor of the theater helps us to look at how people play their roles in face-to-face interaction and to assess whether they succeed at controlling the lines of interaction. Does someone play his or her role smoothly through enacting a standard script? How does the audience respond? When might scripts break down?

Goffman's metaphor of the theater can readily be applied to customer service work with its actors, roles, scripts, front stage performances, and audiences. Customer service representatives who reveal irritation with complaining callers or imply negative judgments of them fail at performing their roles. Such responses are not part of the script. A customer service representative may state the standard script in response to a complaining customer but find it doesn't work. What does the representative do? Thompson et al. (2001:936) report the following advice from a British bank's ("Telebank") telephone customer service training program:

> If a customer is stupid you need to become quite clever in your acting abilities ... enthusiasm and tone give away your mood, if you are five minutes from the end of a shift or having a bad day ... you'll have to fight these reactions, shut them out, push them out.

Even though Telebank's customer service agents only had phone contact with customers, they were on front stage during the call. Their role required nuanced tone, words, and patience. Telebank recruited trainees for their communication skills and then dictated how they should act (Thompson et al. 2001:936). One manager stated that the personalities and communication skills of their service representatives distinguished Telebank from other banks. A customer service representative (2001:935) also noted differences between Telebank and other call centers:

> It's [emotional control] inside certain people. We build it up. I've worked in four call centres so far, from Sky, right through BT, Virgin, to this place, over a period of four years. We used to get emotional on Sky especially, but now I don't. Whatever situation I'm in, I can stop what I'm doing and put on a face.

The representative's "face" dissolves when the call ends and he or she retreats to the backstage – until the next call.

Goffman's (1959) distinction between front stage and backstage draws attention to the *spatial* and *temporal* dimensions of scenes and acts as well as how and when performances are enacted. Space and time matter. Think about the times you have been placed on "hold" by an irritated or overworked telephone customer service agent.

Who gets front stage space and time, for how long, and who is relegated to backstage? What is time like between performances? What happens when the backstage becomes visible from front stage?

For many dramaturgical analysts (e.g. Brissett and Edgley 1975; Edgley 2003; Goffman 1989), meaning emerges through action: what people do conveys more about what they mean than what they say.

> *For many dramaturgical analysts meaning emerges through action: what people do conveys more about what they mean than what they say.*

When discussing his methods, Goffman (1989:131) said, "I don't give hardly any weight to what people say," but he acknowledged connecting what they said with the events that concerned them. In addition, Goffman took careful note of their gestures, facial expressions, and body language. Dramaturgical analysts observe **nonverbal behavior** and how people appear to express it.

For these dramaturgical analysts, the definition of the situation arises in how people act. In the following excerpt, Elaine Keane (2011b) found that students believed their affluent peers used their appearance simultaneously to distinguish themselves from others and proclaim their membership in a distinct clique. Keane (2011b:459) writes:

> Deirdre… felt that those "… who have all the lovely clothes and the labels and who are definitely from a higher class … *like to let people know that.*" Eileen … spoke of "your very obvious upper-class people" wearing "all designer clothes … *as badges.*"

The designer clothes become identity badges. Clothes can make silent but dramatic statements. In the dramaturgical perspective, they become props. Clothing and appearance more generally make an immediate impression and assert claims about social and personal identity, whether or not these claims are calculated.

Eileen's statement illustrates Charles Edgley's (2003:144) point about studying how people *express* themselves in their everyday interactions. Observing people in their own worlds teaches us about the meaning of their behavior. Quite possibly, students who wear designer clothes as badges treat the college scene as a stage on which they play leading roles in striking costumes that proclaim their distinctiveness. If so, these students appear on front stage of everyday life; moreover, they claim center stage. Of course, they, like everyone else, may also express themselves in ways of which they are unaware, but their audiences see. Our accents and grammar, voice and tone, facial expressions and gestures, bodily poses and movements, – and apparel – may all reveal our identities and intentions without our awareness.

Dramaturgical analysis can lead you to ask other numerous questions. Who's on center stage? When? What kind of impression do the actors and the scenes make? What stands as a good performance? How do the supporting actors play their roles? Who's on cue? What role does the audience play? What happens when actors are backstage?

Interaction can become strategic as people try to manage the impressions they give and the expressions they give off (Goffman 1959, 1967, 1989). In a word, they engage in **impression management**, and thus aim to project a particular **presentation of self** and situation and to control anticipated or actual encounters.

> *Interaction can become strategic as people try to manage the impressions they give and the expressions they give off (Goffman 1959).*

Impression-management is not limited to individuals. In the following excerpt from Lisbeth A. Berbary's (2012) study of discipline in a sorority, Yarah tried to impress her errant sorority sister, Roommate Y, who has been placed on social probation, with the importance of maintaining the sorority's image. In dramaturgical terms, Yarah was having a back-stage conversation with Roommate Y about her frontstage behavior at parties.

ROOMMATE Y:    But, it's not like I'm getting wasted and letting people take pictures of me making out.

YARAH:    No, but I mean sometimes you drink a lot…

ROOMMATE Y:    Well sometimes, but not to the point where…

YARAH:    And there are times you have started making out at the bar.

ROOMMATE Y:    Wow, tell me how you really feel.

YARAH:    I'm just trying to help you, don't get mad….

ROOMMATE Y:    *I know. Sometimes it's just hard to deal with all these people watching you and always having to follow some kind of rules. It's like having a magnifying glass on you.*

YARAH:    Yeah, but I mean our reputation is everything. You can make an impression on people here faster than you realize. If one girl makes a bad impression on people, it can make a bad impression of all of us. Not that I think you are doing that, but that is why we have to watch each other.

ROOMMATE Y:    Yeah, I know and I don't want to be that girl. But I just don't think my behavior is anything like your big sis [Sorority sister whose behavior led to formal scrutiny].

(Berbary 2012:610–611; Emphasis in original)

Roommate Y tried to give an account which simultaneously explains her behavior and excuses her from being subject to discipline. But can her definition of the situation persuade others? Dramaturgical analysts have paid considerable attention to the accounts people devise to justify or excuse their behavior, which we detail in Chapter 6. Convicted criminals often develop elaborate justifications for violent acts (Scully and Marolla 1984). Yet on occasion, ordinary acts are called into question (Mills 1940; Scott and Lyman 1968). Thus, you may be called upon to devise quick reasons for explaining why your paper was late or why your test answers resemble those of another classmate (Albas and Albas 1993, 2003). At this point, your motivation has arisen as an issue and you might become self-conscious about explaining what you did.

Dramaturgical analysts say much of our everyday life is routine and thus we account for what we do only when our actions are challenged or interrupted. Then we state a motive to provide a reason that explains our actions. In short, motives provide a way of explaining or justifying actions when they are called into question.

## Conclusion

Where have we gone in this chapter and where will it take you? This introduction to symbolic interaction acquaints you with the perspective and offers some of its main conceptual tools such as meaning-construction, self-concept, definition of the situation, the looking-glass self, and impression management. We explained the premises of symbolic interactionism and explicated its logic. Symbolic interactionism focuses on seeing both self and situation as embedded in processes. This perspective assumes an optimistic view of human nature and emphasizes the active, innovative, and social aspects of human existence. The perspective acknowledges subjectivity while recognizing the constraints imposed by the world.

The value of the symbolic interactionist perspective is how we can understand everyday life through using it. Our stories and anecdotes and, moreover, how we analyze them, show you how we use symbolic interactionism. The concepts we have introduced can be applied in numerous situations and contexts. Revisit this chapter for its concepts as you traverse the pages of this book. You will see the perspective and its concepts in new light. But symbolic interactionism offers more than concepts to apply. It gives you a perspective from which you can develop *new* concepts to understand your everyday worlds and worlds beyond your everyday life. You can use the symbolic interactionist perspective as a starting point to make your own discoveries about yourself, your life, and the world. Learn about the perspective and explore using it.

## Learning by Using the Symbolic Interactionist Perspective

Now think about how you might use symbolic interactionist concepts to analyze the following excerpts from Tim Clydesdale's (2007) book about college students in the United States, *The First Year Out: Understanding American Teens after High School.* Clydesdale first talked with Barb Miscosky a few days before her high school graduation. Barb's record as a marathon runner earned her a hefty scholarship at what Clydesdale (2007:69) calls, "Ordinary Private College." Barb grew up as the youngest child in the middle-class family with three siblings. She chose her college partly because her parents would be close by but "she felt ready to 'test herself'" and live "without parents all around" (2007:69–70). Clydesdale later interviewed Barb shortly after her first year at college and wrote the following remarks.

---

**Barb Miscosky**

*The First Year Out: Understanding American Teens after High School*

**Tim Clydesdale (2007:70–71)**

She reported passing her test. "I liked being on my own. I liked making my own decisions… I don't think I made a wrong one anywhere." Barb loved her parents, but, living back at home after first year at school, she once again had "someone to answer to." And she preferred just having "to answer to myself." Barb was independent in every way except financially, and her relationship with her parents had reached an awkward moment. "I like being home," she said told me, "but I'd rather not be here – you know what I mean?" Apparently the awkwardness went two ways. Barb said of her parents, "They all missed me. Now they have me again; they don't know what to do with me." An important part of Barb's first year out was navigating this changing relationship with her parents as it was for virtually every other teen I interviewed.

Barb's changing relationship with her parents is not the only relationship you she had to navigate, however. Barb fell in love with another freshman in college, she had to live with her first year roommate, she saw relationships with several "very close friends" from high school grow distant, and she discovered that even her closest friends from college made little effort to stay in contact during the summer. Barb's relationship with her boyfriend was "pretty serious. I guess," but she struggled with how much of herself to reveal to him: "I'm, like, should I bother him with this?" Barb's relationship with her roommate was tolerable, but they had to work at it and they did not become close like another roommate she knew.… Perhaps the most surprising change from Barb, however, was seeing how quickly her college friendships cooled off.… "[Sighs.] I guess I'm close with them [college classmates] because I live with them. It's kind of a forced closeness." Barb recognized that shared context like a college dormitory, fosters friendships, and that without that context, friendships grow distant and whither. Navigating the shifting relationships kept Barb quite occupied during her first year out.

At the same time, the independence Barb sought and so enjoyed during her first year out imposed additional obligations on her: managing the myriad adult gratifications now freely available to her. Adult gratifications were not new to Barb; high school students can obtain access to sex, drugs and alcohol. But the removal of parental and school oversight, together with the legal definitions of 18-year-olds as adults gives teens wide freedom to gratify themselves as they choose. Thus, Barb reported, "I'm partying a lot more" than she did as a high school student, by which she means consuming alcohol more frequently with the other teens at parties of various sorts….

Barb learned her limit by exceeding it a couple times and feeling the consequences. She also chose to restrict herself to alcohol only. "No, no illegal substances for me," she declared…

## Notes

1 Sheila Katz and Elaine Keane each shared published and unpublished research materials with Kathy Charmaz for preparing this chapter. We appreciate having their descriptions of participants and interview excerpts. We thank them for their generosity and for granting permission to quote several of their participants. An abbreviated version of MMM's story appeared in Charmaz and Katz (2017).

2 MMM is this research participant's chosen pseudonym. Katz invited each of her participants to choose their own pseudonyms. MMM's story is from Katz's (2008, 2012, 2013a, 2013b, 2019) longitudinal study of low-income women with children who received welfare assistance in California, which in the United States is limited, stringent, and temporary.

3 The TANF program took form in the 1990s from an uneasy compromise between President Bill Clinton's avowal to institute welfare "reform" and conservative legislators who held 1980s stereotypes of indigent families. These stereotypes denigrated impoverished women, particularly African American single mothers, as dependent, unwilling to work, and motivated to have more children to increase the size of their welfare checks (Katz 2013a, 2019). The program became federal law in 1996 but gave discretion to the states as to how to implement and administer it. Katz's study took place in California, one of the few states in the United States that allowed TANF recipients to seek higher education and, by extension, possibly obtain economic independence.

4 Many mid-twentieth century sociologists referred to individuals as social actors who had roles but did not take the metaphor of the theater further, as Goffman did.

# References

Albas, D. C. and C. A. Albas. 1993. "Disclaimer Mannerisms: How to Avoid Being Labeled a Cheater." *Canadian Review of Sociology and Anthropology* 30(4):451–468.

Albas, D. C. and C. A. Albas. 2003. "Motives." Pp. 349–366 in *Handbook of Symbolic Interactionism*, edited by L. T. Reynolds and N. J. Hermans. Walnut Creek, CA: Alta Mira.

Berbary, L. A. 2012. "'Don't Be a Whore, That's Not Ladylike': Discursive Discipline and Sorority Women's Gendered Subjectivity." *Qualitative Inquiry* 18(7):606–625.

Blumer, H. 1969. *Symbolic interactionism: Perspective and method*. Englewood Cliffs, NJ: Prentice Hall.

Brissett, D. and C. Edgley. 1975. "Introduction." Pp. 1–7 in *Life as Theater: A Dramaturgical Sourcebook*, edited by D. Brissett and C. Edgley. Chicago, IL: Aldine.

Carney, G., T. Scarf, V. Timonen, and C. Conlon. 2014. "'Blessed are the Young, for They Shall Inherit the National Debt': Solidarity Between Generations in the Irish Crisis." *Critical Social Policy* 34(3):312–332.

Charmaz, K. 1980. *The Social Reality of Death*. Reading, MA: Addison-Wesley.

Charmaz, K. 1991. *Good Days, Bad Days: The Self in Chronic Illness and Time*. New Brunswick, NJ: Rutgers University Press.

Charmaz, K. 2008. "The Legacy of Anselm Strauss for Constructivist Grounded Theory." Pp. 127–141 in *Studies in Symbolic Interaction 32*, edited by N. K. Denzin. Bingley: Emerald Publishing Group, Ltd.

Charmaz, K. 2014. *Constructing Grounded Theory* 2nd ed. London: Sage.

Charmaz, K., and S. Katz. 2017. "Subjective Stories and Social Issues: Strategies for Making Connections." *Qualitative Methods in Psychology Bulletin* 23(Spring):8–14.

Clydesdale, T. 2007. *The First Year Out: Understanding American Teens After High School*. Chicago, IL: University of Chicago Press.

Cooley, C. H. [1902] 1964. *Human Nature and the Social Order*. New York: Schocken Books.

Cooley, C. H. 2003. "The Looking Glass Self." Pp. 123–124 in *Inner Lives and Social Worlds*, edited by J. A. Holstein and J. F. Gubrium. New York: Oxford University Press.

Edgley, C. 2003. "The Dramaturgical Genre." Pp. 141–172 in *Handbook of Symbolic Interactionism*, edited by L. T. Reynolds and N. J. Hermans. Walnut Creek, CA: Alta Mira.

Gecas, V. 1982. "The Self-Concept." *Annual Review of Sociology* 8:1–32.

Goffman, E. 1959. *The Presentation of Self in Everyday Life*. Garden City, NY: Doubleday Anchor Books.

Goffman, E. 1967. *Interaction Ritual*. Garden City, NY: Doubleday Anchor Books.

Goffman, E. 1989. "On Fieldwork." *Journal of Contemporary Ethnography* 18(2):123–132.

Hewitt, J. P. 2003. *Self and Society: A Symbolic Interactionist Perspective.* Boston, MA: Allyn & Bacon.

Harper, S. R. 2006. "Peer Support for African American Male College Achievement: Beyond Internalized Racism and the Burden of 'Acting White.'" *The Journal of Men's Studies* 14(3):337–358.

Holmstrom, L. L., D. Karp, and P. S. Gray. 2012. "Why Parents Pay for College: The Good Parent, Perceptions of Advantage, and the Intergenerational Transfer of Opportunity." *Symbolic Interaction* 34(2):265–289.

Katz, S. 2008. "Pursuing a 'Reformed' Dream: CalWORKs Mothers in Higher Education after 'Ending Welfare as We Know It.'" Ph.D. Dissertation, Department of Sociology, Vanderbilt University, Nashville, TN.

Katz, S. 2012. "TANF's 15th Anniversary: Are Low-Income Mothers Celebrating Upward Economic Mobility?" *Sociology Compass* 6(8):657–670.

Katz, S. 2013a. "'Just Give Us a Chance to Get an Education': CalWORKs Mothers' Survival Narratives and Strategies." *Journal of Poverty* 17(3):273–304.

Katz, S. 2013b. "Meanings of Education Quotes." Unpublished data from CalWORKs and Higher Education Study by Sheila Katz. University of Houston, Houston TX.

Katz, S. 2019. *Reformed American Dreams: Welfare Mothers, Higher Education, and Activism.* New Brunswick, NJ: Rutgers University Press. In press.

Keane, E. 2009. *'Widening participation' and 'traditional entry' students at an Irish university: Strategising to 'make the most' of higher education.* PhD dissertation, School of Education, National University of Ireland, Galway.

Keane, E. 2011a. "Dependence-Deconstruction: Widening Participation and Traditional-Entry Students Transitioning from School to Higher Education in Ireland." *Teaching in Higher Education* 16(6):707–718.

Keane, E. 2011b. "Distancing to Self-Protect: The Perpetuation of Inequality in Higher Education Through Socio-Relational Dis/Engagement." *British Journal of Sociology of Education* 32(3):449.

Keane, E. 2012. Differential prioritising: Orientations to higher education and widening participation. *International Journal of Educational Research* 53(1):150–159.

Keane, E. 2013. "Differential Prioritising: Orientations to Higher Education and Widening Participation." *International Journal of Educational Research* 53(1):150–159.

Marx, K. 1852/2016. *The 18th Brumaire of Louis Bonaparte.* Charleston, SC: CreateSpace Independent Publishing Platform.

Mead, G. H. [1934] 1962. *Mind, Self and Society: From the Standpoint of a Social Behaviorist.* Chicago, IL: University of Chicago Press.

Mills, C. W. 1940. "Situated Actions and Vocabularies of Motives." *American Sociological Review* 5(6):904–913.

Norris, D. R. 2011. "Interactions That Trigger Self-Labeling: The Case of Older Undergraduates." *Symbolic Interaction* 34(2):173–197.

Qin, D. and M. B. Lykes. 2006. "Reweaving a Fragmented Self: A Grounded Theory of Self-Understanding Among Chinese Women Students in the United States of America." *International Journal of Qualitative Studies in Education* 19(2):177–200.

Scott, M. and S. M. Lyman. 1968. "Accounts." *American Sociological Review* 33(1):46–62.

Scully, D. and J. Marolla. 1984. "Convicted Rapist Vocabularies of Motives: Excuses and Justifications." *Social Problems* 31(4):530–544.

Snow, D. A. 2002. "Extending and broadening Blumer's conceptualization of symbolic interactionism." *Symbolic Interaction* 25(4):571–575.

Strauss, A. L. 1959. *Mirrors and Masks*. Mill Valley, CA: Sociology Press.

Thomas, W. I. and D. S. Thomas. 1928. *The Child in America*. New York: Knopf.

Thompson, P., C. Warhurst, and G. Callaghan. 2001. "Ignorant Theory and Knowledgeable Workers: Interrogating the Connections Between Knowledge, Skills and Services." *Journal of Management Studies* 38(7):923–941.

Tinker, J. E. 2012. "Resisting the Enforcement of Sexual Harassment Laws." *Law & Social Inquiry* 37(1):1–24.

Tucker, J. 2013. "Students Battling Adversity." *San Francisco Chronicle*. Sunday, April 7, 2013, p. A1. http://nl.Hwsbank.com/nl-search/we/Archives? p_action=doc&p_docid=14584316F0C9E9F8&p_docnum=9&s_dlid= DL0118012919502930394&s.

Turner, R. E. 1976. "The Real Self: From Institution to Impulse." *American Journal of Sociology* 81:989–1016.

# 3

# Socialization

Becoming Ourselves

"At 7:40 A.M. four-year old Cassie sidles in, her hair half-combed, a blanket in one hand, a fudge bar in the other. 'I'm late,' her mother [Gwen] explains to Diane [the childcare worker]. 'Cassie wanted the fudge bar so bad, I gave it to her,' she adds apologetically – though Diane has said nothing....

'Pleeese, can't you take me with you?' Cassie pleads.

'You know I can't take you to work,' Gwen replies in a tone that suggests she's heard this request before. Cassie's shoulders droop in defeat. She's given it a try, but now she's resigned to her mother's eminent departure, and she's agreed, it seems, not to make too much of a fuss about it. Aware of her mother's unease about her long day at childcare, however, she's struck a hard bargain. Every so often she gets a morning fudge bar. This is their deal, and Cassie keeps her mother to it. As Gwen Bell later explained to me, she continually feels that she owes Cassie more time than she actually gives her. She has a time-debt to her daughter. If many busy parents settle such debts on evenings or weekends when their children eagerly "collect" promised time, Cassie insists on a morning down payment, a fudge bar that makes her mother uneasy but saves her the trouble and embarrassment of a tantrum. (Hochschild 1997:4–5)

...At the Spotted Deer Childcare Center, the group of young breakfasters gradually expands, early arrivals watching the entertainment provided by yet more newcomers. Sally enters sucking her thumb. Billy's mother carries him in even though he's already five. Jonathan's mother forgets to wave, and soon after Jonathan kicks the breakfast table from below, causing milk to spill and children to yell. Marie [childcare worker] ushers him away to dictate a note to his mother explaining that it hurts his feelings when she doesn't wave. Cassie still stands at the front door holding her fudge bar like a flag, the emblem of a truce in a battle over time. Every now and then, she licks one of its drippy sides while Diane, uncertain about what to do, looks on disapprovingly. The cereal eaters watch from their table, fascinated and envious. Gwen Bell turns to leave, waving good-bye to Cassie, car keys in hand." (Hochschild 1997:11)

*The Social Self and Everyday Life: Understanding the World Through Symbolic Interactionism*, First Edition. Kathy Charmaz, Scott R. Harris, and Leslie Irvine.
© 2019 John Wiley & Sons, Inc. Published 2019 by John Wiley & Sons, Inc.

In her classic study, *The Time Bind: When Work Becomes Home and Home Becomes Work*, Arlie Hochschild (1997) recounts observing the above incident at the Spotted Deer Childcare Center. The Center served the employees of a Midwestern company that several prestigious sources had identified as "family-friendly."

What do you think is happening here? Which lessons are being imparted? What are the stakes? How might having an audience affect what happens? Four-year-old Cassie and her mother, Gwen, enact a frequent morning ritual about leaving Cassie in daycare. No slouch in the bargaining process, Cassie exerts her will and partly gets her way. Gwen teaches Cassie that ultimately her pleas to tag along will go unheeded. The job comes first, despite Gwen's uneasy feelings about leaving Cassie for long hours at daycare and letting her have the fudge bar.

Cassie teaches Gwen how to save time, trouble, and avoid an even more embarrassing tantrum – and she extracts a high price for avoiding it. Cassie already won the fudge bar before leaving home. The daycare setting makes her victory visible to all – and may embolden her. This setting also provides the stage for making further plays on her mother's regret about not giving Cassie enough time. What moral lessons do the participants in the scene learn? The daycare workers might learn that keeping peace with parents and their employers supersedes questioning parenting practices, despite their effect on an entire class. The other children take in the scene and envy Cassie for getting a fudge bar. Does winning trump "acceptable behavior?" Cassie's peers may be thinking of borrowing her tactics of setting a high price for dodging a tantrum.

Bargaining brings pay-offs. Lessons accrue for both parents and children about valuing parental attention, extorting forbidden rewards, expanding the limits of acceptable behavior, and creating tactics to get one's way. However unintended, Cassie shows children how to be rewarded for stretching adult rules. Simultaneously, her childcare workers could be identifying her as a difficult child. These workers are stuck with managing both blatant and latent lessons given in such incidents, including the loss of adult authority. A helpful solution such as Marie escorting Jonathan away to dictate a note to his mother may not always be available. Cassie may gain a fudge bar this time but may lose the approval of her daycare workers. Gwen gets to leave the scene but loses face as a good mother from the staff's view and, moreover, in her own eyes.

Who is being socialized in this scenario? Everyone.

In this chapter, we look at socialization from a symbolic interactionist perspective. As Hochschild's anecdote suggests, socialization involves more than you might think. We offer an initial definition and briefly compare structural and symbolic interactionist perspectives on socialization. Symbolic interactionism gives you useful theoretical tools to think about socialization, so we extend the discussion of concepts presented in Chapter 2. Then we introduce empirical studies that portray the profound influence of interaction throughout life.

## What Is Socialization?

As a starting point, socialization means learning how our society and specific communities and groups work so we can be part of them. Through socialization we learn the taken-for-granted norms and values of our groups along with the requisite skills, views, and actions to conduct ourselves as bona fide members.

> *Socialization means learning how our society and specific communities and groups work so we can be part of them. Through socialization we learn the taken-for-granted norms and values of our groups along with the requisite skills, views, and actions to conduct ourselves as bona fide members.*

Cassie and the other children learn what's permissible at preschool. Diane and Marie learn the ropes of daycare and what it takes to work with small children. The events say something about moral values and moral rules. Socialization shapes behavior and results in patterned actions, continuity between generations, and orderly groups and societies.

Through socialization we learn the ways of thinking, acting, and feeling of the groups to which we belong and **internalize** them as our own. Socialization involves developing ideas and gaining skills to become functioning members of society. **Primary socialization** occurs in childhood when parents have the most responsibility for shaping their children's behavior to fit the worlds they will enter. Children essentially learn to become human by learning their culture and by developing a self-concept befitting it. Yet, children not only absorb the culture of their parents, they also learn the culture of their peers. As William Corsaro (2003) observes, kids are social; they want to be part of a group.

**Secondary socialization** occurs as people enter new social worlds beyond their childhood families and learn how to act within them. Through secondary socialization, people learn the rules of these new worlds and their roles within them. Schools, professions, workplaces, team sports, neighborhoods, and churches are common sites of secondary socialization.

## Sociological Perspectives on Socialization

Two perspectives of socialization have dominated sociological discourse and are particularly evident in discussions of childhood socialization (Handel 2011; Handel, Cahill, and Elkin 2007; House 1977). The structural perspective assumes adults are the **socializing agents** who impart the norms and values of their societies and groups to children (Inkeles 1968; Parsons and Bales 1955). This perspective sees adults as playing active roles and children as passive recipients of socialization processes.[1]

> *The structural view assumes adults are the socializing agents who impart the norms and values of their societies and groups to children. This view sees adults as playing active roles and children as passive recipients of socialization processes.*

In the structural perspective, socialization proceeds as a one-way process: downward. Children are the products of society and become fully functioning members when they become adults. In the meantime, adults have the task of taming and controlling children through socialization. Parents exert control to enable their children's safe passage to adulthood and, moreover, to prescribe certain actions and proscribe others in keeping with cultural beliefs about appropriate behavior. In this perspective, socializing agents essentially control resources, actions and goals, behavior of those being socialized, and the outcomes of socialization.

Thus, in the structural perspective, effective childhood socialization means internalized social control – **self-control**. External agents no longer need to exert constraints; the properly socialized youth voluntarily follows them. Effective socialization here also means the orderly **reproduction of society**. In short, the structural view of socialization assumes orderly societies and groups, control by socializing agents, continuity of values and beliefs, conformity to rules, and predictable outcomes.

Symbolic interactionist views of childhood socialization contrast with the structural view above. Symbolic interactionists see all socialization, including childhood socialization as a dynamic two-way, somewhat indeterminate process. Granted, adults have more control, but children can talk back and exert their will, as Cassie did. Cassie knew that she had a valuable resource – throwing an embarrassing tantrum in a public setting. The value of a public tantrum increases in settings where negative judgments of her mother's parenting skills can last. Adults and children respond to each other in reciprocal ways. Parents learn about their roles as well as children. Marie and Jonathan give Jonathan's mother a gentle lesson about the symbolic meaning of acknowledging Jonathan in one last wave goodbye. Consistent with its basic premises, symbolic interactionists view both children and adults as active, creative beings who influence the form, the content, and outcomes of their experience of socialization. In this view, conformity to cultural rules is not a given outcome of socialization. Innovation – and rejection – of these rules may occur along the way.

> *Symbolic interactionists see socialization as a dynamic two-way, somewhat indeterminate process. Consistent with its basic premises, symbolic interactionists view both children and adults as active, creative beings who influence the form, the content, and outcomes of their experience of socialization.*

Thus, symbolic interactionists make interaction and interpretation crucial dimensions of socialization. The context, form, content, and emotional tone of interaction affect meanings and outcomes for both presumed agents of socialization and their recipients. For symbolic interactionists, socialization is a lifelong process.

Settings and situations may shape the scenes where socialization occurs but people's interpretations and actions may vary within these scenes. Symbolic interactionists acknowledge that some socializing agents keep tight control over their charges in certain organizations, such as prisons. Yet prisoners sometimes rebel against this control and exert their own influences on prison culture.

So what is socialization from a symbolic interactionist perspective?

- It is a learning process.
- It is a teaching process.
- It is a giving process.
- It is a receiving process.
- It is an unfolding process.
- It is an interactive process.
- It is a two-way process.
- It is an on-going process – it doesn't end!

In short, socialization ensues in the rhythms, events, and interactions of each day, whether or not we are aware of what we are learning and imparting to others.

## Conceptualizing Socialization

### Theoretical Perspectives of Socialization

George Herbert Mead's ([1934] 1962) analysis of the development of self has exerted lasting influence on symbolic interactionist perspectives about socialization. As you saw in Chapter 2, Mead treats the development of self as occurring when children come to possess a "me" and can treat themselves as objects. Hence, they can evaluate their own actions, as they would evaluate other people's actions. To possess a "me," a child adopts and internalizes the views, values, and norms of his or her family and community. For Mead, the self consists of the continuous inner conversation between the impulsive "I" and the reflexive "me."

This conversation develops as children acquire language and thus can use words to make sense of their respective worlds. Mead distinguished between "**gestures**" and "**significant symbols**." He defined gestures as instinctual responses of animals that did not entail language such as a dog's bark or growl when confronted with a strange dog.[2] For Mead ([1934] 1962:42–43), dogs engaged in a "conversation of gestures," as they react to each other but do so without awareness how their gesture influences the other dog.

Awareness and shared language, however, enable a child to assess gestures and responses to them. For Mead ([1934] 1962:47), language allows a conversation of significant symbols. Words and gestures become significant symbols when they evoke the same meaning to those with whom the child interacts as they do in the child. Subsequently, this shared meaning permits children to communicate their views, intentions and experiences and to interpret those of others. In the United States, for example, a gesture may be instantly understood: seven-year-old Tommy beckons his class-mate: Tommy catches Billy's eye across the playground and then Tommy curls his index finger several times to tell Billy to come join him. In the U.S., this gesture is an invitation. However, in other countries, such as the Philippines, it is deeply insulting and only used to call dogs.

*A significant symbol evokes the same meaning to those with whom the child interacts as they do in the child. This shared meaning permits children to communicate their views, intentions, and experiences and to interpret those of others.*

A crucial aspect of shared meanings is that people can thus communicate about ideas beyond the concrete world. The shared meaning calls forth the same response in the other that the child holds. For example, if eight-year-old Emma tells you that no one will play with her during recess at school, you gain a sense of Emma's situation and its meaning to and for her. We can imagine what it is like to be isolated on the playground and Emma's feelings about her peers and school.

As also occurs with adults, the conversation between the "I" and the "me" is continuous but usually occurs so quickly that the child is not conscious of it. When actions and events become problematic, however, then this reflexive process slows down. During such moments, people ponder their past actions and present predicament. The reflexive me allows people to monitor their own behavior, but it also enables them to make at least some choices about what they will do and how they will do it. This purposeful, meaningful action is referred to as "agency." Having agency means that people can make autonomous decisions and engage in independent actions. In short, the "me" gives us possibilities for agency as well as self-control.

Recall from Chapter 2 that Mead ([1934] 1962) saw role-taking as a crucial part of the development of self. Through role-taking, we can imagine the other person's perspective, situation, and role and, thus, understand his or her behavior. From this understanding, we can construct our own response to the other person. As Gil Musolf (1996) points out, children's role-taking and language acquisition develop through interacting with their families, peers, and communities. Interaction, through indicating, responding, cooperating, collaborating, negotiating, resisting, is pivotal for role-taking and language acquisition and thus also for children's agency.[3]

Mead ([1934] 1962) contended that children learn to understand the perspectives and actions of others through moving from a **preparatory stage** to **organized conduct** that involves responding to multiple roles. The preparatory stage occurs before a child's self has developed. It is a stage during which children imitate their parents' and siblings' roles but do not understand their own roles as distinctive. The mother reaches for the baby doll; then the child reaches for it, too. The mother points to the doll and says "baby"; the child echoes saying "baba." In this stage, children can only imitate but do not understand meanings of gestures and words. Mead contends that understanding meanings relies on role-taking. When children cannot yet engage in role-taking, they cannot moderate their own roles in response to those of others. To do so requires words and symbols, which a young child does not possess.

But with time and repeated responses, children begin to learn words and take themselves as objects in their worlds. They come to learn their names and those of others. As they learn to make distinctions among people and things, they start to reflect on their behavior and assess themselves.

The **play stage** accompanies language acquisition as children begin to share meanings of words with their families and people around them. At this point, children learn to mimic roles while playing that they have observed, such as their parents' roles. Thus, they may play at driving a car, cooking dinner, feeding the cat, or disciplining little sister. A child may mirror the same words, tone, and body language of the parent while playing the parental role. During the play stage, children practice the role they adopt, although they often move rapidly from one role to another, such as moving from being Mommy to their preschool teacher within a couple minutes. Mead ([1934] 1962) viewed children in this stage as being able to play one role at a time but not able to integrate multiple roles in the situation. Their rapid changes from one role to a different role indicated to Mead that children's selves had not yet jelled into a distinctive organized whole. Rather, their behavior remains unpredictable and inconsistent during play, as is the extent of their role-taking. Children begin to learn to respond to themselves as others respond to them but lack a clear understanding of the web of relationships embedded in the roles they play. Their understanding grows, however, as they enter and master what Mead calls the game stage.

During the **game stage** children learn to respond to multiple roles simultaneously. Mead ([1934] 1962) argues that participating in games requires a more sophisticated awareness of self and others and their respective roles than occurs in the play stage. Games are organized while play is not. Thus, children must take varied participants' specific roles, assess these roles in accord with the rules of the game and the coaches' directives, and construct their own role in response. In Mead's example of baseball, the child must take the role of each player, to see the scene and the plays from their respective vantage points. Moreover, children come to understand various team members are expected to enact their roles. As we pointed out in Chapter 2, complicated games like baseball or soccer teach children to take the role of the **generalized other**. One of us, Leslie, relates an astute observation by one of her students. He told her that kids as young as three "play" soccer, but as you watch them, you see them all cluster around the ball. Kids that young cannot understand that "playing" soccer means not everyone follows the ball. Only when they're a bit older can they accept that the game of soccer requires taking different positions around the field. Thus, they have learned to respond to the perspectives and actions of all other team members and to construct their own roles accordingly.

Mead's ([1934] 1962) analysis assumes a generalized other shared by all members of society. Norms and values would be shared. However, members of many contemporary societies are part of diverse groups, each with its own set of norms and values that may not be compatible. As a result, people often experience **role conflict**. Think of Imani Evans's (Tucker 2013) situation in Chapter 2. She wanted to be the loving daughter who cared for her mother and also wanted to pursue her education but the respective roles conflicted.

Symbolic interactionists have questioned the usefulness of stage theories of socialization, including Mead's (Cahill 1986; Denzin 1977). Empirical studies from Denzin's (1977) research in preschools to the present also question the notion of fixed stages of child development that assume biological determinism. Rather, the social context matters and the quality of interaction within it shapes the extent to which the child engages in role-taking and gains a developed self.

More recently, Leslie (Irvine 2004), has advanced a significant critique of Mead's analysis of socialization. Through her studies of people and their companion animals, Irvine concludes that Mead relies too heavily on language for self-development. She argues that the subjectivity constituting a "core" self-derives from the coalescence of other factors such as having a sense of the following: agency, bodily coherence, affectivity, and self-history. Companion animals then develop selves and can share meanings and emotions without language.

Any theory of childhood rests on assumptions about what a child is. Think about your own conception of children. Is a child a unique individual? A deficient adult? An untamed little animal? A vulnerable being? A developing person? (see also Esser et al. 2016). The conception we hold about what a child is shapes our expectations of children and the rights we view as due to them.

## Types of Socializing Experiences

In the following pages, we will address how socialization processes play out in varied groups and situations. But first, it may be helpful to think about types of socializing experiences, the range between them, and how they affect the lives of individuals. In the chart in Figure 3.1, we draw attention to two extremes types of socialization processes for individuals who are subject to them: those in which the socializing agents have maximum control in contrast with those in which the people being socialized have maximum agency.

When we think of socialization occurring when the individual is subject to maximum control, we think of situations with harsh constraints, such as prisons, boot camps, cults, and orphanages of yesteryear. Informal socialization occurring in more egalitarian relationships, however, opens possibilities for the person's autonomy to increase. Perhaps no socialization experience reflects all the listed characteristics; however, these characteristics give you tools for understanding a variety of experiences and for noting distinctions between them. For example, for some individuals volunteering for the military may mean a separation from their past lives but remains congruent with key values

| MAXIMUM CONTROL | MAXIMUM AGENCY |
|---|---|
| **Occurs through** | **Occurs through** |
| Imposed constraints | Chosen pursuits |
| Degradation, abuse, punishments | Growth, approval, rewards |
| Forced passivity | Active involvement |
| Severance from past life | Congruence with past life |
| Involuntary participation | Voluntary participation |
| Control over all areas of daily life | Choice in main areas of daily life |
|  |  |
| **Consequences for the individual** | **Consequences for the individual** |
| Lose autonomy | Expand agency |
| Mortification of self | Increased self-respect |
| Loss of past self, identities, health | Gain valued self and identities |
| Anonymous existence | Intimacy |
| Forced reconstruction of self | Development of prior self |
| Lose former worlds; live under constant surveillance and control | Gain access to desired new worlds; strengthen position in earlier world |

**Figure 3.1** Types of socialization experiences.

of the past. For a kidnapped boy forced into serving a militia at war against his people, however, such involuntary severance from his past life likely is encompassing.

The nature of the socialization process matters, as does the conditions under which it ensues. Both affect what being socialized means to experiencing individuals and their stance toward it. Context and situation are important, as is evident from the chart in Figure 3.1. As you can tell, the answers to the following questions would also shape a person's experiences of the socialization process and stance toward it.

- Is the person aware or unaware of the socialization process?
- Is this process awaited or unanticipated?
- Was it something the person desired or dreaded?
- Is the person committed, indifferent, or resistant to it?
- Does the person view the socialization process as momentous or mundane?
- Does the person hold realistic expectations or false hopes?
- Does a person view the socialization process as reversible or irreversible?

The questions point to the significance of how the person defines the situation. This definition is consequential for what occurs. Perhaps most commonly, people see themselves as just living and dealing with what comes up in daily life and what they need and want to do. All the while, little lessons unfold, and choices are made shaping who they are and become. Thus, much socialization occurs without people giving much thought to it. Hence, they may be unaware of how they are being influenced in daily life and how they affect other people.

## Socialization in Childhood

### Infants and Agency

Most researchers who study childhood have treated it as a social construction in which children were active creators of their own lives. Nonetheless, these researchers also considered the contexts and contingencies of children's lives given in their social statuses such as gender, sexuality, social class, race, religion, and health (Esser et al. 2016). Although few symbolic interactionists have studied infancy, several studies indicate that parents and babies make sense of each other's responses. If so, babies are interpreting their situations long before they have language. Chris Nash, Jenny Morris, and Benny Goodman (2008) conducted interviews with mothers of infants from three months to one year of age. The mothers said their babies not only seemed to cry to gain their attention but also reacted to arguments between parents and seemed frightened.

Children develop ways to making their needs known. In her detailed study of eight French-speaking families in Switzerland, Sara Keel (2016) videotaped and analyzed multiple interactions of everyday family life. She chose families with at least two children, one of whom had to be between two and three years old. Keel found that these young children appeared to sense ambiguities and contradictions in their parents' expectations of them and subsequently perceived possibilities for subversion and negotiation. For example, the children made nuanced assessments of their situations and immediate interactions and attempted to gain their parents' concurrence of their assessment, such as permission to skip eating a disliked food. These children attempt to expand their choices and shape what occurs and they learn to do it in effective ways.

Keel found that small children engage in what she calls "**noticing**" to elicit their parent's response. Through fixing their gaze, they may make a request or tell what they notice to obtain their parent's attention and involve him or her in what concerns them. The child attempts to control the interaction and its outcome. In their study in Australia, Sandra Cheeseman and Sumsion (2016) found that even younger children attempt to engage others in meaningful interactions although no words may be spoken. These researchers used visual narratives to get a closer view of infants' perspectives. One of their field workers had played with a 19-month-old girl named Clare the week before. When the field worker returned, Clare used her gaze to engage the fieldworker to participate in the game again. The fieldworker wrote:

> Her recall of the game from the previous week indicates a considerable capacity to make meaning and transfer her knowledge of a game in the outdoors to a similar game in the indoors one week later. Significant here, though, is her ability to demonstrate her memory of the game and use sophisticated body language and eye contact as an invitation to me to notice her recall. In the second encounter, her strong use of eye contact drew me into her intent. It required of me attentiveness and attunement. Attunement in this sense is understood as a sensitivity to the infant's invitation – the willingness to stand back and enable the child to lead the encounter, tentatively seeking possible meaning from the infant's actions. (Cheeseman and Sumsion 2016:284)

In this encounter, note that Clare revealed intention, initiative, and acknowledgment of the relationship. Researchers who study infants and toddlers have paid close attention to interactions between these children and adults, particularly their parents. Children also influenced each other, even in their very early years. They attend to the words and actions of their peers, as we saw in this chapter's opening anecdote about Cassie. Hanne Warming (2011) argues that small children's perspectives are not fixed. Rather their interactions can alter their views to arrive at a mutuality of perspectives. Thus, these interactions change their behavior. Warming (2011:41) offers the following example as evidence from her fieldwork in a Danish daycare facility:

> Tobias is hurt, his knee is bleeding, and he is crying. Balder arrives. He looks at Tobias' knee.
> "Congratulations!" He says in a happy voice. "I've hurt my knee too."
> Tobias smiles, but tears are still running down his chin: "But it hurts!" He snuffles.
> "Mmm, that's true," Balder says perceptively, nodding his head. (Warming 2011:41)

Warming observes that Balder's cheerful view of bleeding knees contrasts with Tobias's and challenges notions that the encounter merely represents individualistic perspectives. Instead through interaction and negotiation of meaning, the boys' contrasting views meld into a shared view. Tobias smiles in response to Balder while still crying. In turn, Balder agrees that bleeding knees do hurt (Warming 2011:41–42). The exchange between Balder and Tobias exemplifies the significance of interaction for establishing meaning of an incident.

## Parents and Children

Parental backgrounds and priorities are played out in child-rearing. In her ethnographic study, *The Color of Love: Racial Features, Stigma & Socialization in Black Brazilian Families*, Elizabeth Hordge-Freeman (2015) brings race into focus in her research about people of African descent in a Brazilian community. She makes racial hierarchies explicit and shows how they are reproduced in ten Afro-Brazilian families. Hordge-Freeman found that skin color and hair texture made a decided difference in how parents treated their children from the time they were born. Dark-skinned children received less attention, fewer resources, and less love than their lighter-skinned siblings. Not only did these children receive less, but also their possibilities for agency shrunk. They experienced inequities within and beyond the family that echoed throughout their lives.

Social class differences in parenting styles and priorities have long been documented in studies in the U.S. (Coles 1977; Cookson and Persell 1985; Kohn 1979). Middle-class parents allow children to make choices, value the child's expressiveness and creativity, discuss and negotiate rules, and explain how, why, and when infractions will result in punishment. In contrast, working class parents are more likely to have firm expectations for obedience and to set limits without explanation.

In the U.S., middle-class parents' time becomes organized around children's activities. Annette Lareau (2011:2) calls middle-class socialization "**concerted cultivation**" in which the parent nurtures the child's talents, encourages his or her opinions, and supports the child's developing skills. Lareau juxtaposes this parenting style with that of "accomplishment of natural growth" (Lareau 2011:3) in which children spend more time with peers. Their relationships with adults are hierarchical and predicated on expectations of obedience to adult dictates. These children are more likely to feel uncomfortable in organizational settings than middle-class children and they are less likely to be successful in school.

Lareau found substantial differences occur between middle-class white children and African American working-class school children. Middle-class children's home involvements resemble school activities and tasks. The social class differences that Lareau documents in school-aged children likely begin far earlier in child care settings and preschools (Nelson and Schutz 2007).

The parents that Danielle K. Estes (2011) studied exemplify Lareau's concept of concerted cultivation. Estes examined how students who pursue higher education view and handle the contradictory time demands of simultaneously being diligent students and good parents. She reports that images of the "bad parent" intensified her research participants' resolve to devote time to their kids. She also finds that the fathers adopted an expanded role that blurred with those of mothers. The student fathers believed they should provide their children with emotional as well as financial support and participate in housework. James, a 36-year-old graduate student said:

> The very first thing is Randy [son]. He is most important. He is our first priority, so any classes he is in, any of these extra things, they're not extras. It's priority. ... We went to great lengths to socialize him ... swimming classes ... gymnastics. We wanted parental bonds. ... I wanted to make sure that there was that kind of emotional beginning.
>
> ... From the time my son was about eight months old until actually the start of this semester [about a year], I've been the primary caregiver of Randy. ... Even when I was going to school full-time, I was purposely setting aside one or two days a week for Daddy day. ... Both of us feel fairly strongly that being a parent is a responsibility. (Estes 2011:207)

Little Randy not only has involved parents but also lives in a safe but stimulating environment and has multiple learning experiences while still a baby. Such student-parents often lack money and time but they make time for diverse interactions with their children.

Yet the struggle of obtaining bare necessities to survive can bar impoverished parents from devoting time to their children. Graduate students may be able to extend the time of their education; parents who struggle to survive cannot make such time extensions. Richardson, Johnson, and Vil (2014) report that many impoverished African-American parents have no resources at all. No trusted family nearby, no fictive kin, no money, and little time. These authors report that exhausted parents of troubled children in New York City could spend no more than 30 minutes a day with them and they mostly watched television together. The parents often worked seven-day weeks with double shifts and were too tired to attend school meetings or take their children on outings. The children lacked parental oversight, help, and sustained interaction. Richardson et al. (2014:15) portray this situation in Harriet Jones' story:

> Harriett Jones, single mother of Hasan (age 14) spent much of her time working. She worked multiple shifts as a manager at a fast-food restaurant to support her two children, leaving little time to supervise and monitor their activities.
>
> "Lately, I've been working almost seven days a week. So I have been worried about Hasan a lot. I told my boss about my concerns regarding my son being unsupervised and my boss told me to take some time off, but I worry about whether my job will still be there when I come back so I don't want to take a temporary leave."

Several of the parents in Richardson et al.'s study made valiant efforts to change the path of their troubled children through choosing new pursuits, changing their schools and enlisting the help of experts. Sly Sr. talked of how he and his wife had tried to introduce positive changes in Sly Jr.'s life:

> First we enrolled Sly in Harlem Boys Prep (an elite private school for black males) because he was a really good singer and dancer.... That school was great, it was a good school. But he was only in that school for a hot minute. He got kicked out for taking a knife to school and threatening to kill another little boy. So we had to put him in the neighborhood public school, which wasn't too good. So I tried to put Sly in the Harlem Boys Club to give him something constructive to do. But then they had to put Sly out of the club because of his temper and he just wouldn't listen.... With Sly, he'll be into something for the first week. For about a week he will be interested. But once he gets with a group of his hoodlum friends, he'll decide that he would rather be out on the street. Running around with a crew of guys, it's more exciting on the streets for him. That way he gets to create and control his own excitement. (Richardson et al. 2014:20)

As Sly Sr. gave up trying to use community resources, he and his wife, Lydia, increasingly leaned toward getting help from the juvenile justice system. Lydia came to view the staff at juvenile court as her "only reliable and trustworthy social tie" (Richardson et al. 2014:21). By then, she said that going to court was "the only activity Sly and I ever did together" (Richardson et al. 2014:21). Yet Sly Jr. continues to be socialized, but not by his parents and teachers.

## Peers and Socialization

Peers form an important source of perspective and reference for children's behavior. They serve what sociologists call a **reference group** (Shibutani 1955), which means any group that we use as a standard for evaluating ourselves, including our views, situations, and actions. A reference group consists of people whose perspective we use to interpret our experiences. We identify with certain reference groups, seeing how well our behaviors, attitudes, and appearances measure up to theirs. Sly Jr., for example, identified with his friends on the street and adopted their views, values, and actions. They became his main reference group overshadowing all others.

*A reference group is any group that people use as a standard for evaluating themselves, their views, their situations, and their own actions.*

Children attempt to make themselves acceptable to their peers and to gain or maintain access to valued peer groups. In their study of homeless kids in San Francisco, Roschelle and Kaufman (2004) discovered that the children learned to hide being homeless. These children had absorbed the shame of homelessness that their peers and the public conferred upon it. One girl, Jamie, said, "I always feel like people are looking at me because they know I am poor and they think I am a loser." When Anne asked how they hid their homelessness, Jamie gave this explanation:

JAMIE: I try and dress like the other kids in my school. When we get clothes from Home Away [the shelter], I always pick stuff that is stylin' and keep it clean so kids won't know I'm poor. Sometimes it's hard though because all the kids try and get the cool stuff and there isn't always enough for everyone. I really like it when we get donations from people who shop at The Gap and Old Navy. I got one of those cool vests last week and it made me feel really great.

ANNE: Is it important for you to keep your homelessness a secret?

JAMIE: Yeah, I would die if the kids at school knew.

(Roschelle and Kaufman 2004:34)

Jamie's clothes and self-presentation keep her identity as homeless hidden, so she avoids being shamed and ostracized. She also maintains continuity with her earlier life when her family had a home but what matters most now to Jamie is how she appears to her peers.

Judgment by peers can have lasting effects. Students like Jamie may only wish to "pass" as ordinary kids, but popularity and clique status can mold formidable hierarchies. As Adler and Adler (1998) contend, popularity equals peer prestige and clique membership among U.S. preteens. They find that boys' popularity rests on their athletic ability, "cool" self-presentation, tough attitudes, popular girlfriends, and *savoir faire*, or the awareness and poise to do the smart or cool thing. Girls' popularity derives from their family's social class status (as marked by their brand name clothes), attractiveness, social shrewdness, personal freedom and permissive parents, and ability to form an elite clique. In these preteen groups, boys' academic performance could not exceed their peers but girls could excel without peer sanctions.

Clique culture solidifies dominance, exclusivity, in-group bonds, and out-group subjugation. An **in-group** is a group with which we identify and believe we share distinctive characteristics whereas an **out-group** is one with whom we do not identify and often seek to denigrate (Tajfel 1982). High-status clique members may extend their control by bullying less-popular children.

*An in-group is a group with which we identify and believe we share distinctive characteristics whereas an out-group is one with whom we do not identify and often seek to denigrate.*

The effects of being bullied are often long-lasting and result in what Robert Thornberg et al. (2013) call "**double victimizing**." The child first internalizes the negative images of self-given in their peers stigmatizing actions and words. The child then distrusts others and experiences self-doubt, self-blame, and resignation. Simultaneously, these children develop self-protecting strategies such as isolating themselves and constricting their actions that often confirm the bullies' claims about them. Thornberg and his colleagues in Sweden find that being bullied in school results in a lingering internal victimizing. Many years after schoolyard bullying had ended, the internal victimizing continues as the adult experiences the same kind of self-doubt and self-blame as experienced in childhood.

When peers pull together, they may replace adults as the suppliers of socialization such as occurs with gangs. Gangs can become substitute families and prescribe a round of life for their members. Street children may draw upon peer support without belonging to a gang. When impoverished children have no parents, other children often become the dominant players in each other's socialization. For street children, socialization means learning ways to obtain food and avoid danger. Phillip Mizen and Yaw Ofosu-Kusi (2010) show how street children in Accra form fragile friendships with reciprocities and pooled resources to survive. Food reciprocities between friends enable children to eat something when they have no money. Sleeping together in intertwined groups increases safety from theft and sexual assault, a major concern of girls and younger boys. Night-time raids by other street gangs make sleeping fraught with danger. One boy said, "if you're going to sleep and have money, it will be stolen before the next day. They use blades to cut your clothes so they can get hold of the money" (Mizen and Ofosu-Kusi 2010:450). The authors also observe:

> For girls, theft takes on a more menacing presence as it fuses with the fear, in the words of Anna (female, 15) "that the boys will come and cut my dress into pieces and try to assault me sexually." By sleeping close to one another the children achieve a greater degree of security derived from the reassuring physical presence of friends and a greater strength in numbers. (Mizen and Ofosu-Kusi 2010:450)

Maureen Kendrick and Doris Kakuru (2012) studied child-headed households in Uganda, which included children 17 and under who lost both parents after relocation and lived on their own. Kendrick and Kakuru report that in 2008, estimates included 1,000 child-headed families. They surmise that these children doubly experienced stigma (see Chapter 6 for an extended discussion of stigma). The stigma of their parents having AIDS first led their families to relocate. Subsequently, the stigma of the parents' death precluded the children from returning to the area where they had extended family.

In their case study of one family of six orphans, Kendrick and Kakuru show how the impoverished siblings dealt with the dilemma between caring for the youngest child or attending school, which had the only available access to resources for orphans. Debbie, the authors' Ugandan research assistant, talks with two of the siblings:

DEBBIE: ... didn't you have relatives to come up and take you people because you are so young? Take me back. [Debbie is asking to know how the siblings were left without relatives]

IBRA: There wasn't anyone who came to assist us or even check on us after the death of our parents.

DEBBIE: They left you in this house?

IBRA: Yes.

DEBBIE: Even that baby?

IBRA: Yes.

DEBBIE: You mean you are the ones who have taken care of him till today or up to where he is? ... Now, tell me about this young one, where do you leave him when you are going to school?

WINNIE: When we are going to school, we leave the young one in the neighborhood with leftovers to eat at lunchtime then pick him up in the evening when we come back.

DEBBIE: Doesn't he cry?

WINNIE: We have nothing [else] to do.

(Kendrick and Kakuru 2012:401–402)

None of the siblings had sufficient knowledge and skill to parent and mentor the younger children. However, each sibling contributed whatever skills and resources he or she had. Together the siblings constructed new knowledge and practices to survive. Kendrick and Kakuru (2012:411) state, "Their strong desire to survive, develop positive social identities, become contributing members of their community, and remain together as a family forced them to invest in new practices, relationships, and knowledge." Thus, these siblings' commitment to each other and active involvement in maintaining daily life prompted them to learn new modes of survival in a desperate situation.

In this case, the siblings shared a definition of family and what being a family meant. Their high degree of commitment and cooperation contrasts with sibling relationships in British sociologist Samantha Punch's (2008:36) study. She writes:

> Sibship is a relationship in which the boundaries of social interaction can be pushed to the limit. Rage and irritation need not be suppressed, whilst politeness and toleration can be neglected: "You can do nasty things to your brothers and sisters without a reason … you can just tease them if you're bored." (Sarah 13, middle child)

In Punch's research, the sibling relationships occurred on the backstage of social life – without visibility and constraint. Younger children and animals may become abused scapegoats of their older siblings. Yet backstage relationships are not always the site for meanness. These relationships can also be a private site for trust, support, reciprocity, and sharing disclosures. Here, the lack of visibility and constraint releases children from their public roles. Friendships between children involve some degree of choice. Korkiama (2011) studied teenagers' friendships in Finland. She contends that teens construct their peer relationships "both on the public frontstage of 'friendships' and on the intimate backstage of 'special friendships'" (Korkiama 2011:112). Fourteen-year-old Jenna divided her peers into acquaintances, friends, special friends, and best friends. Korkiama (2011:108) shows that children enact peer relations on multiple stages, depending on their friendship categories.

> JENNA:  Special friends and friends, … they are totally different. I mean with my friends I can hang out and chat and all, and there's lots of them and they are fun, but … when I take a real friend, it's like, I really want to talk about my problems and I trust her, … I know what I can talk about. With those other friends I don't. So it's trust, it's all that, you can talk about your stuff, it's togetherness and, you don't really have secrets from your best friends, when you are with them, at home or something, we talk a lot on the net using messenger, too, so you shouldn't really keep any secrets. (Adapted from Korkiama 2011:108)

## Adult Socialization

### Involvements and Evolvements

As we enter new situations, we try to learn the requirements for functioning within them. When we face official situations, such as being stopped for speeding or going through security at an airport, we wish to conclude the encounter and exit from the situation as soon as possible without further involvement. In the United States, that possibility may not exist for African Americans, Hispanics, and people with Middle Eastern names. The only African American Republican senator, Tim Scott, reports that while he was driving police officers had pulled him over seven times in one year when he was an elected official (Barrón-López 2016).

Azeem Khan (2013) writes of the embarrassing "random" searches he endures every time he goes through an airport. After an incident, he writes:

> This was supposedly a random search. But it wasn't a random search at all. It was a "you're a Muslim" search. I'm tired of being told that it's a random search every single time. I have fewer rights when I walk into an airport because I'm brown. I always have to feel on edge because I know I'm being looked at suspiciously, and not being I've done anything wrong, but because I'm one of the two million Muslims living in this country in a post 9/11 era.

> I get it. My name is Azeem Khan. It's not James Williams. That's why I got picked. It wasn't random. I understand that. So does the person telling me it's random.

Both Scott and Khan find themselves subject to unwanted and undeserved involvements with authorities. Such incidents proclaim each man's identity as someone whom the officials declined to trust. These incidents become lessons in socialization and symbols of the reduced social worth that these officials accord to each man. The incidents become **negative reference points**.

In contrast, getting a coveted job becomes a positive reference point. At these times, people are attuned to cues and suggestions. In formal organizations like schools and corporations, seasoned members often gladly show and tell newcomers how to behave and what to do. Newcomers likely seek and appreciate such socialization when they are committed to keeping the job. Here, socialization is voluntary, active, and likely contributes to the person's sense of development. The job interview, first day at work, being assigned to unfamiliar tasks all may become long-remembered marker events.

Much socialization in adult life, however, occurs without distinctive markers and clear points of reference. Instead, socialization occurs through everyday decisions and actions. Recall Anselm Strauss's (1959:37) insight in Chapter 2: "Involvements are evolvements." Our involvements testify to who we are, who we are becoming, and who influences this process.

Performing well on the job concerns many workers. Yet they may not always have clear criteria for their actions and ways to assuage a poor outcome. Some decisions hold serious consequences. Ken Kolb (2011) studied victim's advocates and counselors in an organization that served clients who had experienced domestic violence and/or sexual assault. Their efforts to empower clients sometimes went awry. Kolb found that by predefining and redefining unanticipated negative outcomes, both groups could interpret what happened as being beyond their responsibility. The counselors' professional claims of competence, however, insulated them from the negative results more than the advocates (pp. 87–89). Perhaps the counselors' collective and credentialed language of competence increased their protection from nagging self-scrutiny over failing a client who had a negative outcome.

How we handle our involvements matters. When people weigh possible solutions to problems they share, such as those at work, they usually arrive at an agreement about what to do and thus shape their subsequent socialization. Becker (1956) found that medical students soon realized the impossibility of learning all the information presented to them. Subsequently, the students attempted to learn what they predicted will appear on the exams rather than mastering everything. Their solution arose from discussions with their peers, who also adopted this strategy.

Now think about further implications of forging shared solutions. What are the effects on the group? What do you feel about fellow students with whom you solve a knotty problem? Agreements arising from members' active participation build trust and loyalty between them. Hence, a close work group or cohort in training can ignore, redefine, or renegotiate expected standards more easily and effectively than an individual.

Consistency of action, commitment to line of action, and congruence between situations over time make socialization seamless. Matthew Desmond (2006) learned that rookie wildland firefighters had already become individuals whose very beings suited firefighting *before* they joined the United States Forest Service. Desmond (2006:397) states, "Their embodied outdoorsmanship acquired through a rural upbringing – the way a hand grips an axe, the way a foot mounts a trail – is directly bound up with their core sense of self, their masculinity and identity." The work of fighting fires extended their country masculinity while the battles of the Forest Service fit how they defined themselves and viewed the world. Desmond writes:

> They must join in the various symbolic battles in which the Forest Service engages, battles over legitimation and classification, one of the most active and charged of which is the fight against environmentalist groups over the right to manage the forest. And if crewmembers have little trouble comprehending the stakes and choosing sides in such a battle, it is because the principles of vision and division at work within

the US Forest Service align succinctly with the principles of vision and division of country masculinity. (Desmond 2006:405)

Thus, when workers see their values and goals as essentially consistent with their employers, their everyday interactions further solidify pursuing shared goals. The commitment the wildland firefighters already possessed to rural life fit the Forest Service. Commitments produce stability – for both the individual and the organization.

Socialization occurs through interactions at multiple levels, as Ara Francis (2015) shows in her study of trouble in families. Parents' hopes for and expectations of their child were compromised, if not crushed, when they discovered that their child had a difficult problem such as a learning disability, physical disability, mental illness, or drug addiction. These parents often aimed to re-socialize their troubled children but they themselves had to learn new ways of being parents. Their commitment to help changed them. Hence, some parents gained new perspectives and views of themselves as they compared themselves and their situations with other parents.

Francis (2015:116) tells of Steve and Marie's visit to their daughter's therapeutic boarding school. They had sent their 17-year-old daughter to the school because of her cocaine addiction.

> STEVE:   Boy, [Marie] and I, when we flew home on that plane from that first visit when it was parent seminar thing, I mean, we looked at each other and said, "my god, everybody's got a story." I mean, what an eye-opener that was! … I mean, we've been through the mill… [but] it's nothing compared to some of these multi-year, two- and three-year battles with some of these kids.
>
> MARIE:   We felt fortunate.

Francis states that Steve and Marie altered their own narrative by comparing their situation with those of the other parents. She notes that other parents' stories prompted Stephen and Marie to "talk about empathy and gratitude instead of isolation and despair" (Francis 2015:116). Such experiences can become turning points, an awakening in which people see their situations in new light (DeGloma 2014). Parents like Steve and Marie can then develop a new story to redefine their situations and change their course of action.

## Total Institutions and Remaking the Self

Recall Figure 3.1 in which the socialization experience derives from constraints. Erving Goffman (1959) coined the term "**total institution**" to depict a setting in which supervised residents eat, play, and sleep in the same location, separate from the larger community from which they may be barred. In Goffman's analysis, total institutions depict the extreme form of settings which impose strict constraints on the residents' daily life and subject them to an intensive socialization to fit the purpose of the institution.

> *A total institution is a setting in which the residents, eat, play, and sleep in the same location, separate from the larger community from which they may be barred. Total institutions impose constraints on the residents' daily life and subject them to an intensive socialization to fit the purpose of the institution.*

The all-encompassing nature of the total institution disconnects the stable arrangements on which the residents' prior selves had been based and strips their selves from these arrangements. The staff further disconnects residents' selves by confiscating or disallowing their "**identity kits**." These kits consist of items such as make-up, clothes, jewelry, and possessions that people had used to present an identity (Goffman 1961:21). Not only is your shampoo part of your identity kit but also your hairstyle, cell phone, and computer are part of it. The institution replaces new residents' identity kits with its own standardized items issued to all residents. Staff evaluate, sort, and process these individuals to acquire the new self-prescribed by the institution. A large batch of residents are supervised by a small staff who exclude them from decisions about their lives. For example, an army officer may order troops to assemble in trucks but not tell them where they will be transported.

Total institutions include concentration camps, prisons, and nursing homes. Although the above description may sound like mental hospitals of yesteryear, patients, inmates, and students may still find themselves sharply constrained by institutional policies and professional practices while residing in a total institution. In the story below, a woman with lupus erythematosus[4] had entered a hospital to have her medications reevaluated and changed. Her friends took her to the local emergency department because they sensed that her behavior indicated serious medication problems. Instead of having her medications reviewed, she was sent to a mental hospital where her doctor ignored her physical condition. She said,

> I tried to tell him about some of the problems I had with my Lupus and stuff and angered him. [He had ordered her to take off her dark glasses.] And I wore [dark] glasses all the time and I tried to tell him, you know, that if he would turn off the fluorescent lights, I would take off the glasses. And he felt I was just being stubborn. I gave him the name and number of my doctor that makes the glasses and he just ripped it up in front of me and threw it away. And you have to go to group sessions all the time while you're there. I went, I just didn't speak to anybody. But I went. I went to everything they said I had to. And every day he'd say that he was going to lock me up again. After ten days he did. He called me in to this little room and there were these two big guys there and they grabbed me and put me on a gurney and tied me down. And he sent me

to a lockup ward, wouldn't let me make a call or do anything. And my potassium was down really bad and, I mean my whole – I was sick. They weren't giving me the pills that I needed and he just wouldn't even acknowledge that I had Lupus. It was bad. (Charmaz 2011:368)

Not all total institutions are viewed as coercive by those who are subject to their constraints. If they agree with the institutional goals, then they may find the constraints to be acceptable and often, positive. Thus, these individuals may see their respective treatment institutions, religious retreats, or boarding schools as lifesaving as well as life-changing. These fit what Susie Scott (2010, 2015) calls "**reinventive institutions**" where people choose to pursue self-improvement through such involvements as "intense self-reflection, education, enrichment and reform" (Scott 2010:218).

Certainly, individuals' commitment to institutional goals may vary and change. Families may urge an addicted loved one to enter a detoxification and treatment facility as a last resort. Parents may be enthusiastic about a school; their children may be less so. Yet, treatment programs and schools may leave a lasting positive imprint on their charges' sense of self and the direction of their lives. Avi Shoshana (2012) studied graduates of a special state boarding school in Israel. The state invented the concept of the "gifted disadvantaged," and conferred this distinction on selected students chosen for the school. Shoshana found that graduates experienced selfhood as shaped by the boarding school and as a phil-anthropic gift from the state. The graduates expressed their gratitude to the state. Shoshana proposes that attending this boarding school resulted in these gradu-ates experiencing their selfhood as "public property" (Shoshana 2012:186). The following reflection from Amir, a 1973 graduate, illustrates this point:

The meaning of the *new personality* that was created for me by my edu-cation at the boarding school, my persistence, my achievements, my intelligence, it's from the boarding school. Before the boarding school I was one thing, and after it I'm something else, as if there's two types of character, or a *first nature* and a *second nature,* as if the boarding school created me, I'm actually *Made in Israel* [laughs].... My life has gone through a critical movement, call it even a sharp turn, from my person-ality from before [the boarding school] to my personality afterwards. (Shoshana 2012:197)

## Conclusion

Symbolic interactionism treats socialization as a **lifelong** interactive process. Certainly, socialization during childhood is fundamental for learning how to conduct ourselves in our social worlds. But we may alter our conduct to fit our purposes. Interaction is crucial from the start. Infants and toddlers try to influence their parents and caregivers and later attempt to affect their siblings and peers' behavior. And as we have seen in this chapter, influencing others and being influenced by them does not stop.

We attend to expectations for us that we discover in new situations. We may reflect upon how we change from the turning points that mark our lives such as moving to another area of the country, getting married, and entering a profession. We may join groups which exert a powerful socialization such as the military or medical school and be aware of how it changes us as is Amir's awareness of how the Israeli boarding school affected him. Yet much socialization occurs without notice. We may not question how our daily interactions and decisions shape our involvements and evolvement. What may have seemed new and strange when we entered a situation may become taken for granted as we become accustomed to it.

Routine involvements affect our evolvement. Think about how your current and anticipated involvements complement or contrast with your past. Some involvements seamlessly align with our past like the firefighters Matthew Desmond studied. Others contrast with how we see ourselves and the choices we wish to make, such as Azeem Khan's repeatedly being singled out and searched at airports. To what extent do your current involvements reflect your interests and commitments? To what extent do you have control over your involvements and the directions they take you?

## Learning by Using the Symbolic Interactionist Perspective

The two excerpts below are from *Home Is Where the School Is* by Jennifer Lois (2013). See if you can use the concepts about socialization in this chapter to analyze these excerpts.

---

**Home Schooling Mothers' Role Conflict**

*Home Is Where the School Is*

**Jennifer Lois (2013):103, 145**

Some mothers felt the conflict between their roles as teacher and mother. Whitney McKee, the mother of 11-year-old Ritchie, described this tension in detail:

> "When you go from being a mother to being a mother-teacher, it's a real hard adjustment for both of you. My son, who teachers think walks on water and is considerate and polite and kind, ... becomes much more

---

demanding. And things [that] he would never do in school, he's very comfortable [doing] with me …. He falls apart. [He says], 'I can't do it,' and 'I need you.' He knows that I won't reject him, and that my love is unconditional for him, so he can push a little further. His teacher would never tolerate that kind of behavior. He is never rude [to me]. He never says mean things to me. But emotionally, yeah, a little more outbursts. But you just have to keep plowing ahead. … The easy thing would be [to say], 'let's just close the books.' But that's what he wants me to do. So you just keep pushing. And then you think, 'Why did I do this? Why am I here?'"

Whitney was torn between acting as a teacher, who would not tolerate such behavior and as a mother, who would tend to her child's emotional needs. Mothers often reported that emotional dynamics made a typical teacher-student relationship impossible; Whitney did not go from 'mother' to teacher, but to 'mother-teacher.'

…Darlene's husband, a physician in a group practice, 'got shoved out of his practice, and we were in a legal battle.' He could not find work locally, he was "in crisis," and she was 'holding the family together.' He finally found work in a nearby larger city, so they moved and enrolled the children in private high schools there (the public schools were "a mess"). At that point, Darlene "crashed" from the stress and took some time to 'recoup.' She 'was so ready to quit homeschooling [and] so ready to get back into the workforce,' but her daughter

> "lasted two weeks in her new ] private school [because of clique dynamics]…. She got depressed. She went through it so badly that everybody was just like, 'you've got to pull her; we've lost our Alexandra.' Within two weeks! It was pretty shocking…. I sat in on the school, and I went, 'Oh, my gosh, I see what she's seeing.' And it's not fair to her, and so I pulled her and homeschooled her. She didn't want to homeschool, and I didn't want to [do it]…. I really wasn't ready to be tied down again; I was ready to be free. That's how I felt after nine years of homeschooling – my son, and then part time, my daughter…. But you go with the flow. You do what you have to do for your kids."

## Notes

1 The term "socialization" has been strongly connected with the structural perspective. To acknowledge children's agency, now many contemporary researchers, particularly in Europe, view their research as contributing to studies of childhood and children. Debates in the US about the implications of the concept of socialization have ensued for over 20 years as researchers have expressed concern that the concept minimizes children's agency (Corsaro 1985, 1997; Handel, Cahill and Elkin 2007, Handel 2011; Thorne 1993).

2 Like other thinkers of his day, Mead viewed animals and humans as qualitatively different and sharply divided on their ability to manipulate symbols. Now many researchers see the difference between animals and humans as a matter of extent.

3 For a discussion of children's agency, see Oswell (2016).

4 Lupus is a general systemic autoimmune disease in which the person's body attacks its own cells and organs including the skin, joints, muscles, heart, kidneys, and brain. Patients experience overwhelming fatigue, fevers, pain, skin rashes, mouth and nasal sores, difficulty in breathing, inflamed joints, kidney problems, numbness of their fingers, and intolerance to light. Some lupus patients live in darkened rooms. Many avoid direct sunlight, fluorescent lighting, and wear dark glasses.

# References

Adler, P. A. and P. Adler. 1998. *Peer Power: Preadolescent Culture and Identity*. New Brunswick, NJ: Rutgers University Press.

Barrón-López, L. 2016. "Black GOP Senator Talks About Being Pulled Over by Police 7 Times in One Year." *Huffington Post*, July 15, 2016. http://www.huffingtonpost.com/entry/tim-scott-pulled-over_us_5786bfffe4b08608d332eaa0.

Becker, H. 1956. "Personal Change in Adult Life." *Sociometry* 27(March):40–53.

Cahill, S. E. 1986. "Language Practices and Self Definition: The Case of Gender Identity Acquisition." *The Sociological Quarterly* 27(3):295–311.

Charmaz, K. 2011. "Grounded Theory Methods in Social Justice Research." Pp. 359–380 in *Handbook of Qualitative Research*, 4th ed., edited by N. Denzin and Y. Lincoln. Thousand Oaks, CA: Sage.

Cheeseman, S. and J. Sumsion. 2016. "Narratives of Infants' Encounters with Curriculum: The Benediction as Invitation to Participate." *Contemporary Issues in Early Childhood* 17(3):275–288.

Coles, R. 1977. *Privileged Ones: The Well-Off and the Rich in America*. Boston, MA: Little Brown.

Cookson, P. and C. Persell. 1985. *Preparing for Power: America's Elite Boarding Schools*. New York: Basic Books.

Corsaro, W. 1985. *Friendship and Peer Culture in the Early Years*. Westport, CT: Greenwood.

Corsaro, W. 1997. *The Sociology of Childhood*. Thousand Oaks, CA: Pine Forge Press.

Corsaro, W. 2003. *"We're Friends, Right?": Inside Kids' Culture*. Washington, DC: Joseph Henry Press.

DeGloma, T. 2014. *Seeing the Light: The Social Logic of Personal Discovery*. Chicago, IL: University of Chicago Press.

Denzin, N. 1977. *Childhood Socialization*. San Francisco, CA: Jossey-Bass.

Desmond, M. 2006. "Becoming a Firefighter." *Ethnography* 7(4):387–421.

Esser, F., M. Baader, T. Betz, and B. Hungerland. 2016. "Reconceptualizing Agency and Childhood." Pp. 16–30 in *Reconceptualizing Child Agency and Socialisation: New Perspectives in Childhood Studies*, edited by F. Esser, M. Baader, T. Betz, and B. Hungerland. London: Routledge.

Estes, D. 2011. "Managing the Student-Parent Dilemma: Mothers and Fathers in Higher Education." *Symbolic Interaction* 34(2):198–219.

Francis, A. 2015. *Family Trouble: Middle-Class Parents, Children's Problems, and the Disruption of Everyday Life*. New Brunswick, NJ: Rutgers University Press.

Goffman, E. 1959. *The Presentation of Self in Everyday Life*. Garden City, NY: Doubleday Anchor Books.

Goffman, E. 1961. *Asylums*. Garden City, NY: Doubleday Anchor Books.

Handel, G. 2011. "Sociological Perspectives on Social Development." Pp. 135–156 in *The Wiley-Blackwell Handbook of Childhood Social Development*, 2nd ed., edited by P. Smith and C. Hart. London: Blackwell.

Handel, G., S. Cahill, and F. Elkin. 2007. *Children and Society: The Sociology of Children and Childhood Socialization*. New York: Oxford University Press.

Hochschild, A. 1997. *The Time Bind: When Work Becomes Home and Home Becomes Work*. New York:Henry Holt.

Hordge-Freeman, E. 2015. *The Color of Love: Racial Features, Stigma & Socialization in Black Brazilian Families*. Austin, TX: University of Texas Press.

House, J. 1977. "The Three Faces of Social Psychology." *Sociometry* 40(2):161–177.

Inkeles, A. 1968. "Society, Social Structure, and Childhood Socialization." Pp. 73–129 in *Socialization and Society*, edited by J. Clausen. Boston, MA: Little Brown.

Irvine, L. 2004. "A Model of Animal Selfhood: Expanding Interactionist Possibilities." *Symbolic Interaction* 27(1):3–21.

Keel, S. 2016. *Socialization: Parent-Child Interaction in Everyday Life*. London: Routledge.

Kendrick, M. and D. Kakuru. 2012. "Funds of Knowledge in Child-Headed Households: A Ugandan Case Study." *Childhood* 19(3):397–413.

Khan, A. 2013. "Airport Profiling: A Familiar Story for Muslims." *The Huffington Post*. May 19. https://www.huffingtonpost.com/azeem-khan/racial-profiling-muslim_b_3303582.html.

Kohn, M. 1979. "The Effects of Social Class on Parental Values and Practices." Pp. 45–68 in *The American Family*, edited by D. Reiss and H. Hoffman. New York: Plenum.

Kolb, K. 2011. "Claiming Competence: Biographical Work Among Victim-Advocates and Counselors." *Symbolic Interaction* 34(1):86–107.

Korkiama, R. 2011. "Support and Control Among 'Friends' and 'Special Friends': Peer Groups' Social Resources as Emotional and Moral Performances Amidst Teenagers." *Children & Society* 25(2):104–111.

Lareau, A. 2011. *Unequal Childhoods: Class, Race, and Family Life*. 2nd ed. Berkeley, CA: University of California Press.

Lois, J. 2013. *Home Is Where the School Is: The Logic of Homeschooling and the Emotional Labor of Mothers*. New York: New York University Press.

Mead, G. H. [1934] 1962. *Mind, Self and Society*. Chicago, IL: University of Chicago Press.

Mizen, P. and Y. Ofosu-Kusi. 2010. "Asking, Giving, Receiving: Friendship as Survival Strategy Among Accra's Street Children." *Childhood* 17(4):441–454.

Musolf, G. 1996. "Interactionism and the Child: Cahill, Corsaro, and Denzin on Childhood Socialization." *Symbolic Interaction* 19(4):303–321.

Nash, C., J. Morris, and B. Goodman. 2008. "A Study Describing Mothers' Opinions of Crying Behavior of Infants Under One Year of Age." *Child Abuse Review* 17(3):191–200.

Nelson, M. and R. Schutz. 2007. "Day Care Differences and the Reproduction of Social Class." *Journal of Contemporary Ethnography* 36(3):281–317.

Oswell, D. 2016. "Re-Aligning Children's Agency and Re-Socializing Children in Childhood Studies." Pp. 32–44 in *Reconceptualising Agency and Childhood: New Perspectives in Childhood Studies*, edited by F. Esser, M. Baader, T. Betz, and B. Hungerland. London: Routledge.

Parsons, T. and R. Bales. 1955. *Family, Socialization and Interaction Process.* Glencoe, IL: Free Press.

Punch, S. 2008. "'You Can Do Nasty Things to Your Brothers and Sisters Without a Reason': Siblings' Backstage Behaviour." *Children & Society* 22(5):333–344.

Richardson, J. Jr., W. Johnson Jr., and C. St. Vil. 2014. "'I Want Him Locked Up': Social Capital, African American Parenting Strategies, and the Juvenile Court." *Journal of Contemporary Ethnography* 43(4):488–522.

Roschelle, A. and P. Kaufman. 2004. "Fitting In and Fighting Back: Stigma Management Strategies Among Homeless Kids." *Symbolic Interaction* 27(1) 23–46.

Scott, S. 2010. "Revisiting the Total Institution: Performative Regulation in the Reinventive Institution." *Sociology* 44(2):213–231.

Scott, S. 2015. *Negotiating Identity: Symbolic Interactionist Approaches to Social Identity*. Cambridge, UK: Polity Press.

Shibutani, T. 1955. "Reference Groups as Perspectives." *American Journal of Sociology* 60(6):562–569.

Shoshana, A. 2012. "The Self as Public Property: Made in Israel." *Symbolic Interaction* 35(2):186–202.

Strauss, A. L. 1959. *Mirrors and Masks*. Mill Valley, CA: Sociology Press.

Tajfel, H. 1982. *Social Identity and Intergroup Relations*. Cambridge, UK: Cambridge University Press.

Thornberg, R., K. Halldin, N. Bolmsjö, and A. Petersson. 2013. "Victimising of School Bullying: A Grounded Theory." *Research Papers in Education* 28(3):309–329.

Thorne, B. 1993. *Gender Play: Boys and Girls at School*. New Brunswick, NJ: Rutgers University Press.

Tucker, J. 2013. "Students Battling Adversity." *San Francisco Chronicle*. Sunday, April 7, 2013, p. A1. http://nl.Hwsbank.com/nl-search/we/ Archives?p_action=doc&p_docid=14584316F0C9E9F8&p_docnum=9&s_ dlid=DL0118012919502930394&s.

Warming, H. 2011. "Getting Under Their Skins: Accessing Young Childrens' Perspectives through Ethnographic Fieldwork." *Childhood* 18(1):39–53.

# 4

# The Social Body

## Appearances and Experiences

> "I'm pretty happy with [my body] most of the time, but it doesn't help that I live with seven boys. When we go out, I know that girls always look at them, not me, and I think it's 'cause I'm short…. My mates are more good looking, like girls always come up to them, so I feel a bit short and unattractive next to them … So when it comes to girls, I definitely think I'm disadvantaged because I'm short and a bit big." – Nick, 22
>
> "When I look in the mirror, I find myself looking at my reflection quite a lot, even though I don't think I'm a vain person. And when I get up in the morning and get out of bed, especially because I've got a big mirror right there, I do find myself looking in the mirror at my stomach and looking at how flabby it is. [And I] do compare myself to other people. I don't do it very often but I guess subconsciously we do it all the time." – Katy, 20
>
> (Smith Maguire and Stanway 2008:65–66)
>
> "The most important thing I have to say to you today is that hair matters. This is a life lesson my family did not teach me, Wellesley and Yale Law School failed to instill: Your hair will send significant messages to those around you. …Pay attention to your hair, because everyone else will." – Hillary Clinton, half-joking, in a 2001 speech at Yale University. (Karni 2015)

A chapter on the body may seem strange, at first glance. After all, you live in your own skin every day. Presumably, you know a lot about your height, weight, hair color, and skin tone, your daily pains and ailments, your muscles, dexterity, and coordination. What is left to learn? Quite a bit, actually. Anyone who has taken an anatomy course will attest to the numerous intricate details that most people don't know about themselves – starting with the over 200 bones that hold us together.

*The Social Self and Everyday Life: Understanding the World Through Symbolic Interactionism,* First Edition. Kathy Charmaz, Scott R. Harris, and Leslie Irvine.
© 2019 John Wiley & Sons, Inc. Published 2019 by John Wiley & Sons, Inc.

If we add a sociological viewpoint, our bodies become further complicated. Culture, inequality, and other social factors shape how we and others around us perceive, experience, use, and modify our bodies. Our physical selves are deeply connected to the eras and communities we live in.

As the opening excerpts suggest, the perspectives we apply to our bodies shape our identities and self-esteem. Over the course of our lives, many of us will spend countless hours in bathrooms, and thousands of dollars on toiletries, to make sure we look and smell the "right" way. We compare ourselves to specific others, and to prevailing standards of beauty. Intentionally or not, we communicate who we are through our height, hair, skin, teeth, breasts, muscles, and body fat. We carve out a persona, or claim allegiance to an idea or subculture, by adorning tattoos, piercings, and clothing styles. Our physical appearance shapes the kinds of personal relationships we develop, and even the kinds of jobs we may be offered.

In what follows, we'll examine some of the social dimensions of the body, moving from issues that might conventionally be seen as more "outer" to more "inner" – from bodily appearances to bodily experiences. By the end, we hope to demonstrate that our bodies as much social as they are biological.

## Bodily Appearances

Do you have a good body? Chances are, you can answer this question with some precision. Which features of yours are attractive, or a bit ugly? What do people notice when they first see you? What parts of your physique are you proud of? What do you try to hide? Our physical appearance is often a central part of our identities. It is "who we think we are" as we walk into a room, whether with confidence and pride or with self-consciousness and meekness.

From an interactionist perspective, our physical traits do not have inherent meaning. Our families, friends, the media, and others socialize us to think about these traits in particular ways. We learn **body norms** – cultural expectations regarding the appearance and use of our bodies – and these govern or at least guide our perceptions of ourselves and others. For example, weight preoccupies many North Americans' concerns about appearance. Slenderness is often prized, and models are almost unanimously thin. However, this particular preoccupation with weight reflects a cultural assumption, one that does not hold cross-culturally or historically. In impoverished societies, being "plump" can indicate wealth, and a larger-sized spouse is a status symbol (Fallon 1990:84). Fat can also be viewed as a sign of fertility and health, both highly valued traits. So, depending on when and where you are born, you might find yourself constantly counting calories, hitting the gym, and fretting about a stomach that is too flabby or big – like Katy and Nick in the opening excerpts – or you might purposefully pack on the pounds. In the 1880s, many women in the U.S. weighed themselves frequently, to ensure they weren't getting *too thin* (Fallon 1990:86). After WWI, "The curvy ideal was replaced by the flat-chested flappers. Dresses of the 1920s were curveless and the ideal body was almost boylike" (Fallon 1990:87). Women flattened their breasts with tight undergarments. Currently, in the beginning of the twenty-first century, the most idealized female figure seems to be both thin and big breasted (Patton 2006:31). Men's weight suffers somewhat less scrutiny but is by no means irrelevant. For one thing, some heavier men find their "Man boobs" or "Moobs" to be extremely embarrassing.[1] And how's your hair? Hillary Clinton, in the opening excerpt, joked about the seemingly endless commentary that her various hairstyles have elicited over her several decades in government. As much as she might have preferred to be evaluated on other criteria – such as her policy proposals and accomplishments – her audiences periodically diverted their attention to her physical appearance, and her hair, in particular. To varying degrees, the same is true for all of us. Our bodies give off numerous signs that our audiences can highlight and interpret as they see fit. Our bodies ordinarily precede us, much like our reputations.

Like weight, hair is open to multiple interpretations. In western societies, people often view long hair as feminine, and short hair as masculine, but this view represents an arbitrary social convention. In some African and Native American cultures, men grew long hair, decorated with accoutrements (beads, feathers, shells) while women shaved or covered their heads (Fallon 1990:84). Interestingly, the relationship between hair and gender can be reversed for other regions of the body. Most Americans may view long hair as feminine, but only on the head; hair on women's armpits, legs, or upper lips can prompt disparagement and shame. Generally speaking, both men and women need to have just the right amount of hair in all the right places. Too little hair (e.g. partial baldness) is less than ideal, but so too is too much hair (e.g. a bushy "unibrow").

People can ascribe many other intricate meanings to hair. The body can be always viewed through a number of prisms. If a man allows the hair on his head to grow down to his shoulders, is that a sign of rebellion – a challenging of convention? Or, is he conforming to a "rock star," "surfer," or "biker" motif? Perhaps he is simply lazy, or thrifty – saving money on barbers. Christian iconography usually portrays Jesus as having long hair, but evangelical preachers usually opt for a shorter, more "respectable" haircut – such as Billy and Franklin Graham, Jack Van Impe, Joel Osteen, and Pat Robertson. Not one of these religious leaders has donned a Mohawk, or dreadlocks, or blue-tinted highlights, all of which might have defied the expectations of their congregations and audiences.

Cultural norms about bodily appearances operate as **external constraints and internal constraints** (Berger 1963). People surrounding us, who believe in and enforce the norms, often limit, and guide our conduct. Our friends, family, co-workers, and even strangers can issue sanctions – via disparaging looks and comments, ostracism, even violence – as well as positive reinforcement through compliments, and favorable treatment. At the same time, we police ourselves. We usually internalize our companions' beliefs and apply our own sanctions and rewards through our private thoughts and feelings of pride and shame. We let ourselves know – as Nick and Katy do in the opening vignettes – when we exceed, meet, or fall short of our culture's standards. We may be proud of our thick, flowing manes of hair, or ashamed of being too "short" and "flabby," despite the fact that we sometimes have little or no control over those traits. The company we keep thus influences our identities (e.g. "I am cute!" "I am too fat"), the effort we put into our appearances (e.g. dieting, haircuts), and the way we feel about our bodies, even when we are alone in our bedrooms, like Katy.

> **Body norms are cultural expectations regarding appropriate uses and appearances of our bodies.**
> **These norms act as external constraints on how we present our physical selves, in that others scrutinize and reward or punish us.**
> **Body norms also operate as internal constraints because we police ourselves as well.**

Bodily conventions may be largely arbitrary, but they are also **patterned**. As we've already seen, the norms vary historically and culturally. In addition, inequality tends to structure and pervade popular beliefs about the body. Groups with more power and prestige can inflict or enforce body norms on other groups. For example, a good argument can be made that beauty standards reflect and perpetuate gender inequality in society. Compared to men, women face narrower expectations, requiring more time, effort, money, and even pain. In the U.S., women are much more likely to endure surgical cosmetic procedures (e.g. breast implants, liposuction, facelifts) as well as nonsurgical procedures (e.g. Botox injections, chemical peels). In 2013, over 90% of U.S. women, and only 9% of men, underwent such procedures (Dolezal 2015:125–126).

Women's looks are emphasized and scrutinized more than men's. Interestingly, one argument for the wearing of a Burqa is that it protects women from such scrutiny and worry, allowing them to more freely participate in society (Read and Bartkowski 2000:405). Of course, the practice is itself controversial. Some Muslims and non-Muslims interpret the all-enveloping garment as excessive and restrictive. Debates over banning burqas, in France and elsewhere, also exemplify the idea that bodily conventions are matters of power – in this case a struggle over the establishment and enforcement of clothing laws.

Racial inequality can profoundly shape the ways bodies are viewed and judged. In the U.S. and many other countries, a hierarchy of color exists, with whiter features usually deemed "the best." As a consequence of colonization, the slave trade, eugenics, mass media representations of beauty, and other factors, many of us have come to view the body via a racist lens. Darker skin, coily hair, a wider nose, fuller lips, and other features have often been defined as inferior (Hordge-Freeman 2013). Features associated with whiteness operate as an inherited resource – a form of **symbolic capital** that bestows advantages in the legal system, employment, housing, and dating (McNamee and Miller 2014).

Skin-lightening products (such as "Clear Essence" and "Skin Success") are marketed to people of color in the U.S., Ireland, India, Mali, Senegal, South Africa, and other parts of the world (Glenn 2008), for those who hope to "brighten" or "fade" their complexion. Hair, too, is big business. Many African American women have been socialized to believe that straight hair is "good hair" and kinky hair is "bad hair" (Patton 2006:38–39). The 2009 documentary film *Good Hair*, produced and narrated by comedian Chris Rock, highlights the large amount of time, effort, and money that some black women spend to achieve what is (or could be seen as) an arbitrary and repressive standard of beauty. Or, consider Elizabeth Hordge-Freeman's (2013) poignant research – quoted at length in a boxed excerpt – on Afro-Brazilian families living in Salvador, Brazil. Hordge-Freeman observed relatives' and neighbors' reactions to the "problem" of children with wide noses, coily hair, or dark skin tones.

---

### The Color of Love

#### Elizabeth Hordge-Freeman (2013:1512–1513)

Damiana is a 28-year-old pregnant mother with caramel brown skin and naturally straight black hair. She identifies as *uma mulher negra* (a black woman) and often discusses the vivid dreams she has about her unborn child with her black (*preto*) husband:

> I have dreams about what she will look like. Sometimes she is white and sometimes she is *morena* [brown/dark]. I hope she gets her nose and straight hair from me. That's why I sit here all day and watch "*gente bonita*" [pretty people] on television. If an ugly person walks by I try not to even look in their direction.

I spend months in Damiana's home watching novelas with her and documenting her continuous commentary about the hair, nose, and bodies of white actresses. Her explanation of why she watches *pretty people* takes on a specific meaning because colloquially the phrase is understood to mean white people. Hence, her casual use of the term naturalizes whiteness and conflates it with beauty....

Curious neighbors instigate whispers that Damiana may have a *barriga suja* and they exacerbate Damiana's anxieties. Translated as "dirty womb," this is a pejorative term that describes a woman's tendency to produce dark-skinned babies when the baby has the potential to be lighter.

[Later], Damiana is eager to display her newborn daughter who is unanimously viewed as pretty: white skin and straight hair. …While Damiana's neighbors dote on the newborn baby, they also lament her unfortunate feature:

> She's beautiful! …But you know you really have to do something about that nose (laughs) that wide nose [*nariz chato*] of hers. You will definitely have to fix that nose with a clamp [*pegador*]. You need to pinch it down. There's no way around it (everyone nods and laughs loudly).

An initial compliment quickly diverges into a conversation about how to correct the baby's wide nose. Laughter normalizes the racist statements and suggests that they have been spoken in jest. But I discover that Damiana follows their advice and engages in a ritual where she squeezes and holds down the baby's nostrils daily, so that she will not have what is popularly referred to as "*o nariz que o boi pisou*" (a nose that the bull stepped on).

Of course, it must be remembered that white women are equally devoted to bodies and to their hair, and that there can be exceptions to the belief that "whiter features are always better." For example, white women sometimes add a bit of color to their skin through bronzers and tanning beds or add kink into their hair through perms. And people do sometimes recognize and resist hegemonic notions of beauty. Nevertheless, the larger pattern of white, Euro-supremacism remains – alongside the stricter standards for women compared to men. As a result, racial and gender inequality frequently do seem to guide the norms that govern our bodily presentations and evaluations (Craig 2012).

## Coping with Bodily Stigma

### Defining Stigma

One of us (Scott) attended middle school with a boy named Chris, who suffered extensive burns as a young child. Much of his face and body were severely scarred. When Chris participated in playground fun, he was sometimes teased by his classmates, who, rather mercilessly, called him "Crispy." Scott remembers muttering disdain for the diabolical nickname, but a friend assured him that Chris was sometimes "a jerk" and so "deserved it."

Unfortunately, our physical features can be stigmatizing, to various degrees. The standard definition of a stigma treats it as a mark of disgrace or dishonor resulting in devaluation of the individual or an entire category of people.

*The standard definition of a stigma treats it as a mark of disgrace or dishonor resulting in devaluation of the individual or an entire category of people.*

From this perspective, stigmas consist of discrediting attributes and reflect the norms of particular groups. The conventional view of a visible bodily stigma is that it contains inherent meaning, marking a person as different and devalued. Then this stigmatizing attribute elicits discriminatory attitudes and actions from "normal" others. The interactionist view is that the meaning of bodily stigmas is not inherent, and that discriminatory attitudes and actions are based on collective and individual interpretations of them.

**Major stigmas**, such as Chris's scars, are immediately visible, discrediting, and influential in virtually all face-to-face interaction. Other examples include paralysis, missing limbs, extreme obesity, dwarfism, or being the "wrong" race or ethnicity. A major stigma can become a **master status-determining trait**, one that comes to define a person. A master status "tends to overpower, in most crucial situations, any other characteristics which might run counter to it" (Hughes 1945:357). Everybody seemed to think of Chris first and foremost as "the burnt kid." Most likely, he thought of himself in the same way.

Whether or not an attribute automatically confers a master status varies. Certainly, **visibility** is crucial, as are shared definitions of what is discreditable. Intermittently visible major stigmas have different effects, depending on how the person and others view and act toward them. Some people refuse to let a potential master status define them and disrupt their lives. For example, one of us (Kathy) recalls an attorney with a radical mastectomy who swam at a public pool before going to her office. The facility had communal showers and lacked private stalls for getting dressed. Other women at the pool were solicitous toward her and viewed her as courageous for revealing her mastectomy in a quasi-public setting. Another woman also had a mastectomy. In contrast to the attorney, she felt profoundly disfigured and humiliated after the surgery. Each night, she undressed in the dark because she did not want her husband to see her altered body. She believed the mastectomy had robbed her of her femininity. For her, the mastectomy was a master status of which she remained continuously conscious.

**Minor bodily stigmas** can be partially hidden, allowing individuals to "pass" as normal on some occasions – such as using a closed-mouth grin to hide discolored teeth. Or, minor stigmas can simply be less undesirable traits: picture a large birthmark on one's forehead (minor) compared to an amputated arm (major). Nevertheless, minor stigmas can be quite embarrassing, if not detrimental to our personal lives and careers. The range of such traits is extensive:

> Minor bodily stigmas may include "blemishes" potentially perceptible by sight (that is, impaired appearance such as buck teeth, hair lips, moles, scars, acne, psoriasis, scales, baldness, red hair, curly hair, big breasts, flat breasts, tall or short stature, heavy or skinny bodies; missing or damaged body parts, such as chipped or crooked front teeth, missing or malformed digits on fingers or toes, scoliosis, or one leg shorter than another; or impeded bodily movement such as tics, shaking, limping, squinting, unbalanced eye tracking or crossing); by hearing (that is, minor speech problems, such as lisping and mild stuttering, or speech impaired by lack of hearing); by smell (that is, chronic halitosis, body odor, or putrid cysts); or by the presence of an aid or sign of impairment (that is, a toupee, hearing aid, thick glasses, brace, or cane). (Ellis 1998:522)

The same physical trait may be interpreted as a major or minor stigma – or even as a point of pride – depending on the person and context (Goffman 1963:3–4). Baldness may be more embarrassing for a woman than a man, or a lisp more stigmatizing for a high school teacher than a truck driver. An extremely tall person may feel awkward embarrassment in most social settings, but confident and proud on the basketball court. Or, imagine the relentless suspicion that the first black or female airline pilots may have endured, due to co-workers and passengers doubting their aptitude. As racism and sexism have declined somewhat – but absolutely not disappeared (Evans 2013) – the pilots' skin color and sex might now be experienced as more minor than major bodily stigmas.

Human beings expend a great deal of energy **hiding and coping** with their stigmatizing traits. People are "constantly creating strategies to avoid incurring the antagonistic, reductive or judgmental gaze of the other" (Dolezal 2015:46). Consider the techniques used by those suffering from hyperhidrosis, or excessive perspiration. A prolific sweater may never leave the house without considering or adopting a number of measures. For example, to hide pit stains, he or she may wear

- Dark shirts (usually black)
- Quick drying shirts (e.g. polyester)
- An undershirt, to soak up moisture before it reaches the outer layer
- Wool sweaters, which repel moisture
- Pit protectors – absorbent pads that adhere to the skin or are attached to clothing

To prevent undesirable perspiration from occurring, a person may seek medical treatments such as prescription strength antiperspirants, Botox injections, and intensive heat that destroys sweat glands (Google "miraDry"). Or, individuals may decline invitations to participate in certain activities – such as dancing at a party or wedding – or conscientiously stand and sit near a fan. See the boxed excerpt from a blog by a sufferer of hyperhidrosis, Caryn Joan, who describes a few of her life-long experiences coping with the stigmatizing condition.

> *Major bodily stigmas (e.g. a missing arm) tend to be immediately visible, defined as very undesirable, and consistently consequential in social interactions. Major stigmas can become master status-determining traits, coloring almost everything we think and believe about a person.*
>
> *Minor stigmas (e.g. chronically bad breath) are less severe and can often be partially hidden but can still affect our status detrimentally.*

What do you see as a major bodily stigma? Having a severe speech impediment? Using a wheelchair? Being epileptic? The experience of people with major bodily stigmas may differ than our preconceptions about their lives. In their classic study of people with epilepsy coming to terms with stigma, Graham Scambler and Anthony Hopkins (1986:27) challenge what they call the "orthodox" view of epilepsy in the UK. In this view, the public (i) remains ill-informed about epilepsy (e.g. viewing it only as grand mal seizures), (ii) holds negative attitudes toward people with epilepsy, (iii) discriminates against them, and (iv) causes most of the problems experienced by people with epilepsy. In contrast, Scambler and Hopkins found no general stereotype of epilepsy nor firm evidence of intolerant attitudes toward people with epilepsy. Although health professionals reported instances of discriminatory actions having profoundly damaging effects on their patients with epilepsy, the authors could not ascertain their generality.

However, Scambler and Hopkins (1986:33) demonstrated the significant difference between **enacted** and **felt stigma**. Enacted stigma means occurrences of discrimination against people because they are deemed to be unacceptable or inferior. Felt stigma refers to these people's fear of enacted stigma, but also includes deep feelings of shame about having their conditions.

> *Enacted stigma means occurrences of discrimination against people because they are deemed to be unacceptable or inferior.*
>
> *Felt stigma refers to these people's fear of enacted stigma, but also includes deep feelings of shame about having their conditions.*

Scambler and Hopkins (1986:33) argue that "being epileptic" becomes a master status and overriding identity that supersedes "having seizures."

The felt stigma of being epileptic cuts to the core of a person's being and permeates his or her sense of self. In this case, epilepsy becomes an inextricable part of personal identity and a feared social identity and master status.

Rather than resulting from episodes of enacted stigma, Scambler and Hopkins found that felt stigma typically *preceded* it. Hence, people became wary of the possibility of experiencing enacted stigma and often chose concealment as the strategy to avoid it. Young people usually did not disclose their diagnoses to boyfriends or girlfriends but averred they would tell a future spouse. A young woman told Scambler and Hopkins (1986:35):

> The only person I'll ever tell, of the opposite sex… is the man that can accept me as I am now, that will say to me: "Will you marry me?" Then if he says that, I won't say "Yes" until he's understood fully, until he's come to the GP and I've asked the doctor to explain it all to him.

However, "honorable" intentions may go awry. Scambler and Hopkins' data show that people's actions do not necessarily coincide with their earlier intentions. The authors (1986:35) state that a full disclosure of epilepsy occurred in only 33 percent of the marriages that took place after the diagnosis.

## Responding to Being Stigmatized

Concealment is a risky strategy and, of course, some bodily traits cannot be hidden. If so, people may feel pressed to invoke other strategies to reduce the impact of stigma. If called or mocked on their bodily deviance, a stigmatized individual may attempt to **excuse** their condition by telling others that he or she can do nothing about it (Scott and Lyman 1968). If balding or sweating is out of our control, then perhaps you cannot be condemned or held liable for it. If our lisp or obesity is due to a diagnosed illness that is very difficult or impossible to overcome, then others may be more inclined to express sympathy rather than derision. Even a conspicuous tattoo of an ex-partner's name might be excused by putting blame elsewhere. We might claim that others pressured us into getting this tattoo; that intoxication produced a bad decision; that intense love or infatuation (now long passed) caused our irrational exuberance; or that a younger version of ourselves made an impulsive decision we are now stuck with (cf. Irwin 2001).

Such **motive talk** – attributing reasons for our bodily conduct – might prompt tolerance and empathy, but not without costs. The invocation of an excuse implies that a physical trait is still bad. Such an account allays responsibility but leaves unchallenged the assumption that it's undesirable to be short, bald, fat, tattooed, and so on, rather than portraying such states as natural, normal, or valued conditions.

---

**"How Would Life Be Different without HH?"**

https://justalittlesweat.com/page/2

*Caryn Joan, 30 November 2014, downloaded 19 November 2016*

Sometimes I wonder how my life would be different without Hyperhidrosis.

I wouldn't have to worry about the little things like greeting someone new with a handshake or writing with a pen on paper. I wouldn't have to worry about holding a newspaper, either deteriorating the paper with sweat or coming away with print on my hands. I wouldn't have to worry about holding onto a subway rail, taking change back from a cashier, accidentally touching someone's arm with a cold and wet hand, or leaving an embarrassing hand print behind. I wouldn't have grown up with other kids not wanting to hold my hand during square dancing in gym class or as their line partner to go to the lunch room. I wouldn't have had to avoid certain things growing up like playing clapping games with my friends or braiding each other's hair.

Sometimes I think about life without HH and how normal it would have been. I wouldn't have had to be anxious about my underarm sweat stains reaching the hem of my shirt, or going to the nurse's office several times a week just to avoid my embarrassment. Maybe I would have continued taking gymnastics lessons. Maybe I would have joined clogging dance with my sister where there is a lot of hand holding.

Life without HH seems so normal and it's something I've envied for a long time. But thinking of life without HH sure has a lot of maybe's and what if's.

What I do know is that I really can't imagine my life without HH. It is a part of me and it is a part of who I have become. Without HH, I would have taken all of the above for granted. I feel fortunate that I don't.

HH has made me a stronger person. It has given me pride in accomplishing even the smallest of tasks. HH has also made me an observer and someone who cares a lot. It has given me an understanding and appreciation for all people.

So how would life be different without HH? I'm not quite sure.

But I think life with HH has made it better.

---

However, another way of coping with bodily stigmas is to challenge beliefs and claims of undesirableness. Individuals can attempt to redefine their physical attributes in more positive terms – either for themselves or for others. Caryn Joan does this. After listing all the drawbacks of suffering hyperhidrosis, the blogger claims that the benefits outweigh the costs: her stigmatizing condition has given her greater empathy for others, and taught her to take pride in the accomplishment of small tasks. Or, imagine a man with a rapidly receding hairline who quips "I'm not losing my hair, I'm growing more aerodynamic!" Similarly, a portly person can put his or her body fat in a more favorable light by asserting "Yes I'm heavy – that just means there's more of me to love" or "I'm healthy, I exercise all the time – I'm 'fit fat.'" Thus, rather than excusing a bodily appearance, individuals can choose to frame it as a positive (or at least not-so-negative) trait.

**Justifications**, as originally conceived by Scott and Lyman (1968), usually involve an acceptance of responsibility for an act but a denial of some or all of its presumed undesirableness. For example, if challenged on the size, location, or existence of a tattoo, a person may say or imply "Yes, I chose to get that tattoo," while asserting that the image is something positive – a sign of loyalty to or love for a spouse, military unit, gang, or ideal (such as freedom, individuality).

Of course, human beings are creative; they can sometimes employ both excuses and justifications when accounting for bodily stigmas. When criticized for excessive perspiration, a person with hyperhidrosis may claim that "It's not my fault, I was born this way!" and then later add "Perspiration is just salty water" or "What's the big deal – is my sweaty shirt somehow hurting your eyes?" The first statement excuses the condition by denying blame. The latter two justify the condition by highlighting its benign consequences and thereby challenging the implication of harm.

> *Motive talk occurs whenever we assign causes to our own or others' behavior.*
> *Excuses are claims that accept that a condition or action was bad, but deny all or some degree of responsibility for it.*
> *Justifications tend to deny that a condition or action is bad, while accepting responsibility for it.*

Coping with stigma is not necessarily an individual task. Our friends and relatives can help us out – telling us our birthmark only makes us unique, or our lisp is cute and endearing. Support groups can emphasize the advantages of being blind or disabled, while offering techniques for managing daily tasks. Sometimes, people can become politically motivated, and take collective action aimed at destigmatizing bodily conditions. For example, the slogan "Black is beautiful" is a product of an organized effort in the 1960s and 1970s to diminish the negative effects of subtle and not-so-subtle white supremacism (Patton 2006). More recently, some groups have pushed back against the constant demeaning of obese and overweight individuals, by promoting "fat acceptance" or "size acceptance" (Saguy and Riley 2005).

## Interpreting Bodily Experiences

The first two sections of this chapter have elucidated some of the social dimensions of the body by focusing primarily on external appearances and definitions. In the remainder of this chapter, we'll take another tack, and look more closely at the social shaping of "inner" experiences.

Not much could seem more physical or natural than the biological signals and sensations we receive from our bodies. Hunger pangs, for instance, seem like an instinctive response to a lack of food. However, even with this seeming "automatic" sensation, interpretations can vary. One person may view an aching belly as a problem to be remedied as quickly as possible, if not preempted, by ingesting food. A dieter, on the other hand, may learn to relish the pangs as a positive sign that progress is being made. A third person may fail to even notice the pangs (being too preoccupied with work or play) while a fourth wonders if the pain is an indication of a virus or illness of some sort.

As Vannini, Waskul, and Gottschalk (2012:18) write, "Flesh and organs bestow the capacity to sense, but those are merely the raw materials by which we fashion somatic experience."

If you think about it, you may have a passing familiarity with the idea that social and interpretive factors shape our bodily experiences, through the common expression "acquired tastes." Sometimes we do not immediately like the flavor of certain foods and beverages, the first time we sample them. Our friends and relatives may need to encourage us to try again, repeatedly, until we learn to like – or at least tolerate – the flavor. Did you enjoy beer, coffee, wine, or hard liquor (rum, tequila, vodka, whiskey) on your first attempt? Many of us dislike or are ambivalent toward these beverages, at least initially. Through repeated effort, and some **coaching** by our companions, we may eventually develop "a taste" for such drinks.

In general, our family, friends, and other companions socialize us into prevailing food preferences and customs. We may learn that cow muscle (steak) is a real treat, but not horse or dog muscle. Alternatively, our parents may tell us that cows are sacred, or that all meat-eating is unnecessary and cruel. Have you been taught to think of caviar (fish eggs) and escargot (snails) as delicacies, or do they strike you as disgusting? Have you learned to appreciate yogurt and soda, but not Doogh – a Persian beverage that combines the two? Do marshmallows seem ridiculously odd, artificial, and unhealthy, or do you consider them a convenient and delectable dessert?

One of us (Scott) grew up thinking bananas-with-mayonnaise was a common side-dish. Since reaching adulthood, he has met almost no one who has eaten the combination or is eager to try it. His parents also convinced him that lobster was a rare reward for unusually high grades on a report card. Looking back, he could just have easily been convinced that eating the large underwater bug (complete with tentacles) was punishment for misbehavior.

To identify and communicate about food and drink, we learn **taste vocabularies** which we use to provide **somatic accounts** to ourselves and others – such as "yuck," "mmmm," "smooth," or "rich" (Vannini, Waskul, and Gottschalk 2012:56). Connoisseurs may be socialized into subcultures that offer more specialized lingo, such as "peaty" for whiskey or "earthy," "grippy," "silky," and "lively" for wine.

Take a look at the boxed excerpt on this topic, from the book *The Senses in Self, Society, and Culture*. Phillip Vannini recounts an interaction he participated in, while conducting qualitative research at a wine festival. Unlike drinking at a pub, a wine festival calls for thoughtful tasting, rather than mere drinking. The point is not simply to quench one's thirst or become intoxicated. Instead, participants must appreciate and describe the qualities of the wine to each other and to wine pourers, who proudly promote their offerings. Here tasting clearly means far more than a simple biological act. The drinker must employ a comprehensible terminology to selectively characterize a multifaceted experience. The attendee could focus on a wine's temperature, color, or aromas, or its various flavors and texture, in addition to extraneous factors such as its vintage, origination, name, and so on. All the while, the drinker must attend to **dramaturgical** elements of the encounter. Attendees usually try to avoid making offensive comments about pourers' products, at least until out of earshot, to protect others' feelings. To guard their own identity, drinkers try not to say anything stupid, clichéd, arrogant, or otherwise detrimental to the self-image they want to present to others. In short, pourers and drinkers must manage emotions and identities at the same time as they interpret and describe their physiological reactions to the wine.

*Through socialization by our family, friends, and others, we acquire "taste vocabularies" – ways of describing and thinking about flavors that we relish or detest.*

*In verbal and written interaction with others, we use this vocabulary to give somatic accounts of our inner experiences. These accounts tend to be selective, interpretive, and situationally sensitive.*

| Experiencing and Describing Wine at a Festival |
| --- |
| Phillip Vannini, Dennis Waskul, and Simon Gottschalk (2012:54–55) |

"So, what do you think?" my pourer asks me (Phillip).

Here I go – I'm up. I am a bad wine taster. I can tell reds from whites. On a good day, I can find some reluctant certainty in the difference between sweet and dry. But that's as far as my skills can take me. This is not a problem on a normal day. …However, a wine festival requires me to display a set of somatic skills by which the wine's own performance and the performative impression I make are measured. Now, to perform well does not just mean to learn to find and appreciate a material quality [e.g. a flavor] but also to become able to make a quality come to life through a lexicon of sensations and a script to be followed with care. With that vocabulary and script, I can speak with others in tongues.

…As an appallingly indiscriminate wine taster, I am painfully aware of these dramaturgic demands. As the pourer pours, I must listen. As the wine speaks, I must taste. As I taste, I must speak. As I speak, I must make sense. The sense-making of wine is far from being a private … affair moving from the tip of the tongue to the back of the throat. Rather, this joint somatic act begins at the very moment when a pourer and I enter each other's realm of awareness and ends after we have taken leave from each other.

"I like it," I answer after a pause. "It has a spark to it that reminds me of a white my grandpa's brother used to drink at the table."

"Finally, a Pinot that doesn't taste oaky," a tall, middle-aged woman standing next to me exclaims, overtaking the conversation. "I just had some Australian wines and they all tasted like oak. Let me try some more of your whites," she asks the wine pourer in front of us. He obliges. Gingerly pulling her wine glass back, she lurches her large, bumpy nose into the cup and whiffs at it. Then, lifting the glass with her right hand well above her shoulder, and gazing at the wine that is now dimly illuminated by the ceiling lights, she swishes it briskly before bringing it back to her mouth….

"No oak in that one, eh?" inquires the wine pourer.

"Not a hint," she consents, "and it's got enough legs to make me wanna chase after it all night long!"

Legs. I had to look that one up the first time I heard it. When a wine has legs a small film of liquid seems to hang on the vertical walls of the glass after swishing, then climbs down slowly to rejoin the rest of its body. Performing wine calls for expressions like this. Wines have legs, a body, a nose, and other human-like qualities that skilled anthropomorphizing tasters attribute to them. …Moreover, performing wine transforms the personal sensations of taste into communal qualities that may, then, be shared with others who possess the same sensual language [and] rituals….

The substances we consume have material qualities that we briefly sense – such as flavors, aromas, and textures – but they can also have longer-lasting consequences on our physiology. After a large meal, we may feel very full for an hour or more. Is this a good thing? Do we feel satisfied, perhaps even lucky, grateful, or blessed? Or, do we feel indifference, disgust, shame, or guilt about our "overindulgence?" Depending on the perspective we apply, the pressing feeling in our stomachs may be given very different meanings.

Interestingly, similar arguments can be made about the intoxicating effects of the legal and illegal drugs we ingest. In his classic study on "Becoming a Marijuana User," Becker (1953) argued that the experience of being high is ambiguous and open to interpretation.[2]

Marijuana-produced sensations are not automatically or necessarily pleasurable. The taste for such experience is a socially acquired one, not different in kind from acquired tastes for oysters or dry martinis. The user feels dizzy, thirsty; his scalp tingles; he misjudges time and distances; and so on. Are these things pleasurable? He isn't sure. If he is to continue marijuana use, he must decide that they are. Otherwise, getting high, while a real enough experience, will be an unpleasant one he would rather avoid. (Becker 1953:239)

To become a recreational marijuana user, Becker argued, required three essential steps. First, a potential user needs to learn from others how to consume the drug. Getting high from smoking a joint or bong differs from absorbing nicotine via cigarettes. The smoke must be held in one's lungs, by holding one's breath. Without this knowledge, a user will not experience significant effects. Second, a user must learn what physiological changes to look for. What will the drug do to you? As with ingestion techniques, Becker found that users learned what effects to look for, by watching and listening to their companions. As two of his interviewees explained:

I didn't get high the first time... I don't think I held it in long enough. I probably let it out, you know, you're a little afraid. The second time I wasn't sure, and he [smoking companion] told me, like I asked him for some of the symptoms or something... So he told me to sit on a stool. I sat on – I think I sat on a bar stool – and he said, "Let your feet hang," and then when I got down my feet were real cold, you know. And I started feeling it, you know. That was the first time.

I heard little remarks that were made by other people. Somebody said, "My legs are rubbery," and I can't remember all the remarks that were made because I was very attentively listening for all these cues for what I was supposed to feel like. (Becker 1953:238)

The third step to becoming a recreational marijuana user was to define the effects, once noticed, as pleasurable. Is it a good thing that one becomes hungry? That your legs are rubbery and your feet cold? An inexperienced user might be tempted to interpret such consequences as "scary" or more "weird" than "fun." This response is especially true if a user has a "bad trip," where smoking results in paranoia or other negative reactions. Becker argued that more experienced users usually helped novices focus on the positive effects (e.g. relaxation, euphoria) and downplay less enjoyable consequences. Again, our point is that physiological sensations "are merely the raw materials by which we fashion somatic experience" (Vannini, Waskul, and Gottschalk 2012:18). For symbolic interactionists, people *make sense* out of the information their senses provide, using the vocabulary and perspectives they learn from others.

Let's be clear: symbolic interactionists do not believe that bodily sensations are completely and utterly malleable. Some foods, drugs, and sensations may be easier than others to ignore or interpret as we see fit. For example, it probably takes more work to learn to enjoy bourbon than ice cream. However, we have met people who dislike the way ice cream "coats the tongue," as well as its fattening consequences. And there are those who learn to associate pain with pleasure and intimacy, as in sadomasochism (Newmahr 2008) or in collaborative "boot camp" exercise classes.

Moreover, even if a substance like marijuana were simply and automatically pleasurable, users would not be relieved of their meaning-making obligations. The experience of taking the drug could and would likely still be framed in multiple ways: as risk taking, as rebellion, as conforming or giving into peer pressure, as a mundane habit, as a special reward, and so on.

## Conclusion

Clearly, the body is a biological entity. Our DNA, our skeleton, our organs and skin, are all significant factors in our lives, regardless of what we think about or do to them. Nonetheless, the body is also a social phenomenon. Cultural expectations govern how we present and adorn our bodies. Bodily stigmas, both major and minor, can bring shame and social ostracism. We police each other and ourselves as we enforce the rules. We are not cultural robots, however. Individuals and groups can revise, adapt, or rebel against prevailing body standards.

Social influences penetrate more than skin deep. As we saw in this chapter, our inner experiences are also subject to culturally-informed, situationally-sensitive interpretations. Many possibilities are available to think about and describe the physiological changes elicited by food, beverages, drugs, injuries, and other phenomena. This discretion implicates us in the daily construction of the meaning of our bodies.

## Learning by Using the Symbolic Interactionist Perspective

The more you practice applying the interactionist mindset, the easier it should be for you to recognize how – under the influence of cultural assumptions and interactional settings – we play an active role in policing and creating our somatic experiences. Try to apply some of this chapter's premises and concepts, as you read the following excerpt from Richard Rodriguez's well-known autobiography. For example, consider these ideas: meaning is not inherent; body norms; norms as external and internal constraints, and as arbitrary yet patterned; major and minor stigmas; master status; enacted and felt stigma; coping strategies. Can you highlight similarities and differences between Rodriguez's story and other examples discussed in this chapter? Do you have a major or minor bodily stigma? Can you draw a parallel or contrast between your situation and Rodriguez's?

---

### Hunger of Memory

### Richard Rodriguez (1982:121, 133–134)

When I was a boy the white summer sun of Sacramento would darken me so, my T-shirt would seem bleached against my slender dark arms. My mother would see me come up the front steps. She'd wait for the screen door to slam at my back. "You look like a *negrito*," she'd say, angry, sorry to be angry, frustrated almost to laughing, scorn. "You know how important looks are in this country. With *los gringos* looks are all that they judge on. But you! Look at you! You're so careless!" Then she'd start in all over again. "You won't be satisfied till you end up looking like *los pobres* who work in the fields…."

When I was around seven years old, I was at a public swimming pool with the whole family. …I caught my mother's eye. I heard her shout over to me. In Spanish she called through the crowd: "Put a towel on over your shoulders." In public, she didn't want to say why. I knew.

That incident anticipates the shame and sexual inferiority I was to feel in later years because of my dark complexion. I was to grow up an ugly child. Or one who thought himself ugly (*feo*). One night when I was eleven or twelve years old, I locked myself in the bathroom and carefully regarded my reflection in the mirror over the sink. Without any pleasure I studied my skin. I turned on the faucet. (In my mind I heard the swirling voices of aunts, and even my mother's voice, whispering, whispering incessantly about lemon juice solutions and dark, *feo* children.) …I began soaping my arms. I took my father's straight razor out of the medicine cabinet. Slowly, with steady deliberateness, I put the blade against my flesh, pressed it as close as I could without cutting, and moved it up and down across my skin to see if I could get out, somehow lessen, the dark. All I succeeded in doing, however, was in shaving my arms bare of their hair. For as I noted with disappointment, the dark would not come out. It remained. Trapped. Deep in the cells of my skin.

## Notes

1 See https://thesocietypages.org/socimages/2016/05/06/the-story-of-my-man-boobs/; Monaghan (2008).
2 For the sake of consistency, we have changed Becker's spelling from "marihuana" to "marijuana."

## References

Becker, H. S. 1953. "Becoming a Marihuana User." *American Journal of Sociology* 59(3):235–242.

Berger, P. 1963. *Invitation to Sociology*. Garden City, NY: Anchor Books.

Craig, M. L. 2012. "Racialized Bodies." Pp. 321–331 in *Routledge Handbook of Body Studies*, edited by B. S. Turner. New York: Routledge.

Dolezal, L. 2015. *The Body and Shame: Phenomenology, Feminism, and the Socially Shaped Body*. Lanham, MD: Lexington Books.

Ellis, C. A. 1998. "'I HATE MY VOICE': Coming to Terms with Minor Bodily Stigmas." *Sociological Quarterly* 39(4):517–537.

Evans, L. 2013. *Cabin Pressure: African American Pilots, Flight Attendants, and Emotional Labor*. Lanham, MD: Rowman and Littlefield.

Fallon, A. 1990. "Culture in the Mirror: Sociocultural Determinants of Body Image." Pp. 80–109 in *Body Images: Development, Deviance, and Change*, edited by T. F. Cash and T. Pruzinsky. New York: Guilford Press.

Glenn, E. N. 2008. "YEARNING FOR LIGHTNESS: Transnational Circuits in the Marketing and Consumption of Skin Lighteners." *Gender & Society* 22(3):281–302.

Goffman, E. 1963. *Stigma: Notes on the Management of Spoiled Identity*. Englewood Cliffs, NJ: Prentice Hall.

Hordge-Freeman, E. 2013. "What's Love Got to Do with It? Racial Features, Stigma and Socialization in Afro-Brazilian Families." *Ethnic and Racial Studies* 36(10):1507–1523.

Hughes, E. C. 1945. "Dilemmas and Contradictions of Status." *American Journal of Sociology* 50(5):353–359.

Irwin, K. 2001. "Legitimating the First Tattoo." *Symbolic Interaction* 24:49–73.

Karni, A. 2015. "Hillary's Hair: She's in on the Joke." Retrieved November 20, 2016. http://www.politico.com/story/2015/05/hillary-clinton-hair-118381.

McNamee, S. J. and R. K. Miller. 2014. *The Meritocracy Myth* 3rd ed. Lanham, MD: Rowman and Littlefield.

Monaghan, L. F. 2008. *Men and the War on Obesity: A Sociological Study*. London and New York: Routledge.

Newmahr, S. 2008. "Becoming a Sadomasochist: Integrating Self and Other in Ethnographic Analysis." *Journal of Contemporary Ethnography* 37(5):619–643.

Patton, T. O. 2006. "Hey Girl, Am I More than My Hair? African American Women and their Struggles with Beauty, Body Image, and Hair." *NWSA Journal* 18(2):24–51.

Read, J. 'N. G. and J. P. Bartkowski. 2000. "To Veil or Not to Veil? A Case Study of Identity Negotiation among Muslim Women in Austin, Texas." *Gender and Society* 14(3):395–417.

Rodriguez, R. 1982. *Hunger of Memory: The Education of Richard Rodriguez: An Autobiography*. New York: Bantam Books.

Saguy, A. C. and K. W. Riley. 2005. "Weighing Both Sides: Morality, Mortality, and Framing Contests over Obesity." *Journal of Health Politics, Policy and Law* 30(5):869–921.

Scambler, G. and A. Hopkins. 1986. "Being Epileptic: Coming to Terms with Stigma." *Sociology of Health & Illness* 8(1):26–43.

Scott, M. B. and S. M. Lyman. 1968. "Accounts." *American Sociological Review* 33:46–62.

Smith Maguire, J. and K. Stanway. 2008. "Looking Good: Consumption and the Problems of Self-Production." *European Journal of Cultural Studies* 11(1):63–81.

Vannini, P., D. Waskul, and S. Gottschalk. 2012. *The Senses in Self, Society, and Culture*. New York: Routledge.

# 5

# Health, Illness, and Disability

---

"A 20-year-old undergraduate receives a phone call from her ex-boyfriend. He nervously informs her that he has just been diagnosed with genital warts and is in the process of having them "frozen off" with liquid nitrogen. He explains that he called her because there was a chance that he might have had *this* when they had last *been together*. He adds that he is not sure that she is at risk because he had not known the symptoms until recently. She quickly thanks him for calling, hangs up the phone, and sits in stunned silence.

   She thinks to herself: *How could this have happened to me? I'm not a slut: I've only had sex with three guys and always used condoms. I talked with both my ex-boyfriends and current boyfriend before we ever had sex – they told me about their sexual histories and sexual health. These guys had all tested negative for HIV, so they were "safe" – healthy and trustworthy – right? My high school sex educator focused on HIV/AIDS, so I've only been worried about fluids being transmitted. Is it possible to get a disease even when you're using condoms?*

   A series of scary questions runs her mind. *Do I have warts, too? How could I? My last annual gynecological exam was less than six months ago, and my Pap smear results were normal. Wouldn't my doctor have noticed if I had warts? Could I have warts that are so tiny that I've never notice them? Have I already infected my current boyfriend?*" (Nack 2008:1–2)

---

After receiving the distressing news, this young woman looks at her life – and her health – from a new and unwelcome vantage point. The news raises questions about her past, present, and future. She reassesses her earlier actions and those of her partner and healthcare practitioners. What she had thought were responsible actions to maintain sexual health now become open to question. A future that had looked promising has become problematic.

---

*The Social Self and Everyday Life: Understanding the World Through Symbolic Interactionism*, First Edition. Kathy Charmaz, Scott R. Harris, and Leslie Irvine.
© 2019 John Wiley & Sons, Inc. Published 2019 by John Wiley & Sons, Inc.

In this chapter, we look at how health, illness, and disability affect people's lives and their understanding of their experiences. We tell the stories of people who experience physical limitations and how they learn to live with them. Our analysis takes the worlds people live in into account as well as how they make sense of their situations. We look at meanings and actions concerning health but give most attention to how definitions of having serious illness arise, whose definitions count, and the consequences for a person's self, identity, and relationships. How does the structure of healthcare affect people with illnesses and disabilities and their families? As we explore such topics, think about what health, illness, and disability means to you.

## Meanings of Health, Illness, and Disability

Meanings of health, illness, and disability reflect times and trends both in the popular imagination and in professional practice. Health, illness, and disability are contested concepts. Nonetheless, people often assume their definitions of these concepts are obvious truths. Before we begin, consider several distinctions we sociologists make. We treat **illness as a social phenomenon** and focus on individuals' experience of being sick, including their situations and relationships as well as bodily sensations. Disease, in contrast, is a medical term referring to a pathological process or state. You can have an illness without being diagnosed with a disease and you can have a disease without experiencing illness – at least for a while. Disability is also more complex than you might think. You may have thought of disability as an impairment, abnormality, or dysfunction inhering in the individual. This definition assumes a standard of normality from which disability deviates. Yet whether and to what extent social and environmental obstacles limit people's lives also shapes whether their conditions are disabling.

*Sociologists view illness as a social experience, disease as a medical term referring to a pathological process or state, and disability as including those obstacles and environmental barriers which limit or deny access to people whose bodies are different.*

Not surprisingly, meanings of health, illness, and disability vary. For many people, health means the absence of discernible symptoms or impairment, and illness means their presence. This view omits the possibility of having an asymptomatic disease. For others, health means a fragile state requiring constant monitoring and effort to ward off illness and decline and to protect their bodies from invasion by germs and contaminants. Still other people see health as directly related to aging. For them, the young are healthy; the old are not. They see loss of well-being, frailty, and disability as predictably accompanying old age. Even so, Kathy has interviewed elders who believe that God chose them to suffer because He knew they could endure it. In contrast, some people from minority groups now talk about how stigma, difference, and deprivation have undermined their health.

Disproportionate risk of illness reflects the structure of people's lives, as Shim (2014) reveals in her study of risk and inequality among minority people with heart disease. Her participants viewed their constant awareness of racial difference as taking a heavy toll on their health. In one interview (2014:98), Mr. Barrister said, "I can't look at myself outside of being told that I'm Black. I'm told that that's the way I *must* see myself." When asked whether this experience had affected his health, he said:

> Yes, I think it has, because it's conditioned everything that I am, unfortunately... I can certainly say it has affected [me] because these things stress me out.... It's really difficult.... It's affected everything.... You can't relax.... You always have to have a mask.... Your emotions are negatively affected, *day in and day out* by the fact that you are Black and not a single day goes by that you are not reminded of this. (pp. 98–99)

Mr. Barrister locates his experience of health and illness within an ever-present oppressive frame shaped by derogatory judgments of his racial identity. What health and illness means to individuals reflects such experiences. Meanings of health and illness are also intertwined with tacit assumptions about the body, its functioning, care, and limits. Some people view their bodies and, by extension, their health, as requiring careful and constant maintenance, while others assume their health is invincible. Cynthia Duer, a middle-aged woman recalled how she viewed her body before she developed a disturbing tremor:

> Wonderful! [laughing]. Capable. Athletic. Golfer. Gardener. Yeah, I thought I was invincible. You know nothing – everything happens to everybody else, couldn't possibly – I'm too tough for anything to happen to me. I've got too many obligations; forget about it. You don't think anything... it's not you. It's always the other guy. (Charmaz 2002:35s)

People like Cynthia may not think or do much about their health but may subscribe to common beliefs distinguishing health from illness, such as the absence of symptoms. Similarly, individuals may share notions of what maintaining health involves but may not be able to act on them. Habits, priorities, and the demands of daily life intervene. Thus, you hear people say things like, "I know I should exercise but I leave too early and get home too late." "Our jobs are so demanding that we have no time for shopping and cooking." Such explanations do not disavow the value of exercise or healthy food but indicate people's reasons for how the structure of their lives overrides acting on their preferences (Harris 2017).

Whose definitions of health, illness, and disability prevail? Women are the health monitors in perhaps most families across the globe, particularly of their children. Although Cynthia paid little attention to her own health for much of her life, she monitored and guarded the health of her family. Cynthia protected her daughter Kate whose precarious health began in infancy when she was diagnosed with life-threatening Type 1 diabetes (Charmaz 2002). At that time, Kate's doctors estimated that she only had a 50–50 chance of surviving to adulthood. Cynthia's main purpose in life became keeping Kate alive and as healthy as possible. Her constant vigilance had saved Kate through numerous crises. By age 19, Kate had begun to create an independent life. For Kate, maintaining health meant preserving autonomy and engaging in ordinary activities while managing a serious chronic illness.

Meanings of health, illness, and disability are intertwined with images, experiences, and expectations of our bodies and those of others. Cynthia's earlier image of her body as athletic and invincible contrasted with her view of Kate's as fragile and vulnerable. Waskul and Vannini (2006) remind us that we interpret what we see when we look at another person's body. Simultaneously, this person imagines what we might be seeing, thinking, and feeling and then responds to his or her imagined interpretation. Waskul and Vannini (2006:5) echo Cooley's (2003) concept of the looking-glass self and name this process the **looking-glass body**. They emphasize that the looking glass body requires reflexivity because is an imagined reflection of the other's judgment, not a direct reproduction of this judgment. For these authors, this reflexivity is fundamental to what embodiment means.

> *Waskul and Vannini's concept, the "looking-glass body," refers to the process of interpreting what we see when we look at another person's body. Simultaneously, this person imagines what we might be seeing, thinking, and feeling and then responds to his or her imagined interpretation. The looking glass body requires reflexivity because is an imagined reflection of the other's judgment, not a direct reproduction of this judgment or observations of another person's body.*

In their depiction of the looking glass body, Waskul and Vannini emphasize the interactions between self and other. Yet, we too make telling appraisals of our own bodies that inform our views and interactions, as well as what we do and don't do to maintain health.

## Maintaining Health

Maintaining health involves beliefs about the body and its care. What does it take to maintain health? How do people decide to follow some conventional health practices but not others? Cynthia's story reveals how complex meanings and actions about health and illness can be and suggests how assumptions about the body underlie health decisions. You can also discern this kind of complexity around health decisions among families who face less dramatic situations but are concerned with maintaining healthy bodies. We describe two such situations here to illustrate this point: making healthy food choices and deciding whether to vaccinate children.

In her study of families and food at a California high school, Priya Fielding-Singh (2017) learned that parents who differed by social class shared views about what constituted healthy food and its importance for maintaining health. In all families, teenagers asked for foods that their parents deemed to be unhealthy. However, families with high socioeconomic status, parents declined their children's requests. Low-income parents granted them except when unaffordable. Yet Fielding-Singh argues that neither affordability nor accessibility played major roles in parents' choices among the low-income families she studied. Instead, she contends that the symbolic value of giving children their preferred foods outweighed these parents' concerns about health. They used food to maintain emotional bonds and to compensate for being unable to give their children other consumer goods and amenities. Miranda's comment to Fielding-Singh exemplifies this view:

> Everything, literally every dime I get goes to food. Every dime. But what do you do? I just buy it for them. It's for my babies. I love them more than anything on the planet. I don't care. They want it. They'll get it. One day, they'll know. They know I love them and that's all that matters. So what? It's food. I don't care. If she wants a $2 candy bar, I get it for her if I have it [the money]. (Fielding-Singh 2017:434)

Fielding-Singh's research illustrates how other priorities eclipse shared views of healthy practices. In contrast, Reich's (2014, 2016) study reveals conflicting definitions of healthy practices. Current arguments about the value of vaccinations illustrate parents' claims about health and which actions to take to protect it. Reich found that mothers decided whether, when, and how to vaccinate their children. In her study, mothers who refused vaccinations focused on their children rather than the collective benefits of vaccination. These mothers discounted professional advice. Instead, they claimed their expert knowledge[1] about their children, healthy meals and living, and concerns about serious health risks from vaccinations outweighed requiring them. The mothers believed healthy living also meant preventing their children from being exposed to other kids and people they thought might pose health risks to their children. Reich (2014:696) notes that the women rely on racialized accounts of disease when evaluating potential infection and protecting their children from exposure.

Mothers who did not vaccinate their children believed their family's health practices provided better immunity than vaccination. The mothers overlooked how their children benefited from the vaccinated immunity of others. They also downplayed or discounted arguments that not vaccinating their children increased community risk, including those of children whose medical conditions precluded being vaccinated (Reich 2014:688). Marlene, an interview participant, explains, "I have just made the best decisions – I think we've made the best decisions we could have gathering as much information as we could" (2014:698). As Reich underscores, mothers who refused to vaccinate their children based their decisions on individualized criteria that placed the primacy of their child and their knowledge of their child above both medical guidelines and community health.

Passionate arguments for and against vaccinations have been raised in the media and between friends. Friendships end and parents clash. For example, co-authors Harry Collins and Trevor Pinch (2005:viii) wrote that their opposing views about vaccination "twice came within a whisker of ending the entire project" of collaborating on their book about the fallibility of medicine. Or, consider Michigan single mother, Rebecca Bredow. She vehemently rejected her ex-partner's wish to vaccinate their 9-year-old son (Brever and Phillips 2017). Bredow cited her religious beliefs and intention to protect the health of her children as reasons for refusing to vaccinate the boy. She served a five-day jail term for failing to follow a court order to vaccinate her son and vowed she would go to jail again to save her son from vaccinations. To her chagrin, the judge awarded temporary custody to the boy's father who had their son vaccinated while she served jailtime.

Our discussion of contrasting food choices and conflict over vaccination points to looking at which health decisions people make, how they make them, and why they act on their decisions. Who is responsible for health? Who *should* be responsible for health?

## Individual vs. Social Responsibility for Health

Health practitioners, social scientists, and members of the public have long engaged in debates about responsibility for health. As Robert Crawford (2006) notes, people who live in a **health-valuing culture** evaluate themselves and others according to their relative success or failure in enacting conventional health practices. Thus, conceptions of taking responsibility for health become measures of self and identity. This type of health consciousness fits notions of individual responsibility for health with its attendant values of agency, rationality, and moral accountability.

Are individual or collective actions most important for maintaining health? As you will see, advocates of each position consider different concerns. Yet both positions assume that risk and hazard reduction and moral accountability are worthy goals to promote health, although they often address different forms of each.

## Individual Responsibility for Health

In many debates about responsibility for health, people give priority to individual responsibility. Values concerning autonomy, health consciousness, risk reduction, and personal accountability support nurturing **individual responsibility for health**. Robert Crawford (2006:402) states, "Personal responsibility for health is widely considered the sine qua non of individual autonomy and good citizenship. Individuals are expected to acquire medical knowledge." Proponents of individual responsibility argue that people achieve good health through their own efforts. From this perspective, people pursue well-being by making sound choices and taking sensible actions. Here, good health means work, not merely the absence of discernible disease. To earn good health, people must seek and apply reliable health information about the mind and body. Diverse although sometimes contradictory instructions for accomplishing such well-being emanate from self-help books, internet resources, personal trainers, commercial diet plans, health education classes, and health insurance plans.

### Gender and Individual Responsibility for Health

Values supporting individual responsibility for health may contradict other deeply held cultural norms. Cynthia's story above indicates how values about maternal responsibility can override a mother's concern with her own health. Similarly, men's adherence to cultural norms of masculinity can both bolster and undercut attending to health. To the extent that men's quest for health merges with their conceptions of masculinity then their incentives increase to pursue individual responsibility for health. Interest in fitness and sport may spur some men – and women – to participate in a health regimen. A quest to be competitive, however, can lead to risky decisions. In his study of Welsh bodybuilders, Monaghan (2001, 2002) details how the athletes gained and shared knowledge of illicit drugs to increase their competitiveness and subsequently account for using them. One man viewed taking steroids as constructive because he aimed to build his body in contrast with taking risky recreational drugs such as cocaine or heroin (2002:699). Others – like Bill, an older retired competitive bodybuilder – embraced the risks despite their potential consequences.

> BILL: When you use steroids [to the extent necessary to win competitions] you really have to weigh up the pros and cons, and you might be shortening your life. You might cause problems in later life [...] A sensible person would weigh up the pros and cons and I've often – in my "I don't give a fuck" time type of attitude, I would think I have sort of justified it all by saying that I would rather be a meteor and flash brightly through the sky than be a little twinkling star for seventy years and do

nothing which is a bit – dramatic, isn't it? [...] I feel that if I die tomorrow I know that my life's been eventful if nothing else. It certainly hasn't been humdrum, and it hasn't been boring [...] Bodybuilding's opened doors to me. (Monaghan 2001:117)

Other studies echo Bill's stance on risk and show how men's shared values conflict with taking responsibility for their health. For example, Noel Richardson's (2010) study of men's responsibility for health in Ireland confirmed that young men took risks. He found that fatherhood, aging, and health crises prompted men to attend to their health. However, his younger research participants engaged in risky behavior such as heavy drinking with other men. Richardson argues that these young men attempted to prove their masculinity and aimed to avoid judgments of being effeminate. The norms of comradeship overshadowed values supporting individual responsibility for health.

Richardson's findings also suggest the men saw health as women's concern. A comment by one middle-aged respondent, Kiernan, provides an example of this viewpoint:

KIERAN: With women, health always comes around in conversation ... but with men it never does, ever.
INTERVIEWER: And why is that?
KIERAN: I don't know, you just don't talk about them things. Like I would switch off if my wife is talking to her friends about [pause] I won't say the gory details, but the more intimate it is, the more interested they are in talking about it and the less interested I am in talking about it. (Richardson 2010:427)

This type of gender divide in talking about health could influence the health practices, if any, men adopt and the extent to which they reflect individual responsibility for health. The contradictory pressures/norms described here likely leads to all sorts of complicated overlaps and divergences in gendered health behavior.

### Extending Individual Responsibility through Online Participation

New digital health programs focus on involving individuals to take responsibility for making lifestyle changes to improve their health. These programs address medical and health practices using mobile electronic devices (e-health). Numerous programs scrutinize individuals' health practices through technological monitoring and electronic health coaching. The coaches may oversee a group of clients, lead discussions, and comment on individual clients' progress – or lack of it. Typical stated goals of such programs include educating, empowering, and encouraging clients to take responsibility for their health (e.g. Adams and Niezen 2015; Vorderstrasse et al. 2016). The programs affirm and extend beliefs in individual responsibility for health through **technological bodily surveillance**.

Clients for these programs are frequently referred by their physicians or health plans. These clients may already have serious illnesses or be defined as "at risk" for contracting them. The programs aim to instill lifestyle changes in clients to improve their health and thus reduce risks. In effect, the programs market **identity goals** with promise of realizing a **preferred identity** symbolizing "assumptions, hopes, desires and plans for a future now unrealized" (Charmaz 1987:284) as well as health tips and tracking. In their study of the development of e-Coaches in the Netherlands, Adams and Niezen (2015) observe, however, that the greatest benefits of risk reduction accrue to the health care system and society by reducing costs of caring for chronically ill people.

Such programs rely on monitoring and measuring computerized information and client reports. For example, clients' daily weight can be sent directly to the health program through a computerized scale and footsteps can be electronically recorded with a smart phone or fitness device. The program can record clients' completion of computerized lessons and urge participation through reminders. Clients may be asked to track everything they eat and drink, record exercise activities, and participate in electronic discussion and support groups. Relying on client-initiated reports does allow room for fibbing about actions and neglecting to record infractions. A client's desire to put forth an approved self-presentation can override creating accurate reports. Trained e-coaches may respond directly to clients' reports as well as set goals and initiate discussion groups.

The intrusiveness of e-monitoring clients is a clear concern. Adams and Niezen (2015:514) cite the following warning in a call for research proposals for e-health program development:

> Coaching solutions collect a wealth of information about their coachees. In particular, unobtrusive, longitudinal monitoring can give rise to all kinds of acceptance issues and ethical concerns. Continuous monitoring can give rise to a feeling of "big brother is watching you" and, even unintentionally, intimate information may be acquired. Therefore, long-term monitoring needs to be organized in such a way that it is acceptable to the individual as well as to society at large. e-Coaching solutions should operate in a manner that is ethically responsible and acceptable for envisioned users.

Here, Adams and Niezen imply that even strong advocates of individual responsibility for health also must consider their social responsibilities. This point adds a new concern for those who have long advocated social responsibility for health. For them, reducing good health to individual responsibility is too limited a focus. Thus, they look critically at social structure. To them, maintaining health necessitates collective actions.

## Social Responsibility for Health

Social responsibility for health means casting a wider net than individual actions to avoid illness and injury and to assume moral accountability. Instead, social responsibility for health includes the environment and addresses such issues as clean air, water, and food, all of which of residents of developed countries may take for granted. Social responsibility for health means providing sanitation, food and drug standards, disease prevention measures, and occupational safety as well as health promotion and health education. Hence, it includes regulatory standards to protect health, such as establishing and enforcing levels of unacceptable toxicity, and thus can lead to conflict with corporate environmental practices.

In short, social responsibility for health involves institutional and organizational policies and practices. Making health care available to all is foremost among advocates of social responsibility for health. In this view, access to health care should be a right, not a privilege, for all members of the society, like public education. Advocates of social responsibility for health argue that accessible health care programs, as well as invisible, taken for granted resources not only contribute to the well-being of individuals but also of society. For example, making nutritious food available to pregnant women increases the health of their babies – and reduces the need for expensive care later. Making nutritious meals available to children improves their ability to learn in school and, by extension, become productive citizens.

Although other developed nations offer institutionalized national health services or comprehensive health insurance plans to their citizens, the United States relies heavily on privately purchased or employer-sponsored health insurance plans. The availability of employer-sponsored health insurance is perhaps the most crucial form of social responsibility at the organizational level in the United States. Some organizations also offer health programs to their employees ranging from health education to health promotion, including access to on-site fitness facilities and cafeterias, as well as benefits such as paid sick leaves, parental and eldercare absences, and access to counseling during life crises.

Advocates of social responsibility for health argue that prioritizing individual lifestyle and health behavior overshadows acknowledging environmental, societal, or genetic sources of ill health. Nonetheless, arguments for individual responsibility for health constitute a persuasive narrative many health professionals and lay people readily adopt.

# Individual Responsibility and Neoliberalism

### How Individual Responsibility for Health Complements Neoliberalism

Individual actions such as acquiring health knowledge and pursuing e-health strategies not only fit conceptions of individual responsibility for health but also fit larger neoliberal political agendas. Neoliberalism consists of political and economic perspectives and practices that support individual freedom, self-sufficiency, competition, individual accountability, and efficiency (Charmaz and Belgrave In press.) Proponents of neoliberalism believe their views are not only economically effective but also enhance the well-being of individuals. In short, neoliberalism presupposes that individuals who endorse and enact its values can achieve well-being. Neoliberalism ignores or minimizes disadvantages imposed by gender, race, class, age, or health status.

> **Neoliberalism consists of political and economic perspectives and practices that support individual freedom, self-sufficiency, competition, individual accountability, and efficiency. Proponents of neoliberalism believe their views are not only economically effective but also enhance the well-being of individuals.**

Through elevating individual responsibility, neoliberal policies, and practices minimize social responsibility for health. Advocates of neoliberalism support efforts to influence individual choices and practices. If so, then health promotion means educating individuals to make responsible health decisions. In her study of sex education, Elliott (2014) describes latent and explicit lessons Mrs. Fox, a middle-class white high school teacher and mother of teen-aged children, imparted to her predominantly African American and Latino students. Elliott (2014:217–218) writes that Mrs. Fox told the students:

> If one of her teen children got pregnant, she would not be like "those parents" whose children become teen parents and are allowed to live at home. Instead, Ms. Fox said, "I would get them an apartment and they can live there and raise that child. They're not going to raise that kid under my roof – they're going to be responsible for that kid." By positioning her white middle-class family's response as superior, Ms. Fox reveals underlying cultural assumptions about race and teen parenting – especially the notion that poor Black and Latino families condone teenage pregnancy.

Most of Mrs. Fox's students could not handle the responsibilities of parenthood alone. Nor could their impoverished families set them up in an apartment. Elliott (2014:213) states, "Sex educators' spoken and unspoken lessons in personal responsibility put forth a limited version of the good sexual citizen, what I call the responsible sexual agent, which is based on and reproduces social inequalities. The responsible sexual agent is self-sufficient, self-regulating, and consequence-bearing." Elliott (2014:213–214) argues that the sex educators' depiction of personal responsibility deflects considerations of social responsibility and absolves adults, schools, and governments of dealing with the consequences of teens' sexual activity.

On a larger scale, neoliberal perspectives influence arguments about explicitly rationing healthcare. In this perspective, patients' personal responsibility for making good health decisions becomes a major criterion for rationing healthcare (Buyx 2008). Proponents of rationing often make the following assumptions: (i) unhealthy lifestyles are a matter of choice; (ii) people have equal access to resources, including knowledge, to lead healthy lives; and (iii) therefore, those who lead unhealthy lives merit having less access to medical treatment than those who have followed healthy practices. Yet as Rebecca C. H. Brown (2013:697) contends, those who experience greater social deprivations more likely have less freedom to make healthy choices. And Alena Buyx points out that certain measures need to be enacted before personal responsibility could justifiably be used as one criterion for rationing. Among these measures are removing toxins from the environment, improving health literacy, and regulating addictive substances and certain foods.

### Moral Failure and Victim-Blaming

When people attribute well-being and good health to individual choice, then what are the implications for people with deteriorating health? Illness and disability become viewed as a **moral failure** rather than caused by a disease, injury, or genetic predisposition (Edgley 2006; Galvin 2002). The weight of moral failure can seep in and shape a person's sense of self. One of Garthwaite's (2015) research participants in the United Kingdom, Sarah, was a middle-aged woman who had received sickness benefits for 15 years. Sarah disclosed her sense of moral failure about not working in the following statement:

> I make any excuse to not to go a party, not that I'm invited to many but at church it might be someone's Golden wedding anniversary and if I go and there's people I don't know and they ask me what I do, what do you think I say? I say "I'm a piece of shit." What else do they want me to say? I say "I'm one of the dregs of society, I'm one of the ones wasting your tax." (Garthwaite 2015:6)

Judgments of moral failure by self and others are magnified by cultural norms of adult responsibilities and good citizenship. Galvin (2002:108) states that remaining physically incapacitated "clashes too uncomfortably with the image of the 'good citizen' as someone who actively participates in social and economic life, makes rational choices and is independent, self-reliant and responsible." Conversely, conceptions of individual responsibility for health fit comfortably in the United States with its value on individualism and independence. Thus, many North Americans look no further than people's irresponsible choices and habits to explain illness and disability.

Adopting this stance encourages **victim-blaming**, which assumes people's poor choices make them vulnerable to illness. In its most stark form, victim-blaming assumes that people get the diseases they deserve or desire. By extension, victim blaming fosters stigmatizing attitudes and actions toward these individuals (Goffman 1963). During McClean's (2005) research at a spiritual healing center in the United Kingdom, one staff member discussed a man whom she was treating for eczema. She said:

> ...He had visited me a number of times over the past three years and every time the same problem occurs. He has quite a bad skin complaint – eczema – and he has said that he has spent thousands of pounds on different drugs and therapies and nothing has helped him and I know that's because he blames it on everyone else except himself, and now he wants the eczema, I think. It isn't going to go away because he seems to want it. (McClean 2005:637)

The staff member's moral judgment of victim-blaming is quite direct. Victim-blaming also includes less direct assertions but insidious judgments. Here, other people question how a person could have avoided becoming ill or disabled and form judgments about what the person "should" have done to avoid it.

*Victim-blaming assumes people's poor choices make them vulnerable to illness or disability. In its most stark form, victim-blaming assumes that people get the diseases they deserve. Yet victim-blaming also includes less direct assertions but insidious judgments. Victim-blaming occurs when people question how a person could have avoided becoming ill or disabled and form judgments about what the person "should" have done to avoid it.*

Victim-blaming judgements may be made about a person's past behavior from the vantage point of present, often incomplete, information. Whether this information is old or new, accepted knowledge or contested views, victim-blaming allows making invidious comparisons between self and the ill person. Thus, those who blame may assume a sense of moral superiority for making different, "better" choices than the ill person whose deteriorating health "attests" to failing his or her moral responsibilities.

## Experiencing Serious Illness

Recall Cynthia's comment earlier in this chapter. In it, she described the healthy body she had had in the past from the vantagepoint of having disabling symptoms in the present. As Cynthia's statement implies, meanings of health and illness shift when people experience jarring symptoms that mark bodily change and the onset of debilitating illness. Furthermore, experiencing debilitating illness and disability magnifies benchmarks in adult life and often minimizes the time between them.

Definitions of illness reveal a range of meanings that reflect people's knowledge, assumptions, and experiences. When they have no symptoms but receive a diagnosis of a dreaded disease through routine medical tests, they likely experience diagnostic shock. These people often treat their diagnoses as portending serious illness and some people view their lives as over. Other people who have troubling symptoms, however, may embark on a diagnostic quest to find out what accounts for their symptoms.

## The Diagnostic Quest

Until symptoms become disturbing, many people ignore or normalize them by invoking such common reasons as stress or aging. How people – and health professions – respond to symptoms reflects the societies and communities to which they belong. As we pointed out in Chapter 4, we *interpret* bodily symptoms – ours and those of others. In affluent societies, people often assume they will enjoy good health throughout their lives. Hence, they begin a **diagnostic quest** when their symptoms become intrusive. For many patients with unexplained symptoms, diagnosis is a journey rather than a single event. Price and Walker (2015:31) call this journey **diagnostic vertigo** as it consists of distress, ambiguity, and uncertainty, and may not result in a discernible end. In her study of women with fibromyalgia, Barker (2005) reports that her research participants' ambiguous symptoms led them to enter a lengthy diagnostic quest. They moved from specialist to specialist on a symptom by symptom basis. For example, one woman said:

> I've seen neurologists, osteopaths, oral surgeons. I can't think of all the different kinds of medicine that there are, but I have seen pretty much the gamut of referrals. Gastroenterologist, gynecologist, if it's got an "ologist" behind it, I've probably seen them. (Barker 2005:94)

The diagnostic quest also may stretch when patients do not fit the image of a person having a common condition. These patients may find their physicians offering reassurance, but not a diagnosis or treatment. For example, a slender, middle-aged woman looked younger than her years. It took multiple doctor's visits before she received more than a cursory examination for intermittent chest pain. Her doctor had suggested that her symptoms were due to indigestion and anxiety. After he discovered she had a coronary artery blockage, he told her, "You don't look like a patient with heart disease."

Many people with ambiguous symptoms find themselves dismissed when their symptoms either remain unexplained or fit contested conditions such as fibromyalgia or multiple chemical sensitivity. Dumit (2006) interviewed people with contested illnesses that many doctors disbelieved. A woman had been recently diagnosed with Chronic Fatigue Syndrome (CFS) after other physicians had discounted her symptoms. She talked about her diagnostic quest:

> I had to travel nearly 1000 miles to get to a doctor who could diagnose me. My GP [general practitioner] indicated he would abide by the specialist's diagnosis, and he has ...tacitly, though he still will not commit himself to even stating that another doctor has diagnosed me with cfids [CFS] (whether he agrees or not). Nor is he willing to attempt any of even the most common symptoms-management protocols (citing side effects and/or addiction as his reasons for not wanting to try any of them). (Dumit 2006:582)

Unexplained symptoms typically result in people living with **uncertainty**, dealing with questions about legitimacy, and resisting psychological explanations of pain and suffering (Nettleton 2006). These patients must somehow prove the legitimacy of his or her symptoms. Thus, accounting for unexplained symptoms shifts responsibility from the doctor to the patient (Jutel 2011).

Yet patients may neither be given a voice, nor have their earlier diagnoses reconfirmed. Disputed diagnoses and contested treatments can wreak havoc in their lives. Recall the woman's story in Chapter 3, whose long history of lupus erythematosus was ignored during her stay in a psychiatric hospital. During her interview, she talked about how her psychiatrist had discounted her earlier diagnosis, disbelieved her explanations of her symptoms, and rejected her pleas to be given her lupus medications. Karina Hansen, a young Danish woman had a diagnosis of myalgic encephalomyelitis/chronic fatigue syndrome, a chronic degenerative neuro-immune disease.[2] After earlier distressing hospitalizations, she did not want more. Karina gave her parents power of attorney in case she was deemed unable to act on her own behalf (MEpedia 2017). However, she was forcibly taken from her family home and institutionalized for over three years during which a psychiatrist supervised her care. A guardian was appointed; her condition deteriorated, and she could no longer speak clearly. Her doctor stated her treatment was voluntary; her advocates declared it was an involuntary incarceration.

Both women had had diagnoses of physical illness but lost credibility and **moral status**, as revealed by each woman's loss of autonomy. As one of us (Kathy) has argued, "A moral status confers relative human worth and, thus, measures deserved value or devaluation" (Charmaz 1999:367). The amount of respect and autonomy other people accord an individual indicates his or her moral status.

*"A moral status confers relative human worth and, thus, measures deserved value or devaluation" (Charmaz 1999:367). The amount of respect and autonomy other people accord an individual indicates his or her moral status.*

Many people, particularly those with undiagnosed debilitating symptoms, lose moral status with their families and friends, who question whether their symptoms are real. Subsequently these ill individuals may welcome a devastating diagnosis after months and years of seeking help, only to have been dismissed and after losing believability in their intimates' eyes. A woman whose lengthy history of mysterious debilitating symptoms resulted in an extensive evaluation by renowned experts. This woman expressed relief and gratitude for being diagnosed with a deadly condition. At last she had a legitimate condition and evidence that her symptoms were physical rather than psychological.

In stark contrast, Cynthia embarked on a diagnostic quest to confirm that her tremor *was* psychological, rather than an early onset of Parkinson's disease with increasing disability, as her physician believed. Because she discovered that her tremor differed somewhat from descriptions of tremors in Parkinson's patients, Cynthia reasoned:

> I'm at a state where I believe it will be reversed when I get control of my emotions. I think it will calm down and be something besides – because one of the things with Parkinson's Disease is that when people are at rest, they have the rhythmic tremor. And when I'm at rest I have no tremor. When I'm not nervous, I have no tremor. (Charmaz 2002:335)

The thought of having an irreversible, progressive condition clashed with Cynthia's self-concept as a healthy, indomitable woman who overcame hardships. She resisted the prospect of becoming disabled by redefining the meaning of her symptoms. Cynthia aimed her diagnostic quest to enlist physicians to validate her interpretation of the cause of her tremor. Hence, she insisted emotional stress accounted for her symptoms and she had conceivable reasons for seeing herself as stressed. Not only had all she shouldered the weight of monitoring Kate's health and getting her emergency care during many crises, Cynthia had essentially raised her two daughters without her husband's involvement. Simultaneously, she kept his business affairs in order and maintained their household and property. Cynthia described her husband as uncommunicative but wholly dependent on her companionship. Although she gave him considerable attention, conflict reigned in their home. Cynthia's husband disapproved of their older daughter, who lived at home, and refused to be in the same room with her. Subsequently, Cynthia endured the stress of trying to keep peace in the household.

### Biographical Disruption and Loss of Self

The onset of illness or disability can result in what Michael Bury (1982) calls a **biographical disruption**, which rips apart people's taken-for granted assumptions about their bodies, lives, and deaths. Bury's concept captures the profound disruption experienced by many people who have a sudden onset of an illness or disability. This disruption separates their lives before and after it. A formerly unnoticed, functioning body now imposes unwelcome limits. Physical independence may be threatened and with it, personal autonomy. Biographical disruptions force reappraisal and reconstruction of self and identity.

> *A biographical disruption rips apart people's taken-for granted assumptions about their bodies, lives, and deaths. This disruption separates life before illness or disability and life after its onset. A formerly unnoticed, functioning body now imposes unwelcome limits. Physical independence may be threatened and with it, personal autonomy. Biographical disruptions force reappraisal and reconstruction of self and identity.*

A biographical disruption begins when a person has troubling symptoms, suffers an injury, or receives a serious diagnosis. Daily life changes. Treatment regimens and self-care often consume hours of the person's day. Managing the workday can become impossible. Relationships change Losses of economic and physical independence may follow. Louise Locock, Sue Ziebland, and Carol Dumelow (2009) conducted interviews of people in the UK with motor neuron disease (MND) [also known as amyotrophic lateral sclerosis [ALS] or Lou Gehrig's disease], which the authors describe as lying at the boundary between chronic and terminal illness. Symptoms of MND include muscular atrophy, progressive neuro-degeneration, and difficulty in breathing and speaking. One research participant, Martin, was a 23-year-old former construction worker whose MND was a devastating biographical disruption. He said, "I can't even write. What am I meant to do, like, if I can't hold a pen? I ain't going to be able to hold a screwdriver or a drill.... I can't do bowling no more, I can't go go-karting, all the things I used to do, like. And obviously driving, I miss that a lot." (Locock et al. 2009:1049)

Biographical disruptions reveal sharp differences between the self of the past and the experience self and the present. These disruptions elicit questions of "Why me?" and "Why now?" (Charmaz 1980; Shim 2014) A college student described her response to a miserable onset of colitis. She said:

> How tragic! [her situation]. Why me? It's not fair. I get a disease I've never heard of, does anyone else have it? I mean I'm nice to small children and animals. I thought I had good Karma and then I grew up with allergies, get colitis, have back injuries, and have migraines. Why do all these other people who are not nearly as nice and far more deserve to be sick, why not them? (Charmaz 1980:126)

"Why now?" questions pervade a person's consciousness, when the timing seems so wrong and punishing. Consider the situation of a 62-year-old woman who had given loving care to her 80-year-old husband during his many crises with prostate cancer. After he died, she sunk into a depression for several years before becoming involved with new friends and a local charity. Life looked brighter. But then she was diagnosed with breast cancer. All she could think of was "Why now?"

Whether people view the onset of an illness or disability as a biographical disruption depends on how they see themselves, their bodies, and their situations. Yet an individual's age and the context of his or her life matters. Those who had endured hard lives or are elderly often view it as one more difficult but unsurprising obstacle to live with (Cornwell 1984; Sanders, Donovan, and Dieppe 2002). Thus, they see their lives as having biographical continuity, despite illness. Hinojosa et al. (2008) found lower and middle-class older stroke survivors created continuity by seeing their conditions as a normal part of growing old and as consistent with their religious beliefs.

Like Cynthia, people initially may treat their conditions as temporarily interrupting their ordinary lives, but not as causing a permanent disruption. The prospect of being chronically ill and/or disabled can shake people's assumptions about themselves and their place in the world. Kayleigh Garthwaite (2015) interviewed Kirsty, a 33 year-old prison officer, who resisted viewing herself as disabled:

> I found it very difficult to accept that I had a disability cos I've always been fiercely independent. I've never asked for help before, it wasn't in my nature and to have to ask for it was tough. Trying to quantify being disabled was difficult, it was something to get your head round and I still don't think of myself as disabled, I'll still call it an injury rather than a disability. (Garthwaite 2015:4)

As long as Kirsty can define her condition as temporary, she can maintain hope of recapturing the self she had in the past. Many people, however, come to see their lives is changed. People with serious illnesses and injuries find themselves facing existential questions and feeling forced to reconstruct how they see themselves, as occurred with the young woman's story about learning that she had been infected with a sexually transmitted disease.

Disabling illness forces many people to recognize their new limitations and reorganize their lives. For some people, serious illness may be an episode – a **temporary interruption** of life – or the beginning of a long ordeal. Arthur Frank (1991:19) defines having a heart attack at 39 as "an incident, an interlude." He compares his heart attack with experiencing cancer and writes, "I may have bounced back from a heart attack, but with cancer, I was going to have to sink all the way through and discover a life on the other side. Cancer was not going to be an incident; I would have to experience it" (1991:28). And to experience it means one's life is disrupted, if not forever changed.

A college student who aspired to become a professional mezzo-soprano lost her voice after cancer surgery. She said, "My voice was gone, so I was gone, and I never was anything but my voice" (Charmaz 2011:176). For her, **loss of self** (Charmaz 1983, 2011) was complete. What is loss of self?

> Loss of self symbolizes more than bodily losses. It means loss of the ways people know, define, and feel about themselves. Their identifying attributes are gone. The foundations of their lives have weakened or crumbled. Loss of self alters how people compare themselves with others and locate themselves in their worlds. It means losing their way of being in the world – and, moreover, in its most intense forms, losing their personal and collective worlds. (Charmaz 2011:178–179)

Profound loss of self fits what Ciambrone (2007) calls "an assault on the self." Here, illness and disability affect every aspect of the person's life. Brett Smith and Andrew Sparkes (2005) interviewed rugby players who had suffered spinal cord injuries. Eamonn, who was injured 12 years before at age 17, reflected "I never thought it would happen to me. You don't, otherwise you'd never play. So becoming disabled was not what I expected, and when it happened I lost everything. It was, *is*, such a huge crisis and because of it I've lost my life" (Smith and Sparkes 2005:1097).

Although Eamonn's injury marked an irreparable disruption between his past and present, he hoped for a cure and a return to his earlier life. Many people try to create some sense of biographical continuity, which preserves the identities they had long-held (Vann-Ward, Morse, and Charmaz 2017). Their stories often reflect a search for new meaning when old meanings of self, identity, and ordinary everyday life no longer suffice.

What role does realizing a preferred identity play? People with intrusive illnesses and disabilities often put considerable effort into creating biographical continuity and realizing a threatened preferred identity. Their efforts can be depicted by an implicit **identity hierarchy** (see Figure 5.1). Using these concepts, Eamonn hoped for a restored self but saw that any chance of realizing it rested on medical science.

Other people move up and down the identity hierarchy, depending on their situations. Thus, someone may first aim for a supernormal identity and scale down the identity hierarchy if he or she experiences progressive illness. Conversely, a person may initiate small steps toward realizing a valued identity after a long convalescence and gradually move up the identity hierarchy. Almost no one wants to become an invalid.

## Living with Illness and Disability

Learning to live with illness and disability can lead to new meanings and new priorities. People learn how their changed bodies affect their lives and selves as they attempt to conduct their ordinary activities. They may discover that

### Identity Levels of an Identity Hierarchy[1]

➤ **Supernormal social identity**—a quest to be victorious over illness and disability and often to seek accomplishment in worlds which ordinary peers do not. People who pursue a supernormal identity:

- Reject stigmatizing images of illness and disability
- View illness and disability as presenting obstacles
- Take risks to realize preferred identity
- Give enormous effort to pursuing their goals.

➤ **Restored self**—aim to resume one's former life, to reconstruct a similar physical self and to regain the same sense of self as before illness and disability. People who aim for this identity level:

- Often assume that *recovery* should be the *sequel* to illness or injury
- Believe they can and should be the same person as in the past
- Disregard their present situation as reflecting who they are and must become
- Seek confirmation from intimates that they are making progress on restoring themselves
- Understand the rhythm and pacing of their former existence, which becomes a measure of their current efforts.

➤ **Contingent personal identity**—aim for a *hypothetically possible,* but *questionable,* *risky,* and *decidedly conditional* personal identity due to potential further episodes of illness. People who aim for this identity level:

- Assume all plans turn on keeping illness contained
- See their precarious health as making their preferred identity *uncertain*
- Believe their hopes and plans are fragile and tentative
- Hope to preserve most valued identity; will relinquish other identities
- Relinquish hope in attaining either a supernormal identity or restored self.

*People pursue their preferred identities to avoid becoming invalids.*

---

[1]Adapted from Kathy Charmaz (1987).

**Figure 5.1** Identity levels of an identity hierarchy (*Source:* Adapted from Charmaz 1987).

handling daily tasks such as self-care, household chores, and shopping now take enormous amounts of time, when they can do them at all. Newly imposed limitations become apparent when they can no longer maintain the pace and involvements of daily life. Participants in Kathy's studies frequently mentioned how they hadn't realized how much their illness or treatment disrupted their lives until they tried to carry on as they had before. A woman who had breast cancer expected to work throughout her treatment but realized that she could not maintain her earlier pace and productivity. She commented:

> So I had thought that I would work during chemotherapy because I had no idea what chemotherapy was, so I said [to business partners and

customers], "Well, don't worry about it, I'll be around, I'll work," you know. Well, of course, chemotherapy was a disaster and I did try to work a lot....

One of the women Mendelson (2006) interviewed for her study of lupus erythematosus said:

> I have to take a nap every day or I can't function. I can no longer get down on my knees or wrestle with my boys on the floor. I used to go on hikes with my husband, but now I am too tired, I can barely climb stairs now. I have to watch myself in the sun or I get a terrible facial rash and get flu-like symptoms. Every day of my life is a challenge and I am only 32 years old. (Mendelson 2006:991)

This woman's earlier assumptions about her body were broken. People with illnesses and disabilities often talk about how their bodies have betrayed them. Price and Walker (2015:85), who each have an autoimmune disease, view these conditions as diseases of the self, a "failure *of* the self." They portray people's lost trust in their bodies as "I am my own worst enemy" (2015:11–30).

Handling daily obstacles and limitations become a major concern, particularly when a person's physical independence and livelihood are threatened. Meriel Norris, Pascale Allotey, and Geraldine Barrett (2012) interviewed survivors of stroke in Indonesia. These survivors talked about their inability to work as worst outcome of having a stroke, as this 66-year-old man's comment reflects:

> I want to be able to work but I am unable to work freely and ... [Previously] I could break the tree branches, but I cannot do that now. I used to take avocadoes. I used to be able to go from one coffee tree to another, now I can't, I have to take a stick with me. It has a big influence to my condition now. I used to go to the garden in five minutes, but now I reach there in two or three hours.... (Norris, Allotey and Barrett 2012:831)

Such contrasts between past and present are striking, particularly when the biographical disruption is new. Over time, people may come to **normalize** their changed bodies and routines. Normalizing symptoms, disabilities, regimens, and adaptations means treating them as ordinary, although the effort needed to do so may be extraordinary. Normalizing involves making life manageable and concealing limitations to keep up conventional appearances. Yet visible disabilities or symptoms can be difficult to hide, as this woman's lament about having cancer indicates:

> I'm coming out in spots and I don't like the way I look. I look like a little old lady and I don't feel like one usually.... I've never classed myself as

old.... I look at that photo [before cancer diagnosis] and think now that's me... this [talking about the present] is not me. (Hubbard, Kidd, and Kearney 2010:136)

Looking older threatened continuity with this woman's previous identity and sense of self. She could not reconcile her current image with the picture of her earlier self. For her, the photo symbolized who she really was yet simultaneously reaffirmed that she was no longer the same person.

Living with chronic conditions and life-threatening illness, however, is not all disruption and loss. A new medication or surgical intervention may improve life and increase the person's possibilities for constructing a valued self. Lucy Bray, Sue Kirk, and Peter Callery (2014) studied how a surgical intervention – a continent stoma – affected children and youth who had lacked urinary and/or bowel control since birth. A successful stoma permitted inserting a catheter into the patient's bladder or bowel, thus enabling him or her to manage emptying the bladder or bowel. After the surgery, most of the children experienced "**biographical enrichment**" (Bray et al. 2014:829–831). With enriched identities and opportunities, such as being able to sleep over at a friend's house or go swimming 11-year-old Katie told her interviewer:

KATIE:   I am proud of it (stoma); it saved my life.
RESEARCHER:   Why did it save your life?
KATIE:   Because then I would have to stay in nappies and I would try and kill myself.

(Bray et al. 2014:830)

The children welcomed the stoma because it helped them to normalize their lives. They could now fit their daily regimens with their activities and conduct their care in privacy (Bray et al. 2014:830). No doubt these changes also reduced their being subject to stigmatizing taunts and slights. For these children, what previously had often become a major bodily stigma, as we discussed in Chapter 4, became a more minor one and decreased their experiences of enacted stigma.

Biographical enrichment also occurs in less tangible ways. People preserve continuities with the past, experience positive changes, and discover hidden strengths. Despite struggling with illness and disability, people talk about developing patience, compassion, and courage, and taking pride in their new attributes. Those with life-threatening cancer often speak of their heightened awareness and appreciation of life and beauty, as this woman conveys:

I was going to live to 105, it's like now will I live to 60? – probably, probably. But I can't take it for granted the way I used to. It's like there's a compactness and a preciousness and little things have more importance.

When I look at the sunset and realize it's really very beautiful, I don't take things for granted.... Everything has shifted. But it's not all negative. A lot of these are shifts that are quite positive. (Charmaz 2014:2)

## Medicalization, Biomedicalization, and Risk

**Medicalization** refers to defining a problem such as birth, risk of illness, or deviant behavior as within medical jurisdiction. A potentially problematic behavior or condition can be interpreted as (i) an unremarkable, normal part of life, (ii) a sin or moral failure, (iii) a crime, or (iv) a disease. Homosexuality and heavy alcohol consumption, for example, could be put in any of these categories. Medicalization occurs when we interpret and treat a behavior such as drinking as (iv), a disease or mental illness.

> **Medicalization refers to defining a problem such as birth, risk of illness, or deviant behavior as within medical jurisdiction.**

According to Conrad (2005:3–6, 2013), in the past, medicalization occurred when (i) the medical profession defined the problem as justifying medical oversight and interventions, (ii) social movements or interest groups redefined behavior as a medical problem, such as alcoholism, and (iii) professional disputes resulted in medical dominance, such as obstetrics gaining control over birth. Conrad argues that in recent decades new sources of defining medicalization have arisen. Market forces, consumerism, corporate control, medical knowledge, the pharmaceutical industry, as well as expansion of medical specialties such as cosmetic surgery all have contributed to medicalization. Clarke et al. (2003:161–162) contend that medicalization has been intensified and transformed into biomedicalization by an increasingly complex, multi-sited, multi-directional techno-scientific biomedicine. Biomedicalization reaches into everyday life as testing, surveillance, and risk assessment increases.

Individual and public acceptance of medicalization and biomedicalization varies and can change or become contested over time. As Reich (2016) shows, parents who refuse vaccinations attempt to *de-medicalize* what vaccination means and who should decide whether children should be vaccinated. Here, what the public had accepted as a conventional health practice is weakened, and with it, medical judgment. Physicians themselves may tacitly de-medicalize a condition affecting patients they find to be difficult and untreatable, as Sandra Sulzer (2015) suggests. Medicalization expands when the public accepts new medical definitions of illness, risk, and prevention. Concerns about remote risks are used to justify increasing medical testing and surveillance of well-babies who have no known genetic predisposition to disease (Timmermans and Buchbinder 2013).

Life changes when health screening designates people as "at risk" for disease. Screening is for early diagnosis and treatment but also raises new questions about when illness begins. Surveillance follows to track changes in the conditions of those identified as at risk. Chris Gillespie (2012) found people designated as being at risk had difficulty in seeing themselves as healthy. Although the designation of being at risk means fitting a statistical category, this designation resulted in symbolic changes of people's self-images and identities. Gene's statement captures the views of Gillespie's other research participants:

> It's sort of like – it's a combination between a trip wire booby trap and a time bomb.... A trip wire booby trap but if you don't trip the wire, it doesn't go off. So, if you watch your cholesterol, then you should be fine. However, there's the time bomb part... that part you can't do anything about. (Gillespie 2012:200)

Not only did these individuals' current personal identities change, but also their beliefs about what their lives would be. They no longer assumed having dependable bodies and invincible selves. Rather, the bodies they had trusted now posed ominous threat.

## Conclusion

Conventional views of health, illness, and disability treat these concepts as objective facts. After all, scientific medicine decrees what health, illness, and disability mean. This chapter presents a contrasting view. We have looked at how people define health, illness, and disability in their everyday lives. Their definitions reveal varied beliefs that inform their actions. People learn what health, illness, and disability mean for them as they interpret events and experiences occurring to and around them. Maintaining health is neither straightforward nor unquestioned. Rather what you need to do to be healthy and whether you can do it on your own are both contested notions.

Experiencing illness and losing physical function pose problems of making sense of what is happening and of managing life. These problems involve the person and his or her intimates – and beyond. The effects of an intrusive illness or disability spread among households, workplaces, and friendship circles. Controlling symptoms and dealing with regimens may take huge chunks of time but permit people to manage their identities and avoid stigmatizing judgments. Loss of autonomy, impaired bodily control, diminished mental acuity, being designated as at risk of disease, or receiving a diagnosis of a sexually transmitted disease all increase a person's potential for loss of self and being stigmatized. Although each can cast shadows on the self and on the future, experiencing illness, disability, and risk may also bring new lessons about the power of social bonds, generosity, and gratitude.

# Learning by Using the Symbolic Interactionist Perspective

The excerpt below is from *Waiting for Cancer to Come: Women's Experiences with Genetic Testing and Medical Decision Making for Breast and Ovarian Cancer* by Sharlene Hesse-Biber (2014). While collecting data for her study, Hesse-Biber interviewed Holly, a young woman, who had done considerable research about the breast cancer genetic mutation. Holly had given the possibility of having this mutation and subsequent cancer much thought. When their laboratory tests show the mutation, some women have mastectomies before they are diagnosed with cancer to prevent it from developing. Choosing when to seek this surgery is a difficult decision. Read Holly's story and see if you can use concepts from this chapter – such as illness, individual responsibility for health, diagnostic quest, medicalization, and others – to analyze it.

---

**"Waiting and Watching"**

---

**Holly**

*Sharlene Hesse-Biber (2014:85–86)*

I came to be tested because my mother actually was diagnosed with breast cancer about four years ago, and she was only forty-five, and so they were kind of already a little bit concerned. And then it came out that two of her aunts and two of her cousins, all on the same side of the family, all had breast cancer at a fairly young age, so they tested her. She was positive for, um, BRCA$_2$ [a mutated gene that increases susceptibility to breast cancer]. And so then, you know, it was kind of agreed that I would test when I was closer to being twenty-five because they, apparently, don't start additional surveillance until you're at least twenty-five…. So they were kind of like, "if you want, don't want to test yet, there's no real need to." They wouldn't do anything differently either way.

I've been planning on this for almost four years…. In all honesty, I had always kind of assumed it would be positive for some reason, so I just figured, it's probably better to get tested and then I can start with the surveillance, and, you know, make sure that I can prevent cancer. And I don't know if that – I don't know if there was it necessarily reason for it, I always just assumed that would be the case. And I don't know if that was just me having a doomsday scenario, or if it was partially just because I'd heard so much about it. Because my mom had gone through the whole thing, I watch my mom go through all the surgeries and all of the, you know, everything related to her cancer.

[Some people's] mentality is just: 'I'm going to do everything I can right now to avoid getting cancer because I want, you know, to beat it before it even can – before I even have it.' And I do absolutely agree with that, I just don't personally feel that [surgery is] something I need to do right this minute. You know what I'm talking to doctors and they're telling me that, you know, the likelihood of me getting cancer right now is very, very low, even though I do have this gene mutation, I don't feel that I need to, you know, instantly uproot my entire life [by having surgery].

## Notes

1  See the discussion in Chapter 7 to compare these mothers' actions with concepts of "privileged access" and "antiprofessionalism."
2  The symptoms include reduced ability to do ordinary activities, increased debilitating fatigue after physical or mental activity, decreased ability to think clearly, intensified symptoms while standing, and pain.

## References

Adams, S. and M. Niezen. 2015. "Digital 'Solutions' to Unhealthy Lifestyle 'Problems': The Construction of E-Coaches." *Health, Risk & Society* 17(7–8):530–546.

Barker, K. 2005. *The Fibromyalgia Story: Medical Authority and Women's Worlds of Pain*. Philadelphia, PA: Temple University Press.

Bray, L., S. Kirk, and P. Callery. 2014. "Developing Biographies: The Experiences of Children, Young People and Their Parents of Living with a Long-term Condition." *Sociology of Health & Illness* 36(6):823–839.

Brever, L. and K. Phillips. 2017. "The Mother Jailed for Refusing to Vaccinate Her Son Says She Would 'Do It All over Again.'" *Washington Post*. 13 October 2017. http://www.washingtonpost.com/news/to-your-health/wp/2017/10/12/a-mother-was-jailed-for-refusing-to-vaccinate-her-son-now-shes-outraged-hes-been-immunized/?utm_term=.b129cbfa85ab.

Brown, R. C. H. 2013. "Moral Responsibility for (Un)Healthy Behavior." *Journal of Medical Ethics* 39:695–698.

Bury, M. 1982. "Chronic Illness as Biographical Disruption." *Sociology of Health & Illness* 4(2):167–182.

Buyx, A. 2008. "Personal Responsibility for Health as a Rationing Criterion: Why We Don't Like It and Why Maybe We Should." *British Medical Journal* 34(12):871–874.

Charmaz, K. 1980. *The Social Reality of Death*. Reading, MA: Addison-Wesley.

Charmaz, K. 1983. "Loss of Self: A Fundamental Form of Suffering in the Chronically Ill." *Sociology of Health and Illness* 5(2):168–95.

Charmaz, K. 1987. "Struggling for a Self: Identity Levels of the Chronically Ill." Pp. 283–321 in *Research in the Sociology of Health Care: The Experience and Management of Chronic Illness 6*, edited by J. Roth and P. Conrad. Greenwich, CT: JAI Press.

Charmaz, K. 1999. "Stories of Suffering: Subjects' Tales and Research Narratives." *Qualitative Health Research* 9(3):369–382.

Charmaz, K. 2002. "The Self as Habit: The Reconstruction of Self in Chronic Illness." *The Occupational Therapy Journal of Research* 22(Supplement 1):31s–42s.

Charmaz, K. 2011. "A Constructivist Grounded Theory Analysis of Losing and Regaining A Valued Self." Pp. 165–204 in *Five Ways of Doing Qualitative Analysis: Phenomenological Psychology, Grounded Theory, Discourse Analysis, Narrative Research, and Intuitive Inquiry*, edited by F. Wertz, K. Charmaz, L. McMullen, R. Josselson, R. Anderson, and E. McSpadden. New York: Guilford.

Charmaz, K. 2014. *Constructing Grounded Theory*, 2nd ed. London: Sage.

Charmaz, K. and L. Belgrave. In press. "Thinking about Data with Grounded Theory." *Qualitative Inquiry*.

Ciambrone, D. 2007. "Illness and Other Assaults on Self: The Relative Impact of HIV/AIDS on Women's Lives." *Sociology of Health & Illness* 23(4):517–540.

Clarke, A., J. Fishman, J. Fosket, L. Mamo, and J. Shim. 2003. "Biomedicalization: Technoscientific Transformations of Health, Illness, and U.S. Biomedicine." *American Sociological Review* 68(April):161–194.

Collins, H. and T. Pinch. 2005. *Dr. Golem: How to Think about Medicine*. Chicago, IL: University of Chicago Press.

Conrad, P. 2005. "The Shifting Engines of Medicalization." *Journal of Health and Social Behavior* 46(1):3–14.

Conrad, P. 2013. "Medicalization: Changing Contours, Characteristics, and Contexts." Pp. 195–211 in *Medical Sociology on the Move*, edited by W. Cockerham. Dordrecht: Springer.

Cornwell, J. 1984. *Hard-Earned Lives. Accounts of Health and Illness from East London*. London: Routledge, Kegan & Paul.

Crawford, R. 2006. "Health as a Meaningful Social Practice." *Health* 10(4):401–420.

Dumit, J. 2006. "Illnesses You Have to Fight to Get: Facts as Forces in Uncertain, Emergent Illnesses." *Social Science & Medicine* 62(3):577–590.

Edgley, C. 2006. "The Fit and Healthy Body: Consumer Narratives and the Management of Postmodern Corporeity." Pp. 231–247 in *Body/Embodiment: Symbolic Interaction and the Sociology of the Body*, edited by D. D. Waskul and P. Vannini. London: Ashgate.

Elliott, S. 2014. "'Who's to blame?' Constructing the responsible sexual agent in neoliberal sex education." *Sexuality Research and Social Policy* 11(3):211–224.

Fielding-Singh, P. 2017. "A Taste of Inequality: Food's Symbolic Value across the Socioeconomic Spectrum." *Sociological Science* 4(17):424–448.

Frank, A. W. 1991. *At the Will of the Body: Reflections on Illness.* Boston: Houghton Mifflin.

Galvin, R. 2002. "Disturbing Notions of Chronic Illness and Individual Responsibility: Towards a Genealogy of Morals." *Health* 6(2):107–136.

Garthwaite, K. 2015. "Becoming Incapacitated? Long-Term Sickness Benefit Recipients and the Construction of Stigma and Identity Narratives." *Sociology of Health and Illness* 37(1):1–13.

Gillespie, C. 2012. "The Experience of Risk as 'Measured Vulnerability': Health Screening and Lay Uses of Numerical Risk." *Sociology of Health & Illness* 34(2):194–207.

Goffman, E. 1963. *Stigma: Notes on the Management of Spoiled Identity.* Englewood Cliffs, NJ: Prentice-Hall.

Harris, D. 2017. "Just the 'Typical College Diet': How College Students Use Life Stages to Account for Unhealthy Eating." *Symbolic Interaction* 40(4):523–540.

Hesse-Biber, S. 2014. *Waiting for Cancer to Come: Women's Experiences with Genetic Testing and Medical Decision Making for Breast and Ovarian Cancer.* Ann Arbor, MI: University of Michigan Press.

Hinojosa, R., C. Boylstein, M. Rittman, M. Hinojosa, and C. Faircloth. 2008. "Constructions of Continuity after a Stroke." *Symbolic Interaction* 31(2):205–224.

Hubbard, G., L. Kidd, and N. Kearney. 2010. "Disrupted Lives and Threats to Identity: The Experiences of People with Colorectal Cancer within the First Year Following Diagnosis." *Health* 14(2):131–146.

Jutel, A. 2011. *Putting a Name to It: Diagnosis in Contemporary Society.* Baltimore, MD: Johns Hopkins University Press.

Locock, L., Sue Z., and C. Dumelow. 2009. "Biographical Disruption, Abruption and Repair in the Context of Motor Neurone Disease." *Sociology of Health & Illness* 31(7):1043–1058.

McClean, S. 2005. "'The Illness Is Part of the Person': Discourses of Blame, Individual Responsibility and Individuation at a Centre for Spiritual Healing in the North of England." *Sociology of Health & Illness* 27(5):628–648.

Mendelson, C. 2006. "Managing a Medically and Socially Complex Life: Women Living with Lupus." *Qualitative Health Research* 16(7):982–997.

MEpedia, A Crowd-Sourced Encyclopedia of ME and CFS Science and History. 2017. "Karina Hansen." February 14. https://me-pedia.org/wiki/Karina_Hansen.

Monaghan, L. F. 2001. *Bodybuilding, Drugs, and Risk.* London: Routledge.

Monaghan, L. F. 2002. "Vocabularies of Motive for Illicit Steroid Use Among Bodybuilders." *Social Science & Medicine* 55(5):695–708.

Nack, A. 2008. *Damaged Goods? Women Living with Incurable Sexually Transmitted Diseases.* Philadelphia, PA: Temple University Press.

Nettleton, S. 2006. "'I Just Want Permission to Be Ill': Toward a Sociology of Medically Unexplained Symptoms." *Social Science & Medicine* 62: 1167–1178.

Norris, M., P. Allotey, and G. Barrett. 2012. "'It Burdens Me': The Impact of Stroke in Central Aceh, Indonesia." *Sociology of Health & Illness* 34(6):826–840.

Price, L. and L. Walker. 2015. *Chronic Illness, Vulnerability and Social Work: Autoimmunity and the Contemporary Disease Experience*. London: Routledge.

Reich, J. 2014. "Neoliberal Mothering and Vaccine Refusal: Imagined Gated Communities and the Privilege of Choice." *Gender & Society* 28(5):679–704.

Reich, J. 2016. *Calling the Shots: Parents, Public Health, and the Politics of Vaccine Choice*. New York: NYU Press.

Richardson, N. 2010. "'The "Buck" Stops with Me' – Reconciling Men's Lay Conceptualisations of Responsibility for Health with Men's Health Policy." *Health Sociology Review* 19(4):419–436.

Sanders, C., J. Donovan, and P. Dieppe. 2002. "The Significance and Consequences of Having Painful and Disabled Joints in Older Age: Co-Existing Accounts of Normal and Disrupted Biographies." *Sociology of Health & Illness* 24(2):227–253.

Shim, J. 2014. *Heartsick: The Politics of Risk, Inequality and Heart Disease*. New York: NYU Press.

Smith, B. and A. Sparkes. 2005. "Men, Sport, Spinal Cord Injury, and Narratives of Hope." *Social Science & Medicine* 61(5):1095–1105.

Sulzer, S. 2015. "Does 'difficult patient' status contribute to functional demedicalization? The case of borderline personality disorder." *Social Science & Medicine* 142(10):82–89.

Timmermans, S. and M. Buchbinder. 2013. *Saving Babies? The Consequences of Newborn Genetic Screening*. Chicago, IL: University of Chicago Press.

Vann-Ward, T., J. Morse, and K. Charmaz. 2017. "Preserving Self: Theorizing the Social and Psychological Processes of Living with Parkinson Disease." *Qualitative Health Research* 27(7):964–982.

Vorderstrasse, A., A. Lewinski, G. Melkus, and C. Johnson. 2016. "Social Support for Diabetes Self-Management via eHealth Interventions." *Current Diabetes Reports* 16(56):1–8.

Waskul, D. and P. Vannini. 2006. "Introduction: The Body in Symbolic Interaction." Pp. 1–18 in *Body/Embodiment: Symbolic Interaction and the Sociology of the Body*, edited by D. Waskul and P. Vannini. Aldershot: Ashgate.

# 6

# Emotion Norms, Emotion Management, and Emotional Labor

> "Even when I am so well prepared [for an exam] that I have no worry at all, I do not dare let on to the others."
>
> "One is not supposed to be too cocky or too teary-eyed. It is best to be just a touch anxious."
>
> "Openly we wish [classmates] the best of luck. Privately we wish ourselves the best, and them not as much."
>
> "One thing I do is avoid people who are very panicky and nervous before exams. During my first year at university, just before an important exam, I was approached by a 'walking time bomb' [who] …could not remember anything [and] …showered me with questions I was unable to answer. I also panicked. I swore never again to go near anyone whose eyes bulged out of their head with panic."
> (Albas and Albas 1988:263–264, 270)

Do any of these statements – from a study of Canadian college students – resonate with your experiences and observations?

The challenge of taking college exams might generate an array of your emotions. You might feel nervous or fearful about underperforming on the test. A score of "100%!" may lead to your pride and exhilaration. A "D" or "F" might prompt your embarrassment, shame, anger, and dejection. When your classmate earns a higher grade, you may experience a flash of envy. Or, if an astute friend gives you some helpful tutoring, then you may feel gratitude and affection toward him or her.

Emotions pervade exam-taking and virtually all other contexts of our lives. Spending time with friends and family, playing games and sports, watching television, going to work, volunteering – can you imagine any of these activities without emotions? Our daily routines would be flat and robotic without

*The Social Self and Everyday Life: Understanding the World Through Symbolic Interactionism*, First Edition. Kathy Charmaz, Scott R. Harris, and Leslie Irvine. © 2019 John Wiley & Sons, Inc. Published 2019 by John Wiley & Sons, Inc.

the highs of amusement ("LOL!!!"), joy, excitement, infatuation, and love, or the lows of boredom, disappointment, humiliation, and outrage.

Emotions may seem simply rooted in our bodies (and thus an odd topic for sociologists). After all, we *feel* the butterflies of stage fright, the physical effects of lust, and the lethargy of depression. Emotions may also seem "natural." We say "of course" people love their children, become jealous when a spouse flirts with another, or grow angry over disrespectful comments. While not denying the role of the body in the experience of emotions, symbolic interactionists argue that emotions are much more than instinctive or automatic responses.

The point of this chapter is to enable readers to use interactionist concepts to understand some of **the social dimensions of emotions**. As we'll see, emotions are highly social phenomena, shaped by culture, interpretation, social interaction, and inequality.

## Emotion Norms

Looking back at the opening excerpt from Albas and Albas (1988), consider the first three quotations. Each comment addresses how a person *ought* to feel in a particular situation. The students did not simply express emotions whatever came "naturally" to them but harnessed and controlled those feelings to fit into the local culture. The first two comments both indicate that – at least in this setting – it would be deemed inappropriate to appear extremely confident about an exam, even if the students were well prepared. Perhaps such "cockiness" would make one seem arrogant, or damage the self-esteem of classmates struggling to master the material.

The second and fourth quotations indicate that the opposite extreme would also be frowned upon, at least by some. A student should not appear too "teary-eyed" – overly nervous or upset about an upcoming exam. Such a person may seem too unprepared, too emotionally unstable, too needy (requiring sympathy or encouragement), or dangerously contagious.

The third statement highlights the potential inappropriateness of overtly competitive sentiments. Imagine if you responded to an encouraging "Good luck!" from a classmate with the statement "Thanks! I wish myself a lot more luck than I wish you! I care more about my own success than yours!" Such excessive honesty may backfire. Your classmates may come to regard you as rude or antisocial, unless they took your remark as an attempt at humor.

In short, we used this opening excerpt to draw your attention to the phenomenon of **emotion norms**, which consist of cultural expectations regarding how people should feel in particular situations (Harris 2015; Hochschild 1983). Human beings create emotion norms, and thus these norms may vary from group to group, just as behavioral norms do: Should a motorist drive on the left side of the road or the right? Should men wear beards or go clean shaven? Are female breasts something to be hidden or routinely displayed? Are cows sacred or an ordinary food source? Beliefs and customs vary.

Like these social norms, emotion norms may also differ by culture. Are funerals a time to mourn quietly or to celebrate vociferously the life of the deceased? Should an instructor always treat students with patience and respect, or is it preferable to motivate them – like an army drill sergeant would – via hostile and derogatory language? Is a parent forbidden, allowed, or encouraged to angrily disparage ("You little [expletive]!") a misbehaving child?

Emotion norms are not necessarily static. They can change over time, within the same cultural context. Gordon Clanton (2006), for example, has argued that North Americans' understandings of romantic jealousy have evolved. Clanton examined articles appearing in popular magazines and found that an axial shift occurred several decades ago. Between 1945 and 1970, articles more likely portrayed jealousy as a natural and positive emotion – something perhaps to even provoke in one's partner, as "proof of love." After the 1960s, jealousy was much more likely to be described as a negative emotion, associated with low self-esteem or some other personality defect (e.g. an inability to trust). A greater cultural emphasis on personal freedom and self-fulfillment may have led to a shifting emotion norm – that is, less tolerance for experiences and displays of emotion by ourselves and by others around us.

> *Emotion norms are cultural expectations for how people should feel in particular situations. They are socially-acquired rules or standards for evaluating the feelings that we experience and display.*

Emotion norms seem to pervade our lives. Yet, if you haven't thought about them before, don't be too surprised. You may have simply lacked a vocabulary for identifying and talking about them. Moreover, emotion norms are frequently invisible or taken for granted, just as social norms are.

We tend not to notice when we obey a social norm (e.g. about personal space), as long as we don't violate the rule. A conversation might proceed in routine fashion until a close-talking acquaintance moves his or her nose just a few inches from our own. "Back up!" we might think or say. "You're standing too close!" Our confident evaluation would be, to a large extent, based on the socialization we have received regarding "proper" distances between speakers engaged in a casual conversation – socialization which is not universal (Husting 2015).

Similarly, emotion norms may operate imperceptibly until they are broken. If we arrive to an energetic New Year's Eve party, but for some reason feel depressed or lethargic, we might tell ourselves "Come on! Get into the spirit of things! This is supposed to be fun!" Or, fellow attendees might give us a dirty look or tell us not to be such a "Debbie Downer" or "Donnie Downer." These **rule reminders** (Hochschild 1983) imply the existence of emotion norms that govern our emotion experiences and displays.

> *Rule reminders occur when we tell others or ourselves that we are breaking an emotion norm. Reminders can occur through nonverbal as well as verbal cues.*

Steven Ortiz (2011) documented a dramatic example of a rule reminder in his research on wives of professional baseball players. When traveling on the team bus, athletes' wives were expected to share the mood of the athletes. After a difficult game, the players and coaches may feel like a death in the family has occurred. One wife "Sheila" recounted this story about traveling with the "Bobcats" (both pseudonyms):

> One time I was on a trip with the Bobcats… and several wives were on this trip and we had just gotten our brains beat out in Meadowville. And something happened on the bus. It was so funny. And a couple of us were just cracking up, and one of the coaches turned around and said, "In case you girls didn't notice, we just lost three games in a row." I was like, "Oh." But I mean, it was still funny. I couldn't help it. I know you're not supposed to do that. (Ortiz 2011:130)

Or, consider Cox's (2016) research on Launch, an organization that provides academic-success classes and tutorials for low-and moderate-income black and Latino students. Along with intellectual growth, Launch socialized students into a particular emotional style – "a mildly pleasant demeanor and … self-disciplined acquiescence to authority" (Cox 2016:493) – that would help students conform to elite academic settings and professional workplaces. From her field notes, Cox recounts a dramatic instance where a school administrator ("Stacia") explicitly reminded students to be calm and behave amiably toward authorities:

> Two boys walk by talking and jostling each other as they walk, and as I see them pass me, Stacia stands up straighter, arms still crossed across her chest, but more tightly now. She squares her body to them, leans forward slightly, and says in an irritated tone, "Excuse me?" …The boys stop abruptly and turn their heads back…. Stacia says, "Excuse me – you're going to walk by a teacher, you're going to walk by us and not say 'good morning' to us when we say 'good morning' to you?" [One of the boys says,] "I didn't hear you." …Still sounding firm, but softening her irritated tone a little, Stacia says, "You don't walk by and not say 'good morning.'" …Stacia says instructively to them, "When you walk by adults, you greet them, you say 'good morning' to them. Both boys nod obediently and then turn and continue walking down the hall. (Cox 2016:497)

The excerpts from Ortiz and Cox both illustrate **direct socialization** into emotion norms, where others explicitly tell us what the rules are. A more mundane example would be the parental instruction reminding children to express gratitude: "Say thank you!" or "What do we say?"

People can also be socialized into norms via more subtle means. With **indirect socialization**, we merely infer proper emotional conduct by observing the behavior of others around us. For example, coaches and administrators may model expected behaviors and feelings; or, wives of professional baseball players may observe the somber emotional expressions of fellow riders on the bus, and thus learn how to act and feel after a losing game; or, younger students may look at each other and at older students, to discover how to fit in, emotionally, in a new educational setting.

**Emotional deviance** – which occurs when we are judged by ourselves or others to have violated an emotion norm – may be committed for a variety of reasons having little to do with mental illness. We may enter a new situation and be ignorant of the rules. Or, perhaps we question the wisdom or morality of an emotion norm – as when children aggressively "talk back" and refuse to "respect their elders." Our prior socialization may also differ from those of our companions: American college students may feel that cheek kissing is a sign of affection reserved for family members and romantic partners, but when traveling abroad discover that the greeting is often expected even for new acquaintances (Husting 2015). On some occasions we may know and want to conform to emotion norms, but simply aren't able. In the example provided above, when something tickled Sheila's funny bone, she claimed she couldn't help but laugh, even though she knew "you're not supposed to do that" on the team bus, after a serious loss (Ortiz 2011:130).

We can commit emotional deviance in at least five different ways. First, and most simply, we can experience or display the wrong type of emotion. A parent who hates a child may be judged harshly, by him- or herself and by others. Equally condemned (in most but not all settings) would be expressions of romantic love for the spouse one's best friend. Or, consider an example from the news.[1] While participating in a televised interview about the twentieth anniversary of his sister JonBenet's death (a 6-year-old beauty queen who was mysteriously murdered in her home), Burke Ramsey smiled in untoward fashion as he recounted the sad and scary details. Or, for a more mundane example: After attending an early-morning graduation ceremony, a college student may feel sluggish, bored, and irritable during a lunch her parents hosted. Friends and relatives may expect her excitement and gratitude, and take offense at the perceived emotional deviance.

*Emotional deviance occurs when we are judged by ourselves or others to have violated an explicit or implicit emotion norm. We can commit emotional deviance in at least five different ways: we can experience or display the wrong emotion (type), or an otherwise appropriate emotion too strongly or weakly (intensity), for too long or short a period of time (duration), too early or too late (timing), in front of an unsuitable audience or in an improper setting (placing).*

Even if we possess the correct feeling, we may deviate if we do not experience or display it with the appropriate intensity. Imagine proposing to a romantic partner, who responds with a shrug and a brief smile: "Sure, why not. That sounds okay." It's a positive response, but the intensity might be deemed too weak – more appropriate for a lunch invitation than for a lifelong commitment. Or, to return to this chapter's opening excerpt: a student who panics about a small quiz (worth 2% of one's course grade) might be judged as having the correct emotion – nervousness – but far too much of it.

A person can also commit emotional deviance if they feel an otherwise correct emotion for a period of time that is deemed too short or too long. We might evaluate unfavorably a fiancé whose excitement does not carry over into a least a few post-engagement conversations with friends and family members, on subsequent days. The duration in this case probably should *not* be limited to the first 10 or 20 minutes, many of us might say. Conversely, excitement over "acing" a tiny quiz would seem odd, if one's celebrating continued for days or weeks.

The placement of our emotions is also important. Classmates may expect a student to be excited and proud of an "A" on a tough exam. However, they may judge such feelings harshly if the student exhibited this response in front of two classmates who just received a "D" and an "F," or while attending a somber funeral later in the afternoon. Similarly, we might be expected to be upset after a fight with a romantic partner, and seek sympathy, but not from a friend who has just been diagnosed with terminal cancer.

Finally, people may define an otherwise normal or expected emotion as inappropriate if it seems oddly premature or delayed. The timing of a feeling can be seen as "off." One's companions would likely disapprove of revealing exam-nerves before the semester even started, or excitement over a prospective engagement after a first date. "Too soon," people may think or say. Or, an emotional reaction can be deemed tardy. Imagine a situation where the death of a parent does not fully "hit" someone until months afterwards – perhaps due to the deceased's absence at a wedding or the birth of a grandchild. The bereaved's companions may wonder why the intense grief was not experienced and displayed at the funeral.

The consequences of violating emotion norms may sometimes be minor. Our friends and relatives may simply tease us, give us withering looks, or gossip secretly about us. Nonetheless, surprisingly large penalties can be dispensed. We may seriously weaken or even lose relationships if our emotional deviance becomes too annoying or troubling. "Poor sports" – who can't help but display anger at losing otherwise friendly games (of tennis, chess, Nintendo, etc.) – may be shunned. Unwelcome anger may lead to fewer opportunities for advancement and leadership roles. Individuals evincing excessive anxiety or arrogance, or who smile too little or too much, or laugh or cry in untoward ways, may not endure past a first date or a preliminary job interview. Criminal defendants and politicians easily offend jurors and voters, if they do not meet their audiences' expectations of the "correct" display of confidence, humility, remorse, and other feelings.

## Emotion Management

Norms, rule reminders, sanctions for deviance – demonstrate some of the ways that emotions are products of culture and interaction as much as they are "physical" or "natural" responses to situations. Different cultures create, impart, and enforce regulations regarding appropriate emotional experiences and displays. These rules vary from group to group, and within the same group over time. They are pervasive and consequential, yet often go unnoticed until they are broken.

Symbolic interactionists have drawn upon this image of society – as a rule-governed body of mutually-policing members – as one viewpoint to explain human emotions. In this section, we'll turn to a second image helpful for organizing our thoughts about the social dimensions of emotions.

We build on dramaturgical perspective introduced in Chapter 2, which draws analogies between our everyday lives and the realm of the theater. From a dramaturgical point of view, we are all actors who employ strategies to manage the impressions we make on our audiences (Goffman 1959). For example, we choose our clothing (costumes), carefully select our words (script), decorate our apartments with diplomas, photographs, and other physical objects (props), all to convince others – or even ourselves – that we are a particular sort of person. We may present ourselves as polite, attractive, intelligent, sporty, spiritual, successful, Goth, preppy, funny, clean, well-liked, and so on. Anytime we purchase and wear an article of clothing, we might wonder – however fleetingly or obsessively – whether it helps confirm or contradict what we want audiences to think about us.

> *Emotion management occurs when individuals attempt to shape their own, or others', emotional experiences and displays.*

The concept of **emotion management** highlights how feelings can be dramaturgical as well. We don't merely "have" emotions as automatic reactions; often, we try to "work on" emotions – to change what we are experiencing and/or displaying, so we can conform to emotion norms, impress an audience, or accomplish other goals.

Actors on a stage sometimes fake feelings at a surface level. A performer in a high school production may have never been married but put on a sad face when portraying a character who has lost a beloved spouse. By dressing in black, forcing a quivering lip, and adopting a gloomy tone of voice, the actor may publicly mourn a loss he or she does not really feel. However, if trained in "method acting," the performer's work may go a bit deeper. By carefully creating a back story for a character, by rigorously imagining what the loss of a spouse would be like, or by recalling the recent real-life loss of a pet, the actor may try to generate "real" feelings of sadness that will come across to the audience.

As we'll see in this section, similar processes frequently occur in our daily lives, through what interactionists call surface acting and deep acting.

**Surface acting** occurs when individuals try to control how they appear to feel (Harris 2015; Hochschild 1983). Sometimes we present an utterly fabricated emotion. Imagine Dan, a college student, receives an undesirable birthday present from his grandmother. Dan might enthusiastically exclaim "Thanks for the great shirt!" while smiling broadly. He might even try on the shirt and praise its color and fit, even while secretly thinking "I will never wear this." Gratitude is likely the unwavering norm when receiving a gift from an elderly relative. To conform to this rule, uphold the image of being a polite person, and protect his grandmother's feelings, Dan may feign an unfelt emotion.

> *Surface acting occurs when individuals manage how they appear to feel. People can alter their facial expressions, bodily posture, tone of voice, verbal expressions, and clothing, in order to convince others that they are experiencing a particular emotion.*

However, surface acting need not be so deceptive. Sometimes we simply modify rather than falsify the display of feelings. Dan may receive a mildly desirable gift and so he may merely exaggerate his enthusiasm ("Wow! It's perfect!") instead of risking a lukewarm response. Or, he may engage in surface acting to ensure his audience perceives an emotion that he believes is real. Now imagine Dan genuinely feels excited about the gift, but someone else in the room distracted his grandmother when he said "Thank you!" Dan may self-consciously re-perform his enthusiastic expression of gratitude two or three times, to be certain of fully conveying his real feeling. Dan may even wear the shirt strategically at the next family gathering, so that his grandmother sees and realizes just how much he genuinely appreciates her thoughtfulness and prizes the shirt.

> *Deep acting occurs when individuals manage how they actually feel. People can manipulate their thoughts, bodies, or expressions, in an attempt to change the emotions they are experiencing.*

**Deep acting** occurs when we manage how we actually feel (Harris 2015; Hochschild 1983). Sometimes we don't want to merely alter the display of an emotion; we want to change how we actually feel, for the benefit of others or ourselves.

**Cognitive deep acting** is probably the most interesting form of deep acting. This strategy occurs when we change our thoughts in order to modify the feelings we have. Recipients of an unwanted or mildly-desirable gift may try to talk themselves into a feeling of enthusiasm or gratitude. They may invoke the refrain "It's the thought that counts!" Or, they may accentuate the positive aspects of the gift when thinking about it ("the size is just right"), rather than dwelling on the negative aspects ("I wish the color were better"). In Dan's case, he might also remind himself of his grandmother's limited resources and come to feel more grateful for her expenditure of time, effort, and money that went into the gift.

Let's look back at this chapter's opening excerpt, from research by Albas and Albas (1988). We can see the fourth quotation as a description of an emotion management strategy. By avoiding panicky classmates, the student attempts to prevent unwanted thoughts – "Is this test going to be really difficult? Am I ready? Do I know everything I need to know?" – that would generate fear or anxiety. Arguably, the student is pursuing a form of cognitive deep acting.

Interactionists have documented scores of similar deep-acting examples across a wide array of settings. Consider these samples:

- Medical students experience nervousness, disgust, and even sexual attraction as they learn to work with live patients and cadavers. To suppress those feelings, or generate more positive ones, they (i) cover or avoid looking at certain body parts, (ii) remind themselves of how much they have learned and accomplished, (iii) focus on how the patient may be feeling, rather than on their own feelings, (iv) joke about their awkward experiences when they are alone with colleagues, in "backstage" settings (Smith and Kleinman 1989).
- Financial advisors may be tempted to feel envious of their clients' wealth, and discontent with their own meager retirement accounts. To combat these feelings, they may (i) repeat the mantra that "Money does not buy happiness" and (ii) purposefully recall some of the unhappy millionaires they have worked with (Delaney 2012:124–125).
- Members of 4-H (a youth development organization) try to avoid feeling sadness or regret about slaughtering the animals they raise, by (i) using terms such as "livestock" and "market animals" rather than personalized names ("Adriana," "Blossom"), (ii) telling themselves "God gave us animals for food," and (iii) focusing on the positive purposes (e.g. college tuition) that the sale of the animal will serve (Ellis and Irvine 2010).
- Flight attendants may try to reduce frustration and increase feelings of tolerance and sympathy by (i) imagining that the cabin is their living room and passengers are guests in their home, (ii) thinking of upset passengers as "mishandled" rather than "obnoxious" or "rude," and (iii) venting negative emotions to fellow attendants, in private, in the galley (Hochschild 1983).

- Homeschooling mothers may feel stressed or annoyed by their multifaceted roles; to improve their mood, they may picture all the good times they would miss out on, if they sent their children to conventional schools (Lois 2013).
- Individuals who experience fear, guilt, or helplessness about social issues – such as climate change, racism, gun violence – may (i) avoid listening to news about the topic, (ii) generate pride or anger by picturing themselves as better than those people who are making the problem worse, or (iii) focus on doing something small but positive (see Norgaard 2006).
- A college student may feel envious of or belittled by an acquaintance who has abundant social connections through the Greek system of fraternities and sororities. To reduce those negative emotions, he may tell himself "I don't have to pay for my friends" (Harris 1997:8).
- The mother of a terminally-ill child, whose mask and feeding tube continually draw unwanted glances from strangers, may try to dismiss feelings of abnormality by telling herself "That's okay! We don't care! Doesn't bother us!" rather than "How embarrassing! So awkward!" (Gengler 2015:624).

All of these behaviors can be seen as cognitive deep acting, because individuals are attempting to change their emotions by changing their thoughts on a situation. Two other forms of deep acting – bodily and expressive – pursue the same goal but adopt a more physical approach.

**Bodily deep acting** occurs when we manipulate our "bodily arousal" – defined in a general sense, not in an erotic way. If we are angry, we may try to calm ourselves down by taking a deep breath and unclenching our fists. Some students in Albas and Albas's (1988) research attempted to reduce exam anxiety by taking baths, jiggling their legs, or chewing pens (to dispel nervous energy). Alternatively, individuals may try to work up their bodily arousal. Self-injurers sometimes assert that they cut, burn, shock, or bruise themselves to overcome emotional numbness (Adler and Adler 2011). Or, individuals may jump up and down, and splash water on their faces, in order to increase alertness and intensity, before an athletic contest, exam, or job interview. Even book authors have been known to carefully modulate their ingestion of caffeine, sugar, tobacco, and other substances, for similar purposes.

**Expressive deep acting** also involves bodily work, but in a more specific way. Individuals pursue this strategy when they manipulate their emotional display in the hope that the real feeling will follow. If we are sad or depressed, we might try to improve our mood by forcing a smile, looking outward and upward instead of hanging our heads, and putting a skip in our step rather than shuffling our feet. Some students told Albas and Albas (1988) that they dress casually during exams to reduce the seriousness and formality of the occasion, and thereby ease their anxiety. Others claimed that they donned their better outfits, in order to appear – and make themselves feel – more professional and confident.

None of these deep acting strategies is guaranteed to work. On some occasions, cognitive, bodily, and expressive deep acting may completely fail to achieve their intended emotional transformations. Other times, they may succeed, but only partially. The same is true of surface acting. We may adjust our wording, tone, facial expressions, posture, and wardrobe, yet fall short of convincing all our audiences, all of the time, that we are feeling the purposefully-displayed emotion. A grandparent might see through our façade and say, "It's OK if you don't like my gift" or even "Don't patronize me!"

With deep acting, the difference is we may not be able to convince ourselves. A financial advisor may remind himself "Money doesn't buy happiness," but does he fully believe his own mantra? Or, after being dumped by a romantic partner, we may try to cheer ourselves up – "I can do better! There are plenty of fish in the sea!" – but doubt the words we tell ourselves.

## Interpersonal Emotion Management

Emotion management is not necessarily, or even primarily, an individual task. Managing emotions can be a group project. After a painful break up, we often don't have to tell ourselves "There are plenty of fish in the sea," because our friends and relatives will do that for us. They may even remind us of all the annoying habits our Ex possessed, in a multi-pronged effort to help us deep act our way out of a funk. Or, imagine a veterinarian who tells pet owners "You did the right thing. …Many people make the mistake of waiting too late" to assuage their guilt following euthanasia (Morris 2012:348). Similarly, picture a river guide who refers to rapids by menacing names ("Hell's Half Mile," "Satan's Gut!") to generate customers' fearful excitement (Holyfield and Jonas 2003). Bill collectors may also attempt to create a sense of alarm but do so by threatening and belittling delinquent customers on the phone (Hochschild 1983). In all these settings, emotions and their management – especially through cognitive deep acting – are not the sole province of isolated persons.

Individuals may simultaneously manage their own emotions as they manage others'. In fact, managing one's own emotions is frequently a means to shape what an audience feels. Consider this example, from Lois's (2003) research with volunteer search and rescuers. Imagine the rescuer's careful use of tone and facial expressions as he conveyed concern and urgency, yet optimism, to an injured climber.

> I remember once… a rock fell on somebody's head and from the front he looked fine, but the back of his head was just half gone. And I remember sitting on the ground with this guy and the helicopter was coming in…. And I was saying, "This is serious, but you've got to keep fighting it. We've got the helicopter on the way," …and he was doing okay. And then

the [climber] who'd knocked the rock off comes running over and went, "Oh my God! Look at the back of his head!" And I remember him just: pppt [passing out]. That was it. He was out. He just, like, panicked and got all shaky and just lay down on the ground. And then the helicopter came. But I remember just thinking how foolish that was. (Lois 2003:123)

The rescuer's controlled demeanor stands in sharp contrast to the climber who screams "Oh my God!" and sends the injured man into a state of shock. Moreover, consider how the rescuer carefully guides the wounded man's thoughts – your condition is serious, but you've got to keep fighting, and help is on the way – to foster a desired emotional state (calm but focused, concerned yet optimistic). Arguably, the rescuer may be engaging in at least three forms of emotion management simultaneously: (i) surface acting, by pretending to be more calm or confident than he is; (ii) deep acting, by changing his own thoughts (or breathing deeply, etc.) in an attempt to create a real feeling of calm rather than a mere facade; and (iii) interpersonal emotion management, by trying to judiciously calibrate the victim's thoughts and feelings.

*Interpersonal emotion management occurs when we try to shape or modify the feelings of others. Two or more individuals may work on emotions collaboratively or as adversaries.*

The climbing example also raises an additional consideration. We can work on emotion management in collaborative or adversarial fashion (Lois 2003:114). Two or more people may or may not agree, implicitly or explicitly, on the desired feelings and the means of generating them. The injured man seems to work with the rescuer's goals; he is a willing collaborator. The injurer – the climber who knocked the rock onto the victim's head, and then created a sense of panic – does not.

The panicked climber accidentally undermined the rescuer's interpersonal emotion management. People may more purposefully and knowingly resist efforts to shape their own or their companions' feelings. If you were to scold a friend for boasting about taking office supplies from his job – "That's stealing! You should be ashamed!" – he might try to resist, proudly. "No, it's smart. And it's justice. My boss doesn't pay me enough." Similarly, detectives may try to create fear and submission in a suspect, by threatening harsh prison time during an interrogation (Rafaeli and Sutton 1991). Suspects, in response, may hurl embarrassing insults at detectives to throw them off their game (Stenross and Kleinman 1989). Or consider a person who wants to dwell or wallow in their sadness over a break-up. They might ignore or argue with our efforts to raise their spirits, even though we think we are trying to help.

Interpersonal emotion management can involve large numbers of people. Politics, for example, is infused with emotion management. Candidates and pundits try to stir up fear, anger, love of country, and other emotions that serve their agendas. Donald Trump famously launched his 2016 presidential campaign by portraying a large but unspecified number of Mexican immigrants as murderers and rapists. He promised to build a long wall to protect Americans from this threat. Many found such remarks to be racist and wrongheaded, but that is beside the point we make here: The candidate was, arguably, and at least in part, attempting to stoke fear and promise a sense of security, if elected. (See Loseke 2009 for a somewhat related analysis of G.W. Bush's speeches on terrorism.)

Social movement activists also attract and motivate supporters via interpersonal emotion management. Deborah Gould (2002), for example, documented how AIDS activists mobilized members of the gay and lesbian community, by encouraging them to convert their grief, shame, and loneliness, into anger and social action. One group, ACT UP, advertised a protest in 1987, by printing this flier:

> WE ARE ANGRY:
> - At the Government's policy of malignant neglect
> - At the irresponsible inaction of this president
> - At the shameful indifference of our elected representatives
> - At the criminal hoarding of appropriated funds by government agencies
> They Waste Our Money, Our Time, Our Lives!
> TAKE ONE DAY OFF FROM WORK...TURN RAGE INTO ACTION!
> (Gould 2002:181)

A social movement depends on participants' continuing commitment to the cause. To retain adherents, leaders may thus use language, music, images, and other methods to prompt indignant and optimistic attitudes, while warding off lethargy and hopelessness.

## Emotional Labor

We can view emotion management as **emotional labor** when we conduct it as part of our jobs. If our paid employment requires or inspires us to use surface and deep acting to shape our own feelings, or the feelings of others, then we are performing emotional labor even if we do not fully realize it. Any occupation will involve overlapping forms of cognitive, manual, and emotional labor, but the latter usually remains unnamed and underappreciated.

*Emotional labor occurs when workers must manage emotions as an implicit or explicit part of their employment. Workers may attempt to alter or disguise their own feelings (through deep acting and surface acting), or they may attempt to shape the emotions of customers, co-workers, and employers.*

Arlie Hochschild's (1983) landmark book, *The Managed Heart: Commercialization of Human Feeling*, developed a vocabulary and highlighted a number of fascinating situations that might reasonably be placed under the umbrella of emotional labor. Her work has inspired research by hundreds of scholars (see Grandey, Diefendorff, and Rupp 2013; Lively 2006; Wharton 2009). In this section, we will focus on employers' control over employees and on inequalities between emotional laborers.

## Controlling Employees' Emotions

Many employers want to ensure that their employees will experience, display, and foster desired emotions in the workplace. Business owners and managers may hire and train workers to set an appropriate emotional tone in interactions with customers, co-workers, and other audiences.

When **hiring**, managers can recruit and evaluate candidates for their emotion management skills as well as for their intellectual acumen or manual dexterity. Open positions are advertised strategically. Solicitations call for applicants who have a "positive attitude," or who are a "people-person" with "strong interpersonal skills." Kotchemidova (2005) searched Monster.com and discovered 200 different jobs with "cheerful personality" listed as a qualification for candidates. If an initial application survives scrutiny, then candidates may be evaluated for their ability to make small talk with new acquaintances during one-on-one and group interviews (Hochschild 1983). Internships may allow employers to scrutinize candidates in even more detail. Scott and Myers (2005) showed how firefighters subtly assess the emotion management skills of potential applicants who go on "ride alongs"; candidates must demonstrate they can handle stress well and act sociably with staff and the public.

Let's consider a large and well-known corporation, Chipotle Mexican Grill (CMG). The leaders of this corporation tell their applicants that they look for 13 characteristics in employees. In a video posted on the "careers" section of CMG's website, co-chief executive officer Monty Moran explains that the company seeks workers who are:

1) Ambitious
2) Conscientious
3) Curious
4) Happy
5) High Energy
6) Honest
7) Hospitable
8) Infectiously Enthusiastic
9) Motivated

10) Polite
11) Presentable
12) Respectful
13) Smart

https://careers.chipotle.com/corporate[2] (alphabetizing and numbering added).

At least seven of these characteristic – items 4, 5, 7, 8, 9, 10, and 12 – can be seen as attempts to articulate the emotion norms to which employees must abide. CMG workers should be happy, polite, and energetic, rather than surly and lethargic, or even competent yet aloof. Moreover, their positive enthusiasm should be "infectious," encouraging customers and co-workers to feel the same way. If a customer is rude, or if a long line impatiently urges workers to move quickly, the worker must remain respectful and hospitable. These guidelines shape how candidates are recruited, interviewed, hired or screened out.

Curiously, CMG claims that these 13 characteristics cannot be taught or learned.[3] Once you are an adult, "you either have them, or you don't," CEO Moran proclaims. The argument is rather stark: once individuals turn 18, they can no longer grow or change. Perhaps this static perspective on human nature is meant to increase profits in three ways: dissuading unhappy people from trying to surface act their way through a job interview; discouraging managers from wasting resources by hiring candidates whose demeanor seems potentially problematic; and encouraging applicants and employees to surface and deep act in silence, as they seek to embody all 13 characteristics "naturally," in the course of their daily work routines.

As the above examples show, employers can use the hiring process to establish norms and guide workers' emotional experiences and displays. Such influence can continue, and be amplified, through **emotion-management training**. Employees can be taught the emotion norms and the surface and deep acting strategies that the company recommends or demands. Instructors, managers, fellow employees – as well as brochures and corporate videos – can be used to socialize workers in an explicit fashion; or, new employees may be indirectly socialized, and infer the desired norms and strategies for conforming.

In a fascinating article, Smith and Kleinman (1989) argued that many medical students are informally socialized into their professions. At the medical school they studied, no courses or modules existed on how to suppress undesirable feelings of anxiety, disgust, annoyance, or sexual attraction that might arise while interacting with cadavers and patients. Students observed their professors' and classmates' behavior and off-hand comments, to discover the norms and the surface or deep acting techniques that might be useful. For example, medical students learned that scientific detachment – viewing patients through the prism of technical terms, as analytical problems to be solved – could be deployed as a form of cognitive deep acting, when unwanted feelings arose.

Other work settings, in contrast, may involve very mindful, explicit, and carefully designed emotion-management instruction (Leidner 1999). For example, David Schweingruber and Nancy Berns (2005) studied "Enterprise," a company that hired young adults to sell educational books door-to-door. Enterprise instituted a rigorous training process, in which they devoted 80% of the time and effort to emotion management (Schweingruber and Berns 2005:688). They carefully prepared workers (usually college students) overcome the job's emotional hurdles – the repeated rejection and rude comments from potential customers, and the stress of working long hours, almost every day of the week, in unfamiliar neighborhoods, through potentially uncomfortable weather, for an uncertain paycheck based on commissions. Enterprise did not want to hire workers who would easily give up. That's costly. So, the company instituted a set of training strategies revolving around "emotional purposes."

Every trainee had to develop a personalized incentive that held more meaning than simply making money. Close relationships were key. The book sellers could focus on making a parent proud, disproving a friend's skeptical predictions of failure, or some other goal with interpersonal significance. Any social bond – even imagined relationships with one's future children – could be treated as "emotional capital" and mined as a motivational resource. Trainers instructed their novice workers to write down their emotional purposes, talk about them with co-workers, and recall them while working on the road. To maintain enthusiasm and passion during difficult days, the trainers encouraged workers to have imaginary conversations with the person(s) at the center of their emotional purposes: "What would they say if I gave up now? What will they say if I choose to endure and thrive?" In addition, emotional purposes were integrated into company meetings and ceremonies, to reinforce their importance and power.

Enterprise augmented emotional purposes with other emotion-management training, primarily designed to foster emotional endurance through cognitive deep acting. For example, trainers told workers that their job had a strong moral element. Enterprise portrayed selling educational books as performing a community service, rather than simply a money-making endeavor. And, by offering customers an example of what a motivated, happy, hard working person looks like, the workers learned they could provide a model that inspired others to lead more fulfilling lives (Schweingruber and Berns 2005).

Most companies do not adopt such a methodical and purposeful training system. Nonetheless, the example of Enterprise can help us spot the less systematic efforts that other employers may engage in. The casual invocation of a business slogan – such as "The customer is always right" or "We owe our jobs to our customers, after all" – may reflect an employer's attempt to set an emotion norm that requires a polite, positive, and deferential demeanor, even in the face of customer discourtesy. Such slogans may change how employees think, so they create "appropriate" feelings (i.e. deep acting), or the slogans may simply motivate workers to fake compliance with the sentiment through surface acting. Any employees who cannot conform would risk being reprimanded or let go.

## The Unequal Distribution of Emotional Labor

In one fashion or another, social inequalities pervade virtually every corner of our lives. Emotional labor is no exception. We have already discussed how employers can exert a great deal of power over employees. Business owners and managers can set emotion norms, encourage or require the use of particular surface or deep acting strategies, and sanction or fire those individuals who cannot conform to their expectations.

This section will focus on another dimension of inequality – the unequal distribution of labor across different categories of workers. Individuals' emotional labor may be more frequent, intense, or under-rewarded, depending on their sex, race, or social status.

The fact that women earn less than men – in general and within identical occupations – often makes the news. Less discussed is the idea that women do more emotion management for their lower wages (Bellas 2001). Many career paths are sex-segregated. Women dominate the field of primary education (K-8), while men are over-represented in construction work. Quite likely, the former occupation requires a larger amount of interpersonal emotion management than the latter. Similar tendencies can be found in other occupations (Guy and Newman 2004). Women gravitate or are steered toward the positions of waitress, nurse, and flight attendant, and men more toward chef, physician, and pilot. Typically, the former involve more opportunities to attend to others' emotional needs – making customers feel safe, respected, happy, calm, and so on.

Of course, some men enter nursing and some women become construction workers. Few occupations are completely sex-segregated. Yet, even when a woman holds the same position as a man, employers may still require her to perform more emotional labor. Such requirements occur in part because the tasks within an occupation may be unequally distributed. For example, co-workers may expect a female police officer to comfort a victim of rape or molestation, while her male partner collects evidence from the scene (Martin 1999). Or, a law firm may not expect male paralegals to provide as many smiles and kind words as female paralegals, even though they work for the same group of lawyers (Pierce 1999).

Women are presumed to be more nurturing, supportive, and servile. These assumptions lead to career paths, and task expectations within a position, but also differential treatment by customers, co-workers, and employers.

Passengers may turn to a female flight attendant as the person to whom one complains (e.g. about a late flight, missed connection) or grumpily resists (e.g. about powering down electronic devices), more than her male counterpart (Hochschild 1983:174). A passenger may ask the male flight attendant to help life a heavy bag, while his female co-worker spends more time on scared or upset passengers. In addition, sexual harassment more likely affects female workers, leading to a great deal of surface and deep acting, as women fend off advances and navigate office politics.

It must be mentioned that, in all likelihood, women come to their workplaces already having performed a greater amount of unpaid emotion management at home. Typically, grandmothers, wives, aunts, and sisters do more of the work that holds families together – comforting children, tending to the sick and aged, promoting positive conversations between relatives, and other feeling-centered tasks (Devault 1991; Sarkisian and Gerstel 2012).

*Race, too, shapes the division of emotional labor.* Consider these heartbreaking excerpts, from Louwanda Evans' (2013) interviews with African American pilots and flight attendants:

> My trip had ended, and I was trying to catch a ride home on another airline.... I was sitting at the gate in my pilot's uniform, just sitting there, and an older white man got up and went to the gate and said, "That nigger better not be flying my plane."
>
> – Tim, pilot

> On a flight to Reagan National Airport from Atlanta, I had an encounter with a [white] male passenger as I moved through the aisle with the beverage cart. I reached his row, stopped the car, and asked, "Can I get you something to drink?" [The passenger responded] "Would you mind getting someone else to bring me my drink? I would prefer you not touch my cup." Initially, I thought that maybe it was something religious and based on my gender because we get that sometimes. But then a white female flight attendant served him his [soda] with no problems. I was shocked and upset, and as a matter of fact, I did not want him to have a drink at all!
>
> – Sue, senior black flight attendant
> (Evans 2013:1)

Unquestionably race relations have improved in the U.S. since the civil rights movement of the 1950s and 1960s. Nevertheless, the U.S. is still plagued by discrimination, segregation, and unequal opportunities for advancement (Feagin 2010; McNamee and Miller 2014). Concordantly, one's race can shape the amount and forms of emotion management needed to navigate interactions on the job.

Adia Harvey Wingfield (2010) found that workplace emotion norms can be racialized, in at least two ways. First, a double standard may exist, as the emotion norms governing employee conduct are variably enforced. For example, not everyone receives the same leeway to violate the common office norm to "remain calm and polite." White workers may be freer to express a bit of anger, as it would likely be interpreted as a sign of passion, candor, or legitimate frustration. Black professionals reported that they could not express such feelings, as others would view their anger as frightening and unprofessional. Jay, a systems engineer for a large corporation, suggested that if he behaved like one of his discontented colleagues, "I'd be labeled as an angry black dude [who] can't get along with coworkers" (Wingfield 2010:259).

Even if organizations did enforce emotion norms in a racially-neutral fashion, minority workers would still need to perform more emotional management than their white counterparts, due to the effects of prejudice. Evans' (2013) research, quoted above, illuminates these effects. If a person encounters discrimination on the workplace – such as the very poor treatment Tim and Sue received – then conforming to the rule to "remain pleasant" likely requires much more effort. Or, consider Wingfield's example from Cedric, a financial analyst for a professional sports team:

> Once at work I had a carton from Boston Market, and one of the guys comes up to me like, "What is that, baby food?" I'm [thinking], why would I be eating baby food at work? So I'm like, "No, its sweet potatoes." He was like, "What?" All confused. I said, "Sweet potatoes, yams, you know." So he's like, "What is that? Is that like soul food?" I'm just like, wow. Stuff like that. You're not mad exactly, it's more like, "This stupid motherfucker…." (Wingfield 2010:261)

Keep in mind that poor treatment in the workplace may aggravate wounds from the prejudice and discrimination experienced outside of work. Receiving hostile looks, being followed by security while shopping at the mall, or being unnecessarily stopped by the police – these unpleasant encounters may combine with workplace insensitivity and make emotion management more of a challenge (see also Wilkins 2012).

Along with sex and race, *social status can impact the distribution of emotional labor*. Individuals have higher **status** when people perceive them to possess more prestige or importance than others. Those with wealth, power, or fame may have high status, somewhat independent of their sex and race. Having high status can minimize the amount of emotional labor one does on the job, in two ways. First, **organizational shields** can protect such individuals from unwanted contact with customers, clients, and others who may seek to express dissatisfaction or receive expressions of confidence, remorse, sympathy, and other feelings (Goodrum and Stafford 2003). For example, a mayor may have assistants and a few layers of bureaucracy between him or her and disaffected citizens or lower level employees. In contrast, angry motorists may confront meter readers almost daily, if not hourly, as they issue tickets. Or, imagine a counter-worker who must absorb the dissatisfaction of customers, while the manager – who caused delays by not scheduling enough workers – can remain behind the scenes.

Secondly, when higher status people interact with others, their thoughts and feelings tend to receive more attention or deference. Their **status shields** protect them from some of the emotional demands that their perceived inferiors may face (Hochschild 1983:172). For example, I (Scott) have sometimes noticed that customers will rather mercilessly complain about a product or service to a minimum-wage worker, only to moderate their tone once a manager appears to help resolve the situation. The lower-paid employee seems to bear the heavier load of emotional labor – the surface and deep acting it takes to mollify customers and maintain an appropriate display of patience, sympathy, and respect. Thus, a pay disparity is subtly, perhaps invisibly, exacerbated by a workload disparity. In similar fashion, the concept of status shields predicts that doctors will be treated more gently than nurses, pilots more deferentially than flight attendants, and deans more cautiously than instructors.

> *"Organizational shields"* are barriers that limit or filter contact with individuals who would require emotional labor, such as customers, clients, or subordinates. *"Status shields"* refers to the protection derived from being perceived as an important or prestigious person; the thoughts and feelings of higher status people tend to be treated more cautiously and respectfully.

Social life is complicated, however. A wide range of variables can influence the intensity and amount of emotional labor a person performs. These variables include one's personal characteristics (e.g. age, beauty, religion) and the larger social context (e.g. political climate, strong or weak job market). The safest approach is to make your own observations, as you apply this chapter's concepts to the settings in which you and your acquaintances are employed.

## Conclusion

In this chapter, we have tried to highlight just a few of the social dimensions of emotions. Although emotions are often thought of as private, physiological, and natural, emotions are – at least equally – social things. Our emotions are in some ways rooted in our bodies, but our "personal feelings" must also conform to culturally-created norms, or risk sanction. Human beings can strategically modify and display their feelings for public consumption. We can fake feelings and make feelings, through surface and deep acting. On many occasions, we may purposely perform our "natural" reactions for our audiences – be they family, friends, classmates, customers, co-workers, or employers. The effort we exert may be underappreciated, and distributed unequally in homes and workplaces, but it is crucial and consequential in our lives.

This short discussion has presented only a brief sampling of interactionist concepts. We hope to whet your appetite and give you some tools to begin analyzing your personal experiences and observations. Please note that we have neglected large swathes of research, by interactionists and sociologists, as well as by psychologists, anthropologists, historians, and researchers from other disciplines.[4]

Scholars have developed many theoretical and methodological approaches for studying human emotion. Many of these are fascinating but can also be somewhat incompatible with each other. This chapter has side-stepped important debates over how best to define emotions, the utility of distinguishing between "affect," "mood," and "primary" versus "secondary" emotions, whether thought precedes or follows emotion (or is separable at all), the difference between constructing feelings "objectively" vs. "interpretively," and other issues. We encourage you to seek out other readings, and wade into these debates, if the topic of emotions piques your interest.

## Learning by Using the Symbolic Interactionist Perspective

Below we offer an excerpt from the book *Gig: Americans Talk about Their Jobs* (Bowe, Bowe, and Streeter 2001). Can you use any of the concepts from this chapter to make sense of Jessica Seaver's description of her waitressing job? Feel free to imagine some of the actions and circumstances that she may leave unstated.

---

**"Waitress"**

**Jessica Seaver**

*Bowe, Bowe, and Streeter (2001)*

I'm 25 and I work five days a week, mostly double shifts. …My main job is I wait tables full-time at Tejas, an upscale Tex-Mex place. The thing I like to bring to it is to make people feel good, make 'em feel comfortable. That's the thing I can do best.

…Tejas is a nice, family owned place. I would never want to work in a stuffy place like a seven-course dining thing. …I don't want to deal with stuffy, snobby people. There's a difference between being a server and being an order-taker. I prefer to be a server and a server has a personality and they use it and that's part of your dining experience.

...It's almost like being an entertainer. One of the hardest things is when customers come in and their nature is just rudeness and you still have to kiss their butt because they're paying your bills. When they're rude, and you know that it's nothing you've done, it's hard to be nice. When you know that no matter what, they wouldn't've been happy anyway – they've had a bad day and they're bringing it with them, when they shouldn't even be going out. When their attitude is just so piss-poor or they're just so high on themselves and they think they're better than you because you're just a waitress – that's what I hate. But I deal with it by knowing that it's part of the job and there's a different situation at every table. So if there's a rude jerk here, there may very well be a great person over there. And so you deal with it.

...Of course, there are also very nice experiences. Last year, I had a small little stockbroking company come for their Christmas party – you know, like 10 employees – and they pushed all these tables together, and the boss was paying for everything. ...We were telling jokes and shooting the shit. I was like part of the party. I was entertaining them and they were hilarious. And at the end of the night ...the dude gives me a [large] tip. He said, "You know what? You were so much fun. Half these people never loosen up. You really made it fun." And that was great.

## Notes

1  "JonBenet Ramsey's Brother Burke Smiles as He Recalls Aftermath of Murder: It Was a 'Chaotic Nightmare.'" Downloaded on September 13, 2016, from http://www.usmagazine.com/celebrity-news/news/jonbenet-ramseys-brother-burke-smiles-as-he-recalls-case-w438909
2  Downloaded 19 September 2016.
3  We wonder: Is there an enterprising undergraduate or graduate student who wants to conduct a research project on CMG? Someone should take a closer look at the hidden emotional labor and indirect socialization that occurs in this work setting, via in-depth interviews and/or participant observation.
4  For example, see Kalat and Shiota (2007); Kemper (2000); Loseke and Kusenbach (2008); Lutz and White (1986); Matt and Stearns (2014); Stets and Turner (2014).

## References

Albas, C. and D. Albas. 1988. "Emotion Work and Emotion Rules: The Case of Exams." *Qualitative Sociology* 11:259–274.

Adler, P. A. and P. Adler. 2011. *The Tender Cut: Inside the Hidden World of Self-Injury*. New York: NYU Press.

Bellas, M. L. 2001. "The Gendered Nature of Emotional Labor in the Workplace." Pp. 269–278 in *Gender Mosaics*, edited by D. Vannoy. Los Angeles, CA: Roxbury.

Bowe, J., M. Bowe, and S. Streeter. 2001. *Gig: Americans Talk about Their Jobs*. New York: Three Rivers Press.

Clanton, G. 2006. "Jealousy and Envy." Pp. 410–442 in *Handbook of the Sociology of Emotions*, edited by J. H. Turner and J. E. Stets. New York: Springer.

Cox, A. B. 2016. "Correcting Behaviors and Policing Emotions: How Behavioral Infractions Become Feeling-Rule Reminders."*Symbolic Interaction* 39(3):484–503.

Delaney, K. J. 2012. *Money at Work: On the Job with Priests, Poker Players, and Hecge Fund Traders*. New York: NYU Press.

Devault, M. 1991. *Feeding the Family*. Chicago, IL: University of Chicago Press.

Ellis, C. and L. Irvine. 2010. "Reproducing Dominion: Emotional Apprenticeship in the 4-H Youth Livestock Program." *Society and Animals* 18:21–39.

Evans, L. 2013. *Cabin Pressure: African American Pilots, Flight Attendants, and Emotional Labor*. Lanham, MD: Rowman and Littlefield.

Feagin, J. R. 2010. *Racist America: Roots, Current Realities, and Future Reparations*, 2nd ed. New York: Routledge.

Gengler, A. M. 2015. "'He's Doing Fine': Hope Work and Emotional Threat Management Among Families of Seriously Ill Children." *Symbolic Interaction* 38(4):611–630.

Goffman, E. 1959. *The Presentation of Self in Everyday Life*. New York: Doubleday.

Goodrum, D. and M. C. Stafford. 2003. "The Management of Emotions in the Criminal Justice System." *Sociological Focus* 36(3):179–196.

Gould, D. 2002. "Life during Wartime: Emotions and the Development of ACT UP." *Mobilization: An International Journal* 7(2):177–200.

Grandey, A. A., J. M. Diefendorff, and D. E. Rupp. 2013. *Emotional Labor in the 21ˢᵗ Century: Diverse Perspectives on Emotion Regulation at Work*. New York: Routledge.

Guy, M. E. and M. A. Newman. 2004. "Women's Jobs, Men's Jobs: Sex Segregation and Emotional Labor." *Public Administration Review* 64:289–298.

Harris, S. R. 1997. "Status Inequality and Close Relationships: An Integrative Typology of Bond-Saving Strategies." *Symbolic Interaction* 20:1–20.

Harris, S. R. 2015. *An Invitation to the Sociology of Emotions*. New York: Routledge.

Hochschild, A. R. 1983. *The Managed Heart: Commercialization of Human Feeling*. Berkeley, CA: University of California.

Holyfield, L. and L. Jonas. 2003. "From River God to Research Grunt: Identity, Emotions, and the River Guide." *Symbolic Interaction* 26(2):285–306.

Husting, G. 2015. "The Flayed and Exquisite Self of Travelers: Managing Face and Emotions in Strange Places." *Symbolic Interaction* 38(2):213–234.

Kalat, J. W. and M. N. Shiota. 2007. *Emotion*. Belmont, CA: Wadsworth.

Kemper, T. D. 2000. "Social Models in the Explanation of Emotions." Pp. 45–58 in *Handbook of Emotions*, edited by M. Lewis and J. M. Haviland-Jones. New York: Guilford.

Kotchemidova, C. 2005. "From Good Cheer to 'Drive-by Smiling': A Social History of Cheerfulness." *Journal of Social History* 39(1):5–37.

Leidner, R. 1999. "Emotional Labor in Service Work." *Annals of the American Academy of Political and Social Science* 561:81–95.

Lively, K. J. 2006. "Emotions in the Workplace." Pp. 569–590 in *Handbook of the Sociology of Emotions*, edited by J. H. Turner and J. E. Stets. New York: Springer.

Lois, J. 2003. *Heroic Efforts: The Emotional Culture of Search and Rescue Volunteers*. New York: NYU Press.

Lois, J. 2013. *Home Is Where the School Is: the Logic of Homeschooling and the Emotional Labor of Mothering*. New York: NYU Press.

Loseke, D. R. 2009. "Examining Emotion as Discourse: Emotion Codes and Presidential Speeches."*Sociological Quarterly* 50:497–524.

Loseke, D. R. and M. Kusenbach. 2008. "The Social Construction of Emotion." Pp. 511–529 in *Handbook of Constructionist Research*, edited by J. Gubrium and J. A. Holstein. New York: Guilford.

Lutz, C. and G. M. White. 1986. "The Anthropology of Emotions." *Annual Review of Anthropology* 15:405–436.

Martin, S. E. 1999. "Police Force or Police Service? Gender and Emotional Labor." *Annals of the American Academy of Political and Social Science* 561:111–126.

Matt, S. and P. N. Stearns, eds. 2014. *Doing Emotions History*. Chicago, IL: University of Illinois.

McNamee, S. J. and R. K. Miller. 2014. *The Meritocracy Myth*, 3rd ed. Lanham, MD: Rowman and Littlefield.

Morris, P. 2012. "Managing Pet Owners' Guilt and Grief in Veterinary Euthanasia Encounters." *Journal of Contemporary Ethnography* 41(3):337–365.

Norgaard, K. M. 2006. "'People Want to Protect Themselves a Little Bit': Emotions, Denial, and Social Movement Nonparticipation." *Sociological Inquiry* 76:372–396.

Ortiz, S. M. 2011. "Wives Who Play by the Rules: Working on Emotions in the Sport Marriage." Pp. 124–135 in *At the Heart of Work and Family: Engaging the Ideas of Arlie Hochschild*, edited by A. I. Garey and K. V. Hansen. New Brunswick, NJ: Rutgers University Press.

Pierce, J. L. 1999. "Emotional Labor Among Paralegals." *Annals of the American Academy of Political and Social Science* 561:127–142.

Rafaeli, A. and R. I. Sutton. 1991. "Emotional Contrast Strategies as Means of Social Influence: Lessons from Criminal Interrogators and Bill Collectors." *Academy of Management Journal* 34(4):749–775.

Sarkisian, N. and N. Gerstel. 2012. *Nuclear Family Values, Extended Family Lives.* New York: Routledge.

Schweingruber, D. and N. Berns. 2005. "Shaping the Selves of Young Salespeople through Emotion Management." *Journal of Contemporary Ethnography* 34:679–706.

Scott, C. and K. K. Myers. 2005. "The Socialization of Emotion: Learning Emotion Management at the Fire Station." *Journal of Applied Communication Research* 33(1):67–92.

Smith, A. C. III and S. Kleinman. 1989. "Managing Emotions in Medical School." *Social Psychology Quarterly* 52:56–69.

Stenross, B. and S. Kleinman. 1989. "The Highs and Lows of Emotional Labor: Detectives Encounters with Criminals and Victims." *Journal of Contemporary Ethnography* 17:435–452.

Stets, J. E. and J. H. Turner, eds. 2014. *Handbook of the Sociology of Emotions*, Vol. II, New York: Springer.

Wharton, A. S. 2009. "The Sociology of Emotional Labor." *Annual Review of Sociology* 35:147–165.

Wilkins, A. 2012. "'Not Out to Start a Revolution': Race, Gender, and Emotional Restraint among Black University Men." *Journal of Contemporary Ethnography* 41:34–65.

Wingfield, A. H. 2010. "Are Some Emotions Marked 'Whites Only'? Racialized Feeling Rules in Professional Workplaces." *Social Problems* 57:251–268.

# 7

# All Our Families

## Diverse Forms, Diverse Meanings

> "Like New Year's Eve and sometimes at night …those little times when I wish someone was there. …If I were to say that to some of my married friends, they would be like 'Well, you need to find a man' but that is not it. Just because I have these little feelings of loneliness does not mean that I want to go out and grab the first guy that looks at me, you know." (Single woman, age 28–34, from Sharp and Ganong 2011:970)
>
> "A lot of people at the kindergarten were teasing and told Anna 'You don't even have a daddy.' And I told her 'You have a daddy, Anna. Everybody has a daddy. There's nobody around without a daddy. He just isn't here.' It [my attempt to make Anna feel better] didn't work." (Single mother in Austria, adapted from Zartler 2014:612)
>
> "My search represented a need for a biological connection. I felt a vacuum … because I was unrelated to people. I didn't have any ties or connections to anyone. My adoptive parents. Even my wife and children. It's different somehow. I wanted an anchor. To connect me. Make me real. I'm much more peaceful now. In the sense that before there were a lot of unknowns. I tended to fill those unknowns with a lot of negatives. Finding them [my biological mother and relatives] removed that. It gave me roots." (Adopted male, age 30, from March 2000:366)

The nuclear family is revered in much of the U.S. and other parts of the world. Canadian scholar Dorothy Smith (1993) proposed a now famous acronym – "SNAF," the Standard North American Family – as a shorthand way of referring to this form of kinship and its idealization. SNAF is achieved when a heterosexual husband, wife, and their biological children live under one roof, with the husband acting as primary breadwinner. Politicians, pundits, and others often assume that this configuration is the most genuine or real form of family. As Smith (1993) might say, their views are "SNAF-infected."

*The Social Self and Everyday Life: Understanding the World Through Symbolic Interactionism*, First Edition. Kathy Charmaz, Scott R. Harris, and Leslie Irvine.
© 2019 John Wiley & Sons, Inc. Published 2019 by John Wiley & Sons, Inc.

North Americans implicitly idolize SNAF when they describe divorced families as "non-intact" or "broken." Hyphenated descriptions, even when relatively benign, can also indicate distance from SNAF. A mother and child may be considered a single-parent family, two gay men may establish a same-sex family, and so on. In contrast, a heterosexual married couple with kids is simply "a family."

Pauline Erera (2002) used the terms variation and deviation to capture American's sentiments on kinship. Diverse forms of kinship are granted more or less respect, depending on their distance from SNAF. **Variations on SNAF** are more tolerable. Examples would be blended families formed by the joining of two divorced parents, or adoptive families, or unmarried-but-cohabitating couples with children. **Deviations from SNAF** elicit harsher reactions. Grandmother-headed, polyamorous, and same-sex families are more likely to be considered morally repugnant or pathological by millions of North Americans who take an "exclusionist" viewpoint (Powell et al. 2010).

SNAF is a cultural touchstone and yardstick, as the opening excerpts demonstrate. We measure our own lives and others' through the prism of SNAF: An unmarried 30-year-old may feel pressure to hurry up and find a partner; a kindergartner may be teased for lacking a father; an adoptee may feel that the family who loved and raised him is not fully real. Similarly, adults who choose to remain single or childfree are discriminated against and assumed to suffer character flaws (Agrillo and Nelini 2008; DePaulo and Morris 2005). Homosexual couples still experience hostile reactions in many communities, and the legalization of same-sex marriage remains controversial in many parts of the U.S.

Advocates of SNAF claim that the nuclear family is a product of evolution, a divine creation, or a steadfast cultural convention. For example, Allan Carlson (2014) portrays the romantic love undergirding SNAF as an inevitable, innate tendency: "Marriage… is natural and self-renewing, rooted in the mutual attraction of man to woman, both of whom feel their incompleteness when existing alone" (Carlson 2014:xiii). Or, consider author and radio host James Dobson. He contends that SNAF was first conceived by God, and should thus be protected and treasured more than other forms of kinship: "The family was God's idea and He does not make mistakes" (Dobson 1998:20, 2006). The 2016 U.S. Republican Party Platform[1] (p. 11), published at the convention that nominated Donald Trump for president, echoes these claims while portraying SNAF as both essential and nearly eternal: "Traditional marriage and family, based on marriage between one man and one woman, is the foundation for a free society and has [been] for millennia."

In this chapter, we will explore the interactionist approach to family, which tends to challenge SNAF assumptions. First, we will highlight cultural relativity. If God or evolution created SNAF, then not everyone got the memo. Anthropologists and sociologists have shown that kinship varies dramatically across cultures and over time. Then, in subsequent sections, we will turn to a more fine-grained examination of meaning-making in discourse and social interaction. From a symbolic interactionist perspective, family is as much idea as thing (Gubrium and Holstein 1990, 2012). Families and their situations are "talked into being" as individuals propose, debate, and act on their respective interpretations. Though these interpretations are diverse, flexible, and idiosyncratic, they are also shaped and patterned by the socially organized settings in which people find themselves.

## The Cultural Relativity of Family

Anthropologists and sociologists tend to hold a different view of kinship than SNAF-advocates. For most of these social scientists, family is not natural, divine, or eternal – it's a human creation (Baca Zinn, Eitzen, and Wells 2015; Harris 2008; Stone 2014). Kinship systems vary. Let's briefly review some forms of cross-cultural diversity. These examples clearly undermine the naturalness, divinity, and ubiquity of SNAF. They also help demonstrate the interactionist premise that the meaning of things – in this case, family – is not inherent.

- Most North Americans trace their heritage bilaterally, through both sides of their families. Not all cultures have done so. Some practice matrilineal or patrilineal decent – assigning kinship through the women or the men. Individuals born to the historical Iroquois would treat as kin those people biologically related through their mothers, grandmothers, aunts, and sisters, but not through their fathers, grandfathers, uncles, and brothers. Those born to the traditional Chinese[2] and the Nyinba of Nepal would do the opposite (Stockard 2002).
- SNAF idealizes monogamous marriage. However, polygamy has been either allowed or encouraged in more than 80% of the societies that anthropologists have studied (Pasternak, Ember, and Ember 1997:86). **Polygyny** – a marriage with multiple wives – was sometimes practiced by !Kung San hunter-gatherers and by elites in China. The Nyinba of Nepal strongly favor **fraternal polyandry** over monogamy. For them, a "family" centers on the marriage between a household's brothers and a single wife. In the unfortunate situation of infertility, or if one of the brothers becomes disgruntled, then a second wife may also marry into the group (Stockard 2002). In contrast, the Moso (living near Lugu Lake in southwest China) prefer to avoid marriage altogether. For centuries, the moral and statistical norm has been for Moso men and women to remain unbetrothed and live with their birth families. Women may invite lovers into their chambers at night, but those men must leave by morning. Any offspring are raised by the woman and her brothers (Shih 2001; Stacey 2011).

- SNAF tends to assume neolocal residence, with spouses occupying their own domicile, such as a house in the suburbs. This arrangement would be unthinkable in some cultures, where the strongly-enforced norm would be for newlyweds to live with the husband's kin (patrilocal residence) or the wife's kin (matrilocal residence). The traditional Chinese and the Nyinba practiced the former, the !Kung San and Iroquois the latter. **Delayed transfer marriage** was practiced in the Guangzhou region of southern China, around the turn of the nineteenth century (Stockard 2002:4). After marriage, young women would remain in their childhood home for three or more years, except for conjugal visits. That way, they could continue to earn money for their parents, by reeling silk.
- SNAF advocates would likely assume that an individual should choose his or her own spouse. Clearly, not all cultures operate that way. Iroquois mothers selected spouses for their children, who received the decision as a gift. The eldest Nyinba brother chooses the woman who will marry him *and* his younger brothers (Stockard 2002). In some cultural settings, individuals may veto their arranged marriages; a young !Kung San girl may successfully halt marital proceedings, if she protests vigorously enough to her parents.
- SNAF venerates first marriages, among young men and women in their twenties. Not all cultures follow suit. A Nyinba male might be a child, an infant, or (in rare cases) not-yet-born when his older brother selects their shared spouse. A !Kung San female would usually be married around age 10, to a man who was approximately twice her age. Marriage can even occur posthumously. Among the traditional Chinese, a deceased daughter could be married to another family's deceased son, in order to connect her to his lineage, and secure her place in the afterlife (Stockard 2002).
- The very terms we use to think about family are not natural, divine, or inevitable. Labels such as mother, father, aunt, and uncle can sometimes be translated to another language fairly easily, as in madre, padre, tía, and tío. But if descent is not traced bilaterally, or if monogamy is not the norm, then those relationships – and even their names – may differ significantly. A matrilineal Iroquois would consider his mother's brother to be an important uncle, from whom he could expect attention and guidance. The brother of the boy's father, however, would belong to a different lineage, and would not serve in that capacity. Or, imagine a Nyinba daughter being raised in a polyandrous household; she would refer to all of her mother's husbands as "father," even if only one of them was her genitor (Stockard 2002).

This list could be extended indefinitely, but we will stop here. These examples are sufficient to make the point that marriage and family can be conceptualized and practiced in a variety of ways. If any one of us was born in a different time or place, we might grow up believing that "of course" fraternal polyandry is the best, "of course" mothers should arrange marriages, "of course" we should reside patrilocally or matrilocally, and so on.

To observe family diversity, we do need not travel to distant lands or collect evidence from bygone eras. People may idealize SNAF in the U.S., but it does not hold a monopoly. In 2010, more than one third of children in the U.S. did not live in families with two married, biological parents (Manning and Brown 2014:49). Approximately one quarter of children born to married parents can expect (by their 12th birthday) their parents to divorce (Manning and Brown 2014:46). Cohabitation is increasingly seen as a legitimate pathway to marriage and as a substitute for a first or second marriage. More couples choose to remain childfree in the U.S. and other Western Industrialized nations (Agrillo and Nelini 2008). North Americans postpone marriage, or avoid it entirely, or stay single after divorce. Consequently, these Americans now spend, on average, more adult years being single than married (DePaulo and Morris 2005:59) – presumably while maintaining relationships with relatives they consider their "families." Geographic separation, or a preference for autonomy and independence, lead some otherwise committed couples to form LAT relationships, or Living Apart Together (Manning and Brown 2014:47). After years of struggle, same-sex marriage has finally been legalized in the U.S. Families now include adoptive families and foster families, as well as those with grandparents raising children (Erera 2002). Transnational families are common, as migrants from impoverished parts of the world seek jobs in wealthier regions that will enable them to send remittances home to kin (Dreby and Adkins 2010). And this list is by no means exhaustive.

## Three Ways of Answering the Question "What Is Family?"

When outspoken SNAF advocates observe family diversity, it only strengthens their resolve. They confidently proclaim what family really is and ought to be: the "traditional" nuclear family, practiced as God or nature intended (Carlson 2014; Dobson 1998). These advocates see variations and deviations from SNAF as weaker imitations or flawed substitutes for the real thing.

As a second approach, many social scientists try to conceptualize family in a way that accurately reflects its diverse manifestations. These scholars ask: Given the variety of kinship systems in the U.S. and globally, can we define family in an inclusive and accurate way? For example, Schwartz and Scott (2007:3) conceptualize family as "any relatively stable group of people bound by ties of blood, marriage, adoption; or by any sexually expressive relationship; or who simply live together, and who are committed to and provide each other with economic and emotional support." Cohen (2015:4) offers a more succinct option: "Families are groups of related people, bound by connections that are biological, legal, or emotional." Such broad definitions are useful and capture a much wider range of kinship practices. Still, problems of exclusion remain. For example, what about pets? Our companion animals may not be "people," but may be loved deeply, as evidenced by photographs, gifts, tombstones, and other indicators. Can't pets be integral members of families? (See the boxed excerpt on Donna; she considered her dog Athena to be the "love of her life," more important than any spouse or romantic partner she ever knew.) On the other hand, another problem is that broad definitions may error by including too much. A group of college students might live together and provide each other with economic and emotional support but deny that they consider each other family. It depends.

In light of these difficulties, symbolic interactionists offer a third approach to answering the question "What is family?" Instead of trying to settle the issue in advance, some researchers **bracket** (or set aside) the issue, to better investigate the diverse meanings that other people give to family in the course of their daily lives (Harris 2008). For these scholars, "Family is a usage, not a thing" (Miller 1991:610). Kinship terminology provides "a set of conceptual resources for accomplishing the meaning of social relations" (Holstein and Gubrium 1999:5). In what follows, we'll explore this point of view. By the end of the chapter, you should be able to analyze virtually any social interaction in which "family" arises as an element of concern.

---

"Athena… was the love of my life." Athena, a German shepherd/Labrador retriever mix, was Donna's companion for 10 years. I asked if she had a picture of Athena on the phone she held. She did not, but it mattered very little, because with obvious admiration and attention to detail, she described Athena's thick black-and-sable coat and her amber eyes, rimmed in black, with the brow spots over them…. Donna became Athena's guardian through a woman named Sita, long a common denominator between homeless people and homeless animals in San Francisco.

About a decade ago, Donna lived with her abusive boyfriend in a garbage-strewn encampment under a freeway. Worn out from addiction and hard living, they began camping in Donna's mother's backyard. Sita and Donna knew each other from the streets, and, as Donna explained, "Sita said, 'You need a dog in your life.'" Sita had rescued three-year-old Athena from death row in a shelter. Although it might not seem that a homeless drug addict in an abusive relationship would make the best guardian for a dog, the match saved two lives. As Donna recalled, "Athena did everything for me. She got me out of an abusive relationship. And it was either the dog or him, and I chose the dog. He used to take my money. My shoes. Everything. The guy used to beat me up, and Sita told me it was either the man or the dog, so I chose Athena. I got the dog. Got rid of the man."

With the boyfriend out of the picture, Donna moved into her mother's house, to a space she described as "the upstairs." But Sita had also said, "You have to be clean to have the dog." Her mother agreed, so Donna faced a decision. "I realized

> Athena meant everything to me," she told me. "I said to myself, 'My dog comes first in my life. Would I rather use drugs, or feed my dog?' And I fell in love with Athena, so I gave up the needle. Gave up the pipe. I gave up liquor. ...I went through withdrawal, and from there, I went to the methadone clinic. Got on methadone. Athena went with me, and everybody loved her, too. Athena was everything, OK? Athena was everything. Everywhere I went, Athena followed." (Irvine 2013:10)

## Family Discourse as Meaning-Making

Anthropological and sociological research present one kind of challenge to the ideology of SNAF by offering evidence that kinship systems may not be natural, divine, or eternal. A closer examination of family discourse presents another kind of challenge: *there are many ways to describe any familial situation.* The existence of kinship bonds – and whether they are close, distant, happy, dysfunctional, stagnant, growing, and so on – are not necessarily simple facts. Rather, kinship bonds are matters of interpretation and claims-making guided by our perspectives, agendas, and interactional constraints. Interactionist researchers have shown that kinship can be routinely talked into and out of being – or portrayed one way and then another – in all sorts of public and private settings (Holstein and Gubrium 1995; Harris 2008).

Consider a poignant example from Gubrium and Holstein's (1990) observations of a support group for mentally-ill patients and their families. In one interaction, a father questions his 22-year-old son's love and motives, portraying him as virtually a stranger.

> You're always willing to drop in any time they toss you out of the [transitional living] home, but you never show us any appreciation at all. You don't keep in touch. You won't even talk on the phone. Or when you do, you're just plain disagreeable. We never know how you're doing or what you're up to. You don't care about your mother's feelings; you don't feel for her at all. Do you realize what she goes through, worrying about you? You know you don't give us a damn thing. You could be a stranger. No consideration. No warmth. Nothing. You only act like a son when you need us. Where's your family loyalty, anyway? (Gubrium and Holstein 1990:58)

The father invokes a few apparent facts – his son is quiet, ungrateful, surly – and claims that these all indicate disregard. The father portrays the young man as having no warmth or loyalty for his parents, as if he is not a member of their family at all. This father constructs a potentially embarrassing and painful portrayal of his son, especially when stated publicly in the context of a support group.

In response, the son disagrees. He crafts an alternative explanation for his behavior, one that casts their familial bonds in a much different light.

> Come on. You know that I care. It's just hard for me. I come by, but I don't want to start you worrying, so I don't say too much. I don't want to complain because I don't want you to think I'm not doing okay. I thought I was doing something good for you by trying to stay out of your hair. We had all that talk about independence... I get pretty screwed up sometimes, so I try to stay away when I might have a bad day. I know what it does to Mom and I don't want to do that to her. I don't want to hurt her. It may not look like it, but I keep away because I thought that was best for you guys. I got my problems and I know that they get to you, but you're all the family I have. (Gubrium and Holstein 1990:59)

In the son's account, he is a loving family member. He endorses his father's claims that he is frequently quiet and out of contact. But he argues that he desires to protect his parents from the effects of his illness. The son reframes absence and silence as signs of family loyalty, love, and a desire to demonstrate independence. Examples such as this one lead Gubrium and Holstein (2012:355) to argue that family can be "constructed and reconstructed as needed... What family essentially is in one turn at talk [may not be] what family essentially is in another."

From a naive or commonsense point of view, family descriptions merely report objective facts or simple truths: "That man is my father. I have three siblings. We are close and communicate frequently." From an interactionist perspective, family descriptions are **reflexive** – *they help create that which they describe.* Any person, relationship, or situation can be understood and characterized in numerous ways. Our descriptions give meanings to ambiguous or indeterminate things.

Recall our earlier anthropological example: a "father" to a Nyinba might seem like an "uncle" to you. Or, perhaps you know someone who calls his or her father by a first name, to convey distance or disapproval. To these we could add hundreds of other descriptions. In addition to "Father" or "George," the same man might be described as an American, a Republican, a human being, a mammal, elderly, Christian, an infidel, my best friend, loving, selfish, self-sufficient, supportive, an idiot, lucky, talented, and so on. We can depict any person, relationship, or situation in a variety of ways, depending on the perspectives we use, the examples we highlight or ignore, and the goals we want to accomplish. We have a great deal of discretion (but not total freedom) to portray families as we see fit.

A notably public example of this discretion is evident in the television advertisements of the Italian restaurant chain Olive Garden. For several years now, their commercials have ended with the tag lines "When you're here, you're family" and "We're all family here." The advertisements (easy to find on YouTube.com) typically show groups of people sharing a meal, smiling, and talking energetically, while being served by friendly waiters. The slogan is a reflexive description. This point is easy to demonstrate – just imagine the different meanings that changing the tag lines would create if they stated, "When you're here, you're a paying customer," "...you're an animal ingesting nutrients," "...you'll probably eat more calories than you would at home," or "...you're supporting a large corporation rather than a locally-owned restaurant." The options are potentially infinite. Each would reflexively give meaning to the situation, rather than simply reporting what is "really" going on.

In Olive Garden's commercials, the use of "family" is **rhetorical** – meant to persuade an audience to think and act in particular ways. Most likely, the goal is to encourage viewers to think of the restaurant as a welcoming, sociable, and fun place to purchase a meal (hopefully, bringing several people with them). In similar fashion, we can see virtually all family descriptions all as rhetorical as well. For example, think of Gubrium and Holstein's discussion of the schizophrenic son, quoted above. In that interaction, the father likely attempted to provoke a behavior-change by getting his son to view his own conduct as cold and unloving. And, we should remember that the opinions and sympathies of the support group members were also in play.

*Family descriptions are...*

- *Reflexive – because they create that which they describe. Our descriptions give meaning to things (people, relationships, situations) that are ambiguous or indeterminate.*
- *Rhetorical – because they are usually intended to persuade other people to think and act in particular ways.*
- *Somewhat flexible and variable – because they are matters of choice. People usually have many options to select from, when deciding how to portray a familial relationship, behavior, or situation.*

If we adopt Gubrium and Holstein's (2012) perspective, we have no need to draw a firm line between language that is meant to be taken literally as opposed to figuratively or metaphorically. Literal[3] and figurative descriptions are both reflexive and rhetorical. Both guide conduct and give meaning to indeterminate states of affairs. For instance, members of fraternities and sororities may (figuratively) call each other "brother" and "sister" – rather than "friend" or "fellow member" – all to create a stronger sense of community and loyalty. A high school or college may encourage similar sentiments when sending newsletters to their "extended family" of past graduates. Such figurative statements may ascribe family bonds casually or with profound sincerity. Either way, they give meaning and guide conduct just as more literal descriptions do.

The same logic applies to the concept of "fictive kin" – those familial relationships that are merely ascribed, rather than rooted in blood or marriage. For decades, anthropologists and sociologists have studied how low-income communities relied on fictive kin as a survival strategy (Nelson 2014; Sarkisian and Gerstel 2012). Faced with tough environmental conditions – such as poverty, scarce job opportunities, discrimination, and meager government assistance – the poor often need more help than wealthier SNAF households. As a result, they turn to non-related friends and acquaintances, who provide essential support. These individuals may act and be described as kin.

Carol Stack (1974) famously studied how members an impoverished Midwestern community, "The Flats," used fictive kin as an essential survival strategy. After paying rent, utilities, and food, most adults were penniless. To cope with these dire circumstances, residents of The Flats created alliances and exchanged goods and favors. They traded "food stamps, rent money, a TV, hats, dice, a car, a nickel here, a cigarette there, food, milk, grits, and children" (Stack 1974:32). Successful, reciprocal trading would reinforce kin bonds, and even create fictive kin bonds between otherwise unrelated people. Poor trading could destroy both types of relationships. In this way, ones "real" kin (those related by blood or marriage) may be supplemented or replaced by others in the community, who may come to be called cousins, sisters, brothers, daddies (Stack 1974:30). Consider one of the respondents Stack interviewed and observed:

> Billy, a young black woman in The Flats, was raised by her mother and her mother's "old man." She has three children of her own by different fathers. Billy says, "Most people kin to me are in this neighborhood, right here in The Flats, but I got people in the South, in Chicago, and in Ohio too. I couldn't tell most of their names and most of them aren't really kinfolk to me. Starting down the street from here, take my father, he ain't my daddy, he's no father to me. I ain't got but one daddy and that's Jason. The one who raised me. My kids' daddies, that's something else, all their daddies' people really take to them – they always doing things and making a fuss about them. We help each other out and that's what kinfolks are all about. (Stack 1974:45)

In their interviews with low-income women in Baltimore, Haney and March (2003) also found that caretaking assumed more importance than formal bonds in assigning kinship.[4] The women applied the label of "father," for example, to grandfathers, uncles, cousins, and brothers – to male relatives who lived with or nearby women and their children, and who participated in caretaking. Allen, Blieszner, and Roberto (2011:1165–1167) would call this **kin promotion**, because the women elevate a more distant relative to the status of a closer relative. They may describe an uncle as a "father," a niece as "a daughter to me," a cousin as "a brother to me," or a sibling as "more like a twin." **Non-kin**

**conversion,** on the other hand, occurs when people turn friends and other non-relatives into kin. Two friends may be described as "going for sisters," as they increasingly support and depend on each other (Stack 1974:58). **Kin loss** and **kin demotion** are also possibilities, as potential relatives are either renounced ("No son of mine") or are downgraded to a lesser familial status (an "Uncle Dad" who takes his children on fun outings but leaves all other child-care duties to his wife or ex-wife[5]).

Adapting to poverty may be an important but not the only factor in assigning kin status (Gubrium and Buckholdt 1982). As our earlier examples have already alluded, we may have many reasons for ascribing or removing family status: to criticize disregard and disloyalty ("You could be a stranger, not a son"), to promote a sense of community ("brothers" and "sisters" in fraternities/sororities or among racial/ethnic minorities), to encourage donations ("As a member of our extended family, we hope you will support your Alma mater"), to entice customers to a restaurant ("When you're here, you're family"), and so on. Whether deemed literal or figural, real or fictive, we can creatively invoke family terminology to signify intimacy or distance, shape conduct, and accomplish a wide range of objectives.

## The Social Shaping of Family Descriptions

So far, we have argued that family is not the eternal, stable entity that SNAF advocates portray it to be. Anthropologists and sociologists have shown that kinship varies cross-culturally and over time. Symbolic interactionists, in turn, emphasize how people can create and recreate family on a daily basis. People can gain, promote, demote, and lose family ties, depending on how they depict, and act towards potential kin. Individuals are not necessarily locked into a single way of understanding any given familial situation or relationship.

Variability and flexibility form only half the story, however. Human beings possess restricted agency. Their social contexts limit, or at least guide and pattern their choices. Consider a metaphor: Jazz musicians improvise spontaneously, but remain sensitive to musical conventions (recurring keys, melodies, beats, riffs) and to subtle feedback from bandmates and audiences. A guitarist who played completely random notes – defying all conventions and expectations – would sound discordant and risk sanctions.

*Family descriptions are...*

- *Somewhat constrained and patterned – because social contexts limit or guide how people depict familial situations. Local agendas and subcultures tend to promote some kinds of descriptions over others. Certain audiences may reject or challenge interpretations that seem odd or unacceptably inaccurate.*

Family discourse operates similarly. Individuals have much discretion in how they interpret familial situations, but it's not as if "anything goes." Our claims are guided by cultural norms at societal and local levels, by actors' and audiences' expectations and agendas, and a wide range of other constraining factors. For example, Olive Garden can label customers as "family," but acting on the label has limited utility. Waiters probably cannot ask patrons (as "family members") for help moving furniture into a new apartment, for one thing. Or, customers can't legitimately complain about having to pay for a "family meal." Our audiences will resist those familial interpretations that sound discordant or out of bounds.

When we decide who counts as family, or what is happening with a family, we do so within **contexts of consideration** (Gubrium and Holstein 1990:117). These contexts set parameters and guide our improvisational discourse in patterned ways.

Clearly, the larger culture is one context that provides basic guidelines. As we've mentioned, Nyinba children learn to refer to their genitor and his brothers as "father," whereas parents usually teach American children to differentiate uncles and fathers (Stockard 2002). And, the rights and responsibilities associated with those labels vary. A Nyinba "father" lives with and financially supports all the children in his household, whereas in the U.S. an American "uncle" would seldom be expected to do so for his nieces and nephews.

Within the larger society, however, additional sub-cultural variations and agendas may exist that encourage some kinds of familial interpretations over others. For example, family therapy clinics adopt different points of view on relationship functioning and treatment. In Gubrium's (1992) study, one agency, Westside House, emphasized the importance of hierarchy and domestic order. Staff learned to believe that parents – especially fathers – needed to establish guidelines and to obtain respect and compliance from children. In therapy sessions, staff deemed it functional if a father sat in a prominent chair and exercised authority via his posture, gaze, total speaking time, and interruptions. The culture at another clinic, Fairview, differed dramatically, and relatively consistently. The staff at Fairview believed families worked best when all members felt free to voice their thoughts and feelings – a more democratic orientation. Thus, the same signs of authority would, in this setting, be interpreted as dysfunctional. "What is going on with this family" would be depicted in variant, yet patterned, ways.

Let's consider a few more examples that demonstrate how familial interpretations are limited and patterned by contexts of consideration:

- An adolescent may list her mother, father, and 12-year-old sister as family members, when submitting student loan applications. However, during an informal conversation with two pet-loving friends, she may describe her cat as "An absolutely essential part of our family!" The former context requires a narrow definition of kinship that is connected to familial finances, while the latter context encourages speakers to define family broadly and include companion animals.

- Conservative politicians – guided by pro-SNAF ideology and legislative agendas, as well as the wishes of their lobbyists and voters – often emphasize family form. Their speeches focus on the importance of legal marriage and parental co-residence. In contrast, low income mothers may be guided by different subcultural beliefs and by the pressing demands of poverty. They may prioritize function over form and view their partners' practical support to be much more essential than legal marriage and co-residence (Haney and March 2003).

- Consider the case of Tyrone Biggs (Holstein and Gubrium 1994:245). A judge presiding over an involuntary commitment hearing needed to decide whether to release or institutionalize Mr. Biggs, who was mentally ill. Given his training and concern with maintaining law and order, the judge wanted to know whether Mr. Biggs had a family who could keep him out of trouble. In contrast, Mr. Bigg's psychiatrist focused on treatment and recovery – on placing patients in loving, less institutionalized environments that might promote healing. The psychiatrist's training and occupational concerns led him to argue that Mr. Biggs should be released to the care of his "family" – his girlfriend, her two children, and her sister. The judge balked, because he did not see "any family there" that would prevent disorderly conduct. Their divergent orientations and agendas led to variant interpretations that were, arguably, somewhat patterned or predictable.

## Who Knows Best about Families?

As we've seen, people debate "Who is family?" and "What is going on with families?" Interpretations sometimes collide. As a result, individuals may weigh the facts of the matter, as well as the standpoints of those making knowledge claims. Put succinctly, they can ask "Says who?"

One strategy for supporting a point of view is to **claim privileged access**. Mr. Biggs (discussed above) could argue that his girlfriend, her children, and her family are a loving, stable, and protective family – and that he knows this because it is *his* family. He has lived with them, and has had many personal experiences that outsiders haven't witnessed or would not understand. Individuals who claim privileged access make statements such as "You just can't imagine what it's like," "You haven't seen what I've seen," and "I don't think anybody else is in a position to tell me I'm wrong" (Gubrium and Holstein 1990, ch. 6; see also Gubrium and Holstein 2009). Imagine if someone told Donna – whom we discussed earlier – that a dog cannot possibly be the most important love of someone's entire life. Donna could protest, "You weren't there! You can't know how much Athena did for me and meant to me!"

Nevertheless, individuals need not be so confident. Sometimes we struggle to comprehend or interpret our own lives. Recall Gubrium and Holstein's (1990:58) example of the father of the schizophrenic son. It's easy to imagine a different context, such as a private conversation with a friend or therapist, where that father might admit that he isn't sure how to interpret his familial situation: "Is my son selfish and cold, like a stranger? Or, is he loving, and just struggling with his mental illness? I'm honestly not sure what to think or do!" In this manner, individuals can **disclaim privileged access**, by disavowing their ability to understand their own familial relationships and experiences. Indeed, confusion about "what is going on" and "what to do" are common reasons for seeking emotional support from others, as occurs when an individual struggles with a disturbed child, a rocky marriage, tensions with in-laws, and other family troubles.

Whether we seek their counsel or not, outsiders may assert that they know best about our families. People claim **objectivity** when they state or imply that their outsider status gives them advantages – such as personal distance or lack of emotional involvement – that provide a better vantage point. Picture an elderly man who cares for his ailing wife, afflicted with dementia. He may think that he is handling the situation well, but a neighbor, friend, or nonresident relative may disagree. Gubrium and Holstein (1990) documented this kind of discord, when they observed Cynthia interacting with her father, in an Alzheimer's support group:

> I don't want to make a big thing out of this, but it's known to happen that what's happening all around you, you just don't realize that it's affecting your life. I'm a bit worried… I go over and find all this stuff all over the place, like a tornado's hit [your house]. Dirty, moldy dishes in the sink. Newspapers all over. You name it. …Dad, I know you say that you're hanging on and doing it, but from what I see all around whenever I'm over, I think something's giving. (Gubrium and Holstein 1990:82)

Cynthia argues that her father is somewhat incapable of understanding the changes occurring right under his nose. Similar arguments can be made to those who can't see the proverbial forest for the trees or who don't realize they are basking in a pot of slowly boiling water – such as a spouse in an abusive marriage, or a parent whose savings are being depleted by an adult child who refuses to work. Of course, those so informed can counter such arguments. In the example of Cynthia, her father insisted that he was not overwhelmed, and that dirty dishes were insignificant compared to the love and attention he gave his wife (Gubrium and Holstein 1990:82).

> *Family descriptions are...*
>
> • *Grounded in explicit or implicit claims about "Who knows best?" about families. There are at least six ways to bolster or undermine the standpoint from which a familial interpretation is made: A person may claim or disclaim privileged access, invoke objectivity or expertise, embrace antiprofessionalism, or assert denial.*

In some circumstances, people may bolster their opinions by claiming **expertise**. An individual can state or imply that others should believe their familial interpretations because they result from formal credentials, academic degrees, or rigorous training. A social worker, for example, could render a judgment on Mike and Cynthia's situation, and offer it "as someone who has an MSW and a CSW-G" (i.e. a master's degree with a certification in clinical gerontology). Expertise may provide a compelling basis for one's viewpoint. Or not. Some individuals may defer to expert opinions, whereas others may not be convinced. Family members can choose to embrace **antiprofessionalism**, by invoking privileged access ("I've been there, you haven't"), or by asserting that the expert's "textbook knowledge" doesn't fit their unique situation. Two or more expert opinions can also be played against each other, as their perspectives and findings may vary (Gubrium and Holstein 1990; Knapp 1999, 2002).

**Denial** is a sixth type of claim that can be made about the source a familial interpretation. For example, a social worker may contend that Mike knows he can no longer car for his ailing wife, but just doesn't want to admit it to himself and to others. In another case, recall the situation of Tyrone Biggs, who wanted to avoid involuntary commitment. The judge or the psychiatrist might have chosen to invoke denial, by asserting that Mr. Biggs did not want to recognize or concede what he knew to be true – that his family could not care for him adequately, and that institutionalization was necessary.

## Conclusion

Certainly, family is a crucial part of people's lives. We can link our most precious moments, and our biggest heartbreaks, to familial relationships. Relatives can provide us with unconditional love and support or crush our spirits and inflict irrevocable harm.

Symbolic interactionists do not deny the importance of family; however, they invite us to think critically about its meaning and functioning. "What is family?" and "What is going on with families?" are matters of interpretation and debate not only among social scientists, politicians, pundits, and professionals, but among laypersons themselves. Interactionists make clear that we cannot simply assume a confident definition or viewpoint when considering these issues. Rather, we should investigate people's wide-ranging discretion in crafting versions of family affairs, as well as the social constraints that limit and pattern those versions.

SNAF advocates tend to offer a myopic view of family, by proclaiming the nuclear family to the most genuine, longest-lasting, and even divine form of kinship. Anthropologists and sociologists highlight cross-cultural and historical evidence that contradicts that ethnocentric assumption, revealing the diversity of ways kinship has been practiced. Interactionists, in turn, demonstrate a further layer of diversity: any single familial situation can be understood and described in many different ways. People talk family into being, and revise, or even renounce it, as they interpret their relationships within specific contexts.

## Learning by Using the Symbolic Interactionist Perspective

Below is an excerpt from *What Is Family?* by Gubrium and Holstein (1990). Can you use any of this chapter's concepts – especially those pertaining to family discourse – to analyze the situation involving Rodney Keats, Esther Franks, and Officer Jones?

| The Case of Rodney Keats |
| --- |
| **Gubrium and Holstein (1990:118–119)** |
| The South City police department's community service officer had just responded to a civilian complaint that a young black man, Rodney Keats, was disrupting a residential neighborhood, ranting incoherently, and brandishing a broomstick at concerned onlookers and passers-by. Officer Jones approached the youth cautiously, talked him into sitting down under a shade tree to discuss the problem, and convinced him to surrender the broomstick. As Jones tried to decipher the circumstances that led to the bizarre, but unsettling incident, she searched for a practical solution to the question at hand: what was she going to do with Rodney? |
|     Keats appeared to be psychologically impaired – disoriented, agitated, and delusional. Local statutes made it possible to transport a dangerous mentally ill person to the county hospital – involuntarily if necessary – for the purpose of observation and treatment. Hospitalization, however, was contingent upon the availability of a bed on the emergency psychiatric ward. Jones knew that only six such beds existed and that, in all likelihood, Rodney would be turned away. The city jail was not equipped to handle persons with psychiatric |

problems and would almost certainly refuse him as well. Under the circumstances, the best Jones might have done was to negotiate some sort of community custody for Rodney, securing the help of a responsible resident to look after him and make sure that he sought immediate treatment at a community mental health center.

To that end, Officer Jones asked Rodney where he lived. He said he lived down the street and directed Jones to a small duplex in a row of modest, slightly deteriorating houses. Jones asked Rodney who he lived with and Rodney responded, "My momma." A middle-aged woman answered the door and, after inquiring into the circumstances of Rodney's "arrest," asked what she could do to "keep Rodney out of trouble." The following exchange took place:

> JONES: Are you the boy's mother?
>
> WOMAN: As much as he's got.
>
> JONES: Well, where is his mother? Where does she live? Does the boy have a family?
>
> WOMAN: She lives across town, but she don't have nothing to do with him.
>
> JONES: Well, who are you?
>
> WOMAN: Esther Franks. I'm his momma.
>
> JONES: Just a minute. Who's the mother? What are you saying?
>
> WOMAN: I'm Rodney's momma. I raised him since he was a baby. He's mine to look after, so I got to claim him.

As Officer Jones considered Rodney's family ties, she sought more clarification of family status. Most importantly, she looked for signs of who was "really" responsible for Rodney's care and supervision. For the moment, it was of little concern to her that the woman had only tenuous kinship ties to Rodney. (She was the former common-law wife of Rodney's deceased uncle.) Jones's immediate purpose was to find Rodney's "family," which, in this situation, meant someone who would care for him in a familial manner.

…After a lengthy discussion regarding Rodney's problems and detailed instructions on how to enroll him in a community mental health program, Jones left Rodney with Esther Franks and returned to the police station. She called the mental health center and made arrangements for Rodney to be seen the next day, telling a therapist that Rodney's "mother" would accompany him on the intake visit. Jones then filed a police report on the incident, indicating that after restoring order to the situation, she left Rodney at home with his "family" and arranged for his "mother" to call her, Jones, if any further trouble arose.

# Notes

1 https://www.gop.com/the-2016-republican-party-platform/. Downloaded 16 August 2018.
2 By this term, Stockard (2002:112n2) means Chinese living in "late imperial times, primarily the nineteenth and early twentieth centuries, prior to the establishment of the People's Republic of China in 1949."
3 The term "literal" implies that words have simple meanings that can be straightforwardly applied, but this is often not the case. For example, does "mother" literally mean the person who gives birth or can it refer to the adoptive parent who raises a child? If a woman marries into a widower's household and helps care for his six-year-old, can she literally become the child's mother? If a paid surrogate is implanted with a fertilized embryo, is she the mother or the person who hired her? In those rare cases where an embryo is created via DNA from two women, are both literally mothers? If a woman behaves horrendously, can her grown offspring legitimately proclaim, "You are no longer my mother!" and cease all contact?
4 To be sure, there are low-income and minority families that do fit the SNAF model. There is family diversity within and across economic class as well as by race ethnicity. Our point is merely to highlight that SNAF terminology can be put to a variety of uses, as people give meaning to their relationships and navigate their circumstances.
5 http://www.huffingtonpost.com/alison-patton/uncle-dad-syndrome_b_2986705.html. Downloaded 17 October 2016.

# References

Agrillo, C. and C. Nelini. 2008. In "Childfree by Choice: A Review." *Journal of Cultural Geography* 25:347–363.
Allen, K. R., R. Blieszner, and K. A. Roberto. 2011. "Perspectives on Extended Family and Fictive Kin in the Later Years: Strategies and Meanings of Kin Reinterpretation." *Journal of Family Issues* 32(9):1156–1177.
Baca Zinn, M., D. S. Eitzen, and B. Wells. 2015. *Diversity in Families*, 10th ed. Boston, MA: Pearson.
Carlson, A. C. 2014. *The Natural Family where It Belongs: New Agrarian Essays*. New Brunswick, NJ: Transaction.
Cohen, P. N. 2015. *The Family: Diversity, Inequality, and Social Change*. New York: Norton.
DePaulo, B. M. and Morris, W. L. 2005. "Singles in Society and in Science." *Psychological Inquiry* 16:57–83.

Dobson, J. C. 1998. *Love for a Lifetime: Building a Marriage that Will Go the Distance*. Sisters, OR: Multnomah Publishers.

Dobson, J. C. 2006. "Media Provides Cover for Assault on Traditional Marriage." Posted October 20 2006 on CNN.com. http://www.cnn.com//2006/US/06/28/dobson.gaymarriage/index.html?section=cnn_topstories.

Dreby, J. and T. Adkins. 2010. "Inequalities in Transnational Families." *Sociology Compass* 4:673–689.

Erera, P. I. 2002. *Family Diversity: Continuity and Change in the Contemporary Family*. Thousand Oaks, CA: Sage.

Gubrium, J. F. 1992. *Out of Control: Family Therapy and Domestic Disorder*. Newbury Park, CA: Sage.

Gubrium, J. F. and D. R. Buckholdt. 1982. *Describing Care: Image and Practice in Rehabilitation*. Cambridge, MA: Oelgeschlager, Gunn & Hain.

Gubrium, J. F. and J. A. Holstein. 1990. *What Is Family?* Mountain View, CA: Mayfield.

Gubrium, J. F. and J. A. Holstein. 2009. "The Everyday Work and Auspices of Authenticity." Pp. 121–138 in *Authenticity in Culture, Self, and Society*, edited by P. Vannini and P. Williams. Surrey: Ashgate.

Gubrium, J. F. and J. A. Holstein. 2012. "Theoretical Validity and Empirical Utility of a Constructionist Analytics." *Sociological Quarterly* 53:341–359.

Haney, L. and M. March. 2003. "Married Fathers and Caring Daddies: Welfare Reform and the Discursive Politics of Paternity." *Social Problems* 50:461–481.

Harris, S. R. 2008. "What Is Family Diversity? Objective and Interpretive Approaches." *Journal of Family Issues* 29(11):1407–1425.

Holstein, J. A. and J. F. Gubrium. 1994. "Constructing Family: Descriptive Practice and Domestic Order." Pp. 232–250 in *Constructing the Social*, edited by T. R. Sarbin and J. I. Kitsuse. London: Sage.

Holstein, J. A. and J. F. Gubrium. 1995. "Deprivatization and Domestic Life: Interpretive Practice in Family Context." *Journal of Marriage and Family* 57:607–622.

Holstein, J. A. and J. F. Gubrium. 1999. "What Is Family? Further Thoughts on a Social Constructionist Approach." *Marriage & Family Review* 28:3–20.

Irvine, L. 2013. "Animals as Lifechangers and Lifesavers: Pets in the Redemption Narratives of Homeless People." *Journal of Contemporary Ethnography* 42(1):3–30.

Knapp, S. J. 1999. "Analyzing Narratives of Expertise." *Sociological Quarterly* 40:587–613.

Knapp, S. J. 2002. "Authorizing Family Science: An analysis of the Objectifying Practices of Family Science Discourse." *Journal of Marriage and Family* 64:1038–1048.

March, K. 2000. "Who Do I Look Like? Gaining a Sense of Self-Authenticity Through the Physical Reflections of Others." *Symbolic Interaction* 23:359–373.

Manning, W. D. and S. L. Brown. 2014. "American Families: Demographic Trends and Social Class." Pp. 43–60 in *The Wiley Blackwell Companion to the Sociology of Families*, edited by J. Treas, J. Scott, and M. Richards. Malden, MA: Wiley.

Miller, G. 1991. "Family as Excuse and Extenuating Circumstance: Social Organization and Use of Family Rhetoric in a Work Incentive Program." *Journal of Marriage and Family* 53:609–621.

Nelson, M. K. 2014. "Whither Fictive Kin? Or, What's in a Name?" *Journal of Family Issues* 35(2):201–222.

Pasternak, B., C. R. Ember, and M. Ember. 1997. *Sex, Gender, and Kinship: A Cross-Cultural Perspective*. Upper Saddle River, NJ: Prentice-Hall.

Powell, B., C. Bohlzendahl, C. Geist, and L. C. Steelman. 2010. *Counted Out: Same-Sex Relations and Americans' Definitions of Family*. New York: Russell Sage Foundation.

Sarkisian, N. and N. Gerstel. 2012. *Nuclear Family Values, Extended Family Lives*. New York: Routledge.

Schwartz, M. A. and B. M. Scott. 2007. *Marriages and Families: Diversity and Change*, 5th ed. Upper Saddle River, NJ: Pearson Prentice Hall.

Sharp, E. A. and L. Ganong. 2011. "'I'm a Loser, I'm Not Married, Let's Just All Look at Me': Ever-Single Women's Perceptions of Their Social Environment." *Journal of Family Issues* 32(7):956–980.

Shih, C-K. 2001. "Genesis of Marriage among the Moso and Empire-Building in Late Imperial China." *Journal of Asian Studies* 60(2):381–412.

Smith, D. E. 1993. "The Standard North American Family: SNAF as an Ideological Code." *Journal of Family Issues* 14:50–65.

Stacey, J. 2011. *Unhitched: Love, Marriage, and Family Values from West Hollywood to Western China*. New York: NYU Press.

Stack, C. 1974. *All Our Kin*. New York: Harper & Row.

Stockard, J. 2002. *Marriage in Culture: Practice and Meaning Across Diverse Societies*. New York: Harcourt.

Stone, L. 2014. *Kinship and Gender: An Introduction*, 5th ed. Boulder, CO: Westview.

Zartler, U. 2014. "How to Deal with Moral Tales: Constructions and Strategies of Single-Parent Families." *Journal of Marriage and Family* 76:604–619.

# 8

## "Always On/Always On Us"

Technology, Interaction, and the Self

> "If I'm upset, right as I feel upset, I text a couple of my friends …just because I know that they'll be there and they can comfort me. If something exciting happens, I know that they'll be there to be excited with me, and stuff like that." (Turkle 2011:175)

> "It was the other night, and I was trying to study and I just kept looking at my phone. God knows how long I've been doing it for, but I just felt the urge to be with it, sometimes I feel like it is just me and it in a bubble. And I don't know what I was waiting for, but I just kept thinking 'someone might call' or 'someone might text.'" (Rippin 2005)

> "45-year-old Chris Dancy is known as the most connected man in the world. He has between 300 and 700 systems running at any given time, systems that capture real-time data about his life. 'I've lost 100 pounds and learned to meditate,' he says. 'I'm much more aware of how I respond to life and take steps to adjust to my environment. I've also formed better habits thanks to the feedback I'm getting.'" (Murphy 2014)

> "I like to put my music on random… I don't like a set playlist in order. There's something about the spontaneity of a random song coming on that I really enjoy…. I don't like it all planned and I like to be surprised as to what song will come on next. Sometimes it gets weird with the song selection, almost like the damn thing was reading your mood and playing a succession of songs that perpetuate a mood. It makes me wonder if the random function on the machine is just an unbiased algorithm or if my iPod is somehow cosmically connected to me." (Bull 2006:139)

Do you have your phone nearby? Crazy question. Who doesn't? Although people have long listed public speaking and death among their greatest fears, a new concern has joined the ranks: *nomophobia*, or the fear of being without a phone

*The Social Self and Everyday Life: Understanding the World Through Symbolic Interactionism*, First Edition. Kathy Charmaz, Scott R. Harris, and Leslie Irvine.
© 2019 John Wiley & Sons, Inc. Published 2019 by John Wiley & Sons, Inc.

(no-*mo*bile-phobia). Its symptoms include anxiety and restlessness. The habit of constantly checking for messages or calls is known as *ringxiety* (combining "ringer" and "anxiety"). Ringxiety and nomophobia are related to *FOMO*: Fear of Missing Out. *Phantom Vibration Syndrome* and *Phantom Ringing Syndrome* refer to the sensation that one's phone is ringing or vibrating (Bragazzi and Del Puente 2014).

These fears and syndromes indicate how what was considered a luxury not long ago has become a necessity (McGuigan 2005). As we have incorporated communication technologies into our lives, both intentionally and unintentionally, they have had profound influence on our behavior and interaction (Rippin 2005). Of course, this applies to *all* technologies; they "configure" their users, changing how people think and act (Woolgar 1990). Consider, for example, how the discovery of fire changed civilization. As a cooking fuel, fire improved the human diet by making a wider variety of foods edible. As a heat source, it enhanced survival in a wider range of climates. As light source, it enabled activity in the dark. Similarly, technologies such as the wheel, the steam engine, paper, electricity, and the microwave, just to name a few, have changed human existence in countless ways. Technology "doesn't just do things *for* us. It does things *to* us, changing not just what we do but who we are" (Turkle 2013; emphasis added).

Communication technologies have profoundly changed how we live. Although telephones have been in people's homes since the turn of the twentieth century, the transition from landlines to mobile phones (or cell phones) changed communication dramatically. Mobile communication technology made it possible to call a *person*, rather than a *place* such as a home or office. Mobile phones mean we are no longer bound to a location, waiting for a call on a landline. Instead, we are "tethered" to our "'always on/always on us' communications devices and the people and things we reach through them" (Turkle 2008:121).

One scholar writes, "My 18-year-old daughter and my 21-year-old son find social life virtually inconceivable without a mobile phone. Maintaining a friendship network and arranging meetings would be just too much hassle without the mobile. Yet, when I was 18 or 21, I had friends too and, somehow, I managed to meet up with them" (McGuigan 2005:46). Look back at the quotes that opened this chapter. The person who was trying to study reports, "I just kept looking at my phone... I just kept thinking 'someone might call' or 'someone might text.'" In another quote, the speaker claims that text messaging made romantic relationships possible.

In short, communication technologies "get inside our heads, position our bodies, and dictate our everyday lives" (Agger 2004:1). Although "dictate" might seem like overly strong language, think for a moment about just one example: how the cell phone has shaped people's physical actions. For some people, "the mobile phone has become a prosthetic, an extension to the body"

(McGuigan 2005:52). One study examines the "stances, gestures and bodily movements" related to cell phone use (Plant 2001:51). It distinguishes users by body language, such as:

- The "Speakeasy": These users throw their heads back while talking, projecting an air of self-assurance and refusing to be distracted by the outside world.
- The "Spacemaker": These users bow their heads and "cocoon" in, or incline their bodies toward the phone.

People's eyes respond in characteristic ways during calls. Some users adopt "the scan," in which the eyes dart around, as if searching for the face of the person on the call. Others adopt "the gaze," focusing on a single point, often in the distance (Plant 2001:53). Users who wear headsets or headphones while making calls have their hands free, but appear to be talking to themselves. Moreover, phones and other handheld devices have given the human thumb new dexterity. Research documents that, among younger people in nine cities worldwide, musculature in the thumbs has surpassed that in the other fingers (Tenner 2004). In Japan, teenagers are called *oyayubi sedai*, or the "thumb generation."

The transition from mobile phones to smartphones meant that phones were no longer solely devices for communicating with other people. A smartphone is a handheld personal computer. It can function as a wallet and a bank, a television and a movie theater, a still and video camera, a shopping mall, a library, and a memo pad. It provides maps and directions, games, and can play enough music to last a lifetime. It also streams popular culture into every aspect of our existence. It entices us with continual advertisements for products, services, and experiences. It bombards us with information about the lives of celebrities and public figures. It shows us news as it happens, around the clock. In short, our phones constantly engage us with others, whether real or virtual.

In this way, the smartphone is a technology of "social saturation" (Gergen 1991). This term refers to technologies that increase our contact with the social world dramatically. As a sponge absorbs water until it reaches saturation, we absorb new information and relationships. Before the era of smartphones, technologies such as the landline and the television also played this role by introducing new possibilities for communicating and relating into people's everyday lives. However, by providing access to the Internet, and by being "always on/always on us" (Turkle 2008), the smartphone has a far greater capacity to "saturate" us with the social world.

Our phones bring us an infinite amount of information and countless new ideas. Up-to-the minute information and new ideas encourage, or even force us, to consider new ways of thinking, new opinions, attitudes, and causes in the moment. Your music streaming service suggests the latest music. A friend on Facebook invites you to sign a petition. You now need to think about anti-bullying legislation, a new disability rights law, clean energy initiatives, or protection for victims of domestic violence. You sign a petition and immediately receive invitations to sign others. An algorithm has linked your response to the petition to countless other causes. You make a purchase online and immediately see that "you might also like" other items you did not know you needed.

Communication technologies increase the number and variety of relationships we engage in. Friends on Facebook might be followers on Instagram or Twitter. These relationships come with new obligations and opportunities. Someone tagged you in a post. A text needs a response right away. What happens if we don't comment or "like" that photo our friend-of-a friend just posted? Will he or she "unfriend" us? A new tweet appears on Twitter; should you retweet? In short, people feel connected, but also pulled in many different directions.

In this chapter, we'll examine how technology participates in the construction and re-construction of the self. Of course, the examples we could use are endless. We'll limit the discussion to three. We'll first consider how the use of social networking sites calls for revising some aspects of the interactionist model of the self. Then, we'll investigate what it means that technology has brought recorded music into everyday life. We'll conclude by examining the practice of self-tracking – the apps and wearable devices, such as Fitbit, that allow people to quantify the self.

## The Cyberbased Generalized Other and the Mediated Looking Glass

Since your phone is (of course) nearby, take a quick selfie. Don't worry about what it looks like, and you don't need to retake it. Your first image will work for our purposes.

Whom do you see in the picture? "Me, of course," you'll probably say. And who took the picture? "I did," you respond. *You* took a picture of *yourself.* That act defines a "selfie," after all. It is an image that says, "here I am. This is me" (Agger 2015). But where is the "self" in the selfie? Is the self in the *image*, or is it in the person *looking* at the image? Is it both?

In Chapter 2, you learned to think about the self as having two phases: the "I" and the "me." Selfies illustrate these phases well (Catalano 2014; Senft and Baym 2015). In response to the question of who took the picture, you said, "I did." The "I," or the active phase of the self, took the picture. The self-image represents the "me," or the phase of the self toward whom the "I" acted. The "I" took the picture. When you look at the picture, you see the "me." You became an object to yourself (Mead [1934] 1962).

Now, think about what you do with most selfies. You don't keep them to yourself. Selfies "need to be constantly disseminated, navigating the globe, posted all over for others to endorse with a two-thumbs-up. A selfie taken but stored isn't the real thing; it needs to be distributed through social media" (Stavans 2017). Therefore, you post your selfies – and other photos you take – to Snapchat, Instagram, Twitter, or Facebook. You want your friends and followers to see what you're doing, where you are, whom you're with, and how much fun you're having, so you "share." As the saying goes, "if it's not on Instagram, it didn't happen." You add a caption and some hashtags and you tag the friends in the picture with you. You wait – not too long, you hope – for comments and likes. Posting to a social networking site provides "instant feedback on our appearance, activities and opinions" (Belk 2014:1107).

Look at your selfie again. What do you think about it? Do you like the way you look in it? For most of us, the answer is either "meh" or a resounding "no!" We judge the image by standards about how we think we "should" appear. We look at it through our perceptions of how other people perceive us. In doing so, we adopt the attitude of what Mead called the generalized other. We also have feelings about how others would perceive us if they saw this selfie. As you saw in Chapter 2, this imagined reflection and emotional response to the judgment of others is what Cooley called the "looking glass self." Long before the invention of social media, Cooley famously said that each person lives "in the minds of others" (1902:208). Today, selfies and social networking provide new insights into these classic interactionist concepts.

In the pre-digital era, the sense of the generalized other developed through face-to-face interaction in real-time groups, such as sports teams, classes at school, neighborhoods, and family activities. As we absorb the "general" attitudes of these social groups, their "voices" contribute to our internal conversations of the self. We know we've encountered the generalized other when we say to ourselves, "*Most people* would [fill in the blank]." The generalized other also appears whenever we report that "*they* say" this or that (Holdsworth and Morgan 2007).

Social networking sites extend the generalized other to include the views and ideals of people and groups with whom we have no face-to-face interaction but encounter primarily – or even exclusively – online (Cerulo 1997; Meyrowitz 1997). Instagram followers may be casual acquaintances, friends-of-friends, and even celebrities or public figures. Some can also be "micro-celebrities" (Senft 2008, 2013) or "influencers" (Abidin 2016), social media users who have gained high numbers of followers.[1] For example, it might not come as a surprise that the pop music star Rhianna had over 11 million Instagram followers in 2015. However, it is hard to explain why an Indiana high school student named Cayla Friesz, known on Instagram as "Freeezy," had 31 496 followers during the same year (Marwick 2015).

Social media offers a sense of society's expectations through a **cyberbased generalized other** (Altheide 2000:9; Milkie 1999; Robinson 2007; Zhao 2005).[2] The cyberbased generalized other expands the number of individuals who have an influence on how we see ourselves. On social media, people who are not physically present to us inform our sense of self. For example, how do you determine whether an image is worthy of posting to social media? How did you learn that the image has to amuse, amaze, entertain, or make friends and followers envious? Through the cyberbased generalized other, you learned that the image has to say, "Aren't I fabulous?" "Look where I am!" or "Look what I have!"

For selfies, micro-celebrities and influencers shape a cyberbased generalized other, particularly for women. For example, Kim Kardashian, whose 2015 book, *Selfish*, contains more than 1200 selfies, offers advice on how to take the perfect selfie. In interviews, she has said "that when it comes to finding her best angles for a selfie, it's all about (i) Keeping her chin down and (ii) Holding the camera up a bit higher than face level, which ensures her features appear more streamlined" (Valenti 2016). The "duckface," or sucking in the cheeks, enhances the cheekbones, Kardashian says. She and her sisters are also known for provocative, glamourous, and nude selfies. Of course, whether this constitutes *oversharing* (Gould 2008) depends on whom you ask (Agger 2004).

Even if you aren't aware of Kardashian's advice, and even if you dislike what she represents, her image has shaped the cyberbased generalized other, particularly for young white women in the middle and working classes. For men, the advice is to "flaunt your style" but "don't be too flashy" (Samuels 2015).

Regardless of gender, the cyberbased generalized other promotes enhancing photos using Instagram's filters. It is also common to enhance selfies using a retouching app, like Perfect365. This illustrates how posting to social media involves **digital impression management** (Kaufman 2014). In Chapter 2, we described this as how people aim to project a particular presentation of self and situation and to control anticipated or actual encounters. People vary their style of dress or manner of speech based on the impressions they want to engender in the audience. In "real time," people encounter their audiences face-to-face. Online, the audience is invisible. Digital impression management refers to the self-presentational strategies involved in an online presence. Social networking sites allow individuals greater control over what they present to others. People can "curate" their online presence, showing only flattering, positive images. The disadvantage, of course is the increased opportunity for misrepresentation. Online dating sites are good examples of this (Ellison, Heino, and Gibbs 2006). People hoping to have face-to-face dates must balance self-promotion with the need for accurate self-presentation.

Along with changing impression management, social media has also modified the looking glass self. Because users continually revise, update, and edit what they post, they have greater control over the presentation of self than face-to-face interaction allows (Zhao 2005).

The practices associated with having an online presence have produced a **mediated looking glass self**, in which the conventions of social networking sites shape the reflections. Users can manage their online reputation by deleting images that elicit few "likes" or receive negative comments. Consequently, the responses one receives on a social networking site are based on an online feed of self-presentations intended to gain affirmation from others. For example, users can intentionally seek positive feedback by post self-disparaging comments along with selfies, such as "Bad hair day," or "I'm so fat." The expectation is "that their online friends will post contradictions affirming that [they] are really fine, good-looking, smart, or normal" (Belk 2014:1107). Those who receive such compliments are expected to reciprocate later, and users can "unfriend" or "unfollow" any contacts who make unwanted comments.[3]

> *Social networking sites revise some of interactionism's main ideas about the self.*
>
> - *The cyberbased generalized other expands the number of individuals who influence on how we see ourselves.*
> - *Digital impression management refers to the self-presentational strategies involved in having an online presence.*
> - *In the mediated looking glass self, the conventions of social networking sites shape the reflections we see.*

## Music as a Technology of the Self

We live in an era of "ubiquitous music" (Holmquist 2005; Kassabian 2013). We hear it everywhere. In addition to what we choose to listen to for our own enjoyment, we hear music in coffee shops, bars, restaurants, offices, waiting rooms, retail stores, and airports. We hear it in movies, TV shows, and commercials. It plays while we wait "on hold" and while we ride elevators. If you think about it, it is difficult to *avoid* hearing music.

Ubiquitous music is tied to the history of recording technology, which changed the way people listen (Radano 1989). Before the availability of commercially recorded discs around the turn of the twentieth century, people heard only live music. It was virtually impossible to listen to music alone (Katz 2010). Listening to music at home meant playing an instrument. In the early 1900s, the "Victrola," an early record player, brought recorded music into middle-class homes. In the 1920s, "needle cut" disc records that played at 78 revolutions per minute (rpm) offered improved sound fidelity. Technological developments then introduced 45 rpm "singles," with one song on each side, and larger 33 1/3 rpm records, known as LPs ("long playing"). Also called "albums," LPs held a number of songs released by groups or individual musicians.

Recording technology allowed people to choose what music they listened to, and to hear it repeatedly. We take this for granted today, but it had a profound effect on the meaning of music for the self. Here is one way of thinking about this effect: "A man may hear Beethoven's Ninth Symphony in concert and be awed. But if he plays a part of the Columbia recording every morning while shaving, he will be less reverent, perhaps, but the music will mean a thousand times more to him" (Katz 2010:21).

After the 1920s, radios became commercially available. Listeners could gather around a radio at home to hear professional musicians and bands. Emerging radio networks created regular programming. The invention of the transistor made small, battery-powered radio possible. Transistor radios could fit in the hand, and during the 1960s and 1970s, listeners could hear music, news, sports coverage, and other programming anywhere.

In the 1970s, the availability of cassette tapes made music more portable. People could record their own "mix tapes" from songs on LPs. The preferred format soon became the compact disc (CD), smaller than the LP and free of its characteristic scratches and pops. Along with cassettes and CDs came personal stereos and portable units called "boom boxes." In 1979, Sony introduced the Walkman, with headphones that made listening personal.

The inferior sound quality of boom boxes and personal stereos meant that they did not always offer a smooth listening experience. Moreover, users had to create mixes in advance or carry CDs or tapes with them, trying to anticipate what they might want to hear later. For example, in studying Walkman users, Bull (2000, 2001, 2005) found that people sometimes stopped listening because no music was better than the "wrong" music. In other words, the available music did not suit their current mood, time, or place. One man explained:

> Since I was 8 years old, I have acquired a CD/LP collection of more than 5000 items over the years. The biggest issue to me has always been what music to take along (on vacation, driving in a car, going out jogging or walking etc.). I made hundreds of compilation tapes (and later CDs), but what I was missing was the flexibility to listen to exactly the right song at the right time. (Bull 2005:347)

The arrival of the Apple iPod allowed users to store up to 10 000 songs and arrange "playlists" of preferred music in any configuration. Users could also use the "shuffle" mode of the iPod to play music at random, allowing the technology to take over. By 2009, growing disc capacities, compression algorithms, and increasing bandwidth increased the streams of delivery dramatically. The Internet broadened people's tastes dramatically. Previously, one's exposure to new music depended on friendship groups, older siblings, or what the radio offered (Bergh, De Nora, and Bergh 2014). Portable MP3 players and then smartphones, combined with earbuds or headphones, and streaming services such as Pandora, Apple Music, and Spotify brought "ubiquitous music" (Holmquist 2005), where everyday life is accompanied by a soundtrack.

Wherever users go, they can take "their" music with them. Access to extensive music libraries solves the problem of finding the "right" song.

In deciding on the "right" music, people simultaneously express their individuality and acknowledge a relationship with others – those who composed, performed, and produced the music. Music feels intensely personal, even while it draws listeners into "emotional alliances with the performers and with the performers' other fans" (Frith 1996:121). Let's consider some examples of how people experience music.

- *Music serves as a timepiece:* It locates the self in time, such as within a particular year or decade we associate with a type of music or a band, or on a specific date, such as a birthday or anniversary (Kotarba 2002). For example, the music of the Beatles evokes the 1960s, and grunge, rap, and hip-hop bring to mind the 1990s. You might recall the music that was popular when you were in high school or a song you danced to at the prom.
- *Music sets the tone for events and experiences*: Music creates the mood for what happens to the self at specific times. When having guests for dinner or brunch, for instance, jazz creates a certain ambience, while classical or world music establishes different atmospheres (see Batt-Rawden and DeNora 2005). Many faith traditions use music as part of worship services.
- *Music shapes how we experience place:* Retail stores use music to create an image and influence shoppers' behavior (De Nora and Belcher 2000). Upbeat music can make a place seem lively and youthful. Classical music evokes sophistication. Music can also make places *uninviting*. As a "non-aggressive deterrent," businesses and shopping districts often play "easy listening" or classical music to stop groups of "undesirable" people from hanging around (Sterne 2013).
- *Music signifies collective identity*: Although the connection to music feels intensely personal, music is inherently social, made for and by people who may not even be present to one another. "Deadheads," or fans of the Grateful Dead, describe the experience of "getting it," or identifying with the music and "the whole traveling circus scene" associated with the band's shows (Jennings 2000:209). Hard core punk music is associated with the Straight Edge youth movement (Haenfler 2006). Fans of bluegrass music believe they "share a special type of bond" (Gardner 2004:166). Among opera fans, only other fans understand their shared "obsession" (Benzecry 2011).
- *Music expresses and helps manage emotions*: In Chapter 7, you learned about "emotion management," which refers to how people "work" on their feelings. Listeners identify feeling states with particular music. They "know what they need" at a particular time (De Nora 2000; Wells 1990). They choose what will calm them down or lift them up. They also know the right music for feeling elated, sad, sentimental, or nostalgic. Music can also "take over" and "express disorganized feeling in a way that was impossible in words" (Willis [1978] 2014:216).

Music gives meaning to events, emotions, experiences, memories, relationships, and other valued aspects of social life. It offers "a sense of both self and others" (Frith 1996:109). Consequently, sociologist Tia De Nora (1999, 2000) described music as a "technology of the self." The self is always in process, developing throughout our lives, and music "works" on the self, constructing, and shaping who we are, who we would like to be, and what we want to feel. Music creates ways of being and feeling. We "know ourselves in and through" our engagement with music (Kassabian 2013:18). As one listener said, "It changes your life," and "changes your outlook on life" (Willis [1978] 2014:215). It also gives you a break from thinking about life and allows you to listen and simply "be." Depending on one's access to technology, the impact of music can be greatly enhanced or diminished. Headphones and earbuds, connected to smartphones and other devices, allow music to be "always on/always on us," to recall Turkle's (2008) apt phrase. A constant soundtrack influences and reflects the experience of self.

> *Music is a "technology of the self," constructing and shaping who we are, who we would like to be, and what we want to feel.*

## The Quantified Self

Benjamin Franklin, a founding father of the United States, kept a notebook with him at all times. He described a practice he began in 1726:

> I allotted a page for each of the [thirteen] virtues. I ruled each page with red ink, so as to have seven columns, one for each day of the week, marking each column with a letter for the day. I crossed these columns with thirteen red lines, marking the beginning of each line with the first letter of one of the virtues, on which line, and in its proper column, I might mark, by a little black spot, every fault I found upon examination to have been committed respecting that virtue upon that day. (Franklin 1916:66)

Franklin (1916:69) wrote of finding himself "so much fuller of faults than I had imagined." He also noted that, due to his record keeping, he "had the satisfaction of seeing them diminish" (1916:69).

Fast forward to a "meetup" in 2012, where a woman named Angela told the other attendees that she had been "working in a job she thought she loved." Recently, however:

> ...she downloaded an app that "pinged" her several times a day, asking her to rate her mood. After a while, she discovered that her mood score when at work was "awful." On the basis of the evidence revealed by her mood data – she was not as happy as she had thought – Angela revised

> her sense of her own job satisfaction and eventually quit. (Nafus and
> Sherman 2014:1784–1785)

In the age of digital technology, the ancient saying "know thyself" has been replaced by "track thyself." Of course, people have long recorded details about their lives and habits for various reasons. They have kept journals and diaries for personal reflection and improvement, as Franklin did. Women have tracked their menstrual cycles for thousands of years. Athletes have recorded times with stopwatches. Dieters have recorded calories consumed, and diabetics have monitored blood glucose. Until recently, Franklin's method of writing things down was the only way to keep such records. Today, however, technologies once available only to computer geeks allow everyone to collect, analyze, and share an overwhelming amount of data about themselves.

A growing number of devices, apps, and wearable gadgets can track and analyze spending habits, the number of steps taken, eating habits and calories consumed, amount of time spent in sleep or online, heart rate, and mood. People can track meditation practices, television watching, driving habits, work productivity, and sexual activity. They can monitor environmental conditions such as air temperature and humidity. Sensors in shoes can measure distance. A "smart" fork embedded with sensors uses a vibration and a blinking light to warn people that they are eating too fast. An activity tracker for dogs notifies owners of how much exercise their pets have had. Some apps make use of "gamification" strategies, offering points, badges, or other rewards for reaching goals or changing habits. Self-trackers often create graphs and charts of their progress. Even a basic wearable device such as Fitbit provides users with visualizations of their data.

Collectively, these practices are known as "self-tracking" or "lifelogging" (Lupton 2014a, 2014b). They involve "capturing a human life in realtime" through "data trails" (Selke 2016:3). Self-trackers or lifeloggers use the capacities of new technologies to generate increasing amounts and varieties of data about themselves with the goal of *self-optimization*: becoming faster, fitter, thinner, smarter, more productive – in short, better in any way imaginable.

One dedicated self-tracker describes the appeal: "Tracking what I am doing and the effects those actions have appeals to the data-loving, gamemaking, goal-oriented part of my brain. Tracking keeps me accountable to myself and allows me to turn what might otherwise be a chore into a challenge" (Parrish 2012). Others remain skeptical. Some consider self-tracking part of a "narcissistic quest for uniqueness and exceptionalism" (Morozov 2013:233). Self-tracking can also consume a lot of one's time (Lanius 2015). Some express concerns about the risks to privacy when personal information is transmitted and stored (Barcena, Wueest, and Lau 2014; Lupton 2015). Questions linger about ownership of the data generated by self-tracking (Lupton 2016; Nafus and Sherman 2014).

Symbolic interactionism directs our attention at other issues. In particular, it focuses on what self-tracking means for the understanding of the self. Self-tracking characterizes bodies and minds in terms of measurable details, such as the number of steps. For example, to measure stress, which might result from facing a dangerous situation or an emergency, self-tracking apps would measure your heart rate (the number of beats per minute), heart rate variability (the spaces *between* heartbeats), and galvanic skin response (electrical changes in the skin). These are known indicators of the mental or physical arousal involved in stress. Self-tracking makes the experience you know as "stress" visible as "slices" of data on these indicators.

In self-tracking, you would not measure these indicators only once. By definition, self-tracking requires accumulating a trail of data; this allows for the "tracking" to occur. Consequently, you would measure your responses repeatedly. As the data accumulate, a profile emerges of how you respond to stress, in this case, or of how many calories you typically consume, hours you sleep, or steps you take each day. Self-tracking involves having a visual representation of the data, whether as little black marks in a column, as in Ben Franklin's notebook, or in the charts, tables, and graphs that apps and programs make possible today. Regardless of method, the result is a version of you comprised of information. This virtual "you" is your **quantified self**, or your **data double** (Haggerty and Ericson 2000; Lupton 2012, 2013a, 2013b; Ruckenstein 2014).

Because the goal of self-tracking is self-improvement and even self-optimization, self-trackers don't just look at the data and say, "That's interesting." Although there are some instances of that – as in having one's DNA tested for genealogical reasons – more often, self-trackers more often seek motivation to improve their lives. The data double allows people to see who they are, what they should change, and who they might become (Rettberg 2014; Ruckenstein 2014).[4] In this way, the data double becomes the "me," or the object being reflected upon by the "I."

The idea that the self is an ongoing process of construction is consistent with symbolic interactionism. The notion that the process of construction involves reflection and self-knowledge also resonates with interactionism.

*The data accumulated through self-tracking creates a new entity known as the "data double" or "quantified self." Self-trackers scrutinize and act upon quantified selves.*

Although tracking the details of one's life might seem highly individualistic, self-tracking can be a highly social activity. Self-tracking involves, and in some cases *requires,* other people. It does so in two distinct, yet related ways.

First, the idea of quantifying the self depends on others. It depends on a set of data that define normal or average, happy or sad, or the ideal number of steps or calories. Imagine, for example, if your teacher assigned you a grade of

"46" on a test. Neither of these numbers would mean anything to you without knowing how other students scored. Is 46 a "good" grade? Is it "average"? Should you worry about receiving a 46? Without collective self-tracking, neither your quantified self nor mine means anything. No one can strive for self-optimization without data from others. Concepts such as "better," "faster," or "thinner" need baselines or starting points. Baselines and starting points require knowing what is humanly possible. For self-trackers, this information frequently comes through crowdsourcing (Lupton 2014a).

Second, self-tracking often requires community to keep people engaged. Many self-trackers share their data with like-minded people. Tracking apps allow people to compare progress with others. Many post their progress publicly through apps that sync with Facebook, Twitter, or other social networking sites. For example, users of the moodtracking website and iPhone app MoodPanda post several times each day. One of the creators described MoodPanda as "a large community of friendly people, sharing their moods, celebrating each others' happiness, and supporting each other when they're down" (Mehta 2012).

Some self-trackers take community to another level. They share their analyses and experiences on the website and in the meet-ups of Quantified Self groups (capitalized).[5] The unofficial motto of Quantified Self is "self knowledge through numbers." Quantified Self gained attention following the 2010 publication of an essay entitled "The Data-Driven Life," which appeared in *The New York Times Magazine* (Wolf 2010). Although the group had begun three years earlier, the essay made greater numbers of people aware of self-tracking (Boesel 2013). Participants also attend conferences to discuss different techniques and devices for self-tracking and the process and practice of "tracking" itself.

Although the phenomenon of web-based self-tracking is a recent development, the technological reshaping of the self has a long history. For example, throughout much of human history, most people existed within small social networks. A farmer or artisan in pre-industrial times would have interacted with only a limited group of people. The family, the village, and the market would have formed the pool of those whose judgments, opinions, and voices mattered for the self (Baumeister 1986). This amounted to a narrow range of influences on who one might become.

Industrialization and urbanization, along with communication and transportation technologies and other developments vastly expanded the number and variety of others that people encountered (Gagnon 1992; Gergen 1991). Social life began to bring people into contact with strangers as never before. These social changes expanded the number and variety of people who mattered for the self. Over time, one's network came to include not only friends and family members, but also strangers, celebrities, and a host of others to whom one has been exposed. These characters "populate" the self, increasing the range of options and possibilities that shape the experience (Gergen 1991).

Compared to the pre-industrial farmer or artisan, the contemporary individual has an infinitely more complex experience of self.

To borrow from Walt Whitman (2005), technology allows each of us to "contain multitudes." Self-tracking quantifies these multitudes, turning them into data. It is up to us to decide how to respond to this technological change. What do you think? Will you use it as a tool, or disconnect and opt out?

*Although self-tracking records data about individuals, it is a highly social activity.*

## Conclusion

It can sometimes seem that technology has brought on the decline of social interaction, but this chapter shows another side of that story. Social media that seem to isolate individuals and make them more narcissistic actually depend on social interaction. New technologies encourage us to rethink assumptions about the self.

In this chapter, we have seen that the person posting selfies to a social networking site interacts with an expanded version of the generalized other. Digital impression management involves self-presentation for an invisible audience, and the mediated looking-glass-self filters the reflections one sees. The person wearing earbuds or headphones may seem cut off from his or her environment, but the act of listening to music involves other people, including those who made the music and others who share one's tastes. As a "technology of the self," music shapes and reflects who people are and who they want to become.

Another technology promises to make the self better, stronger, healthier, smarter, or the best it can be. Self-tracking produces a quantified self, depicted in data doubles that represent the person in numbers. The data double has become a statistical version of the "me," the object of scrutiny and the target of change.

The next time you go online, pay attention to the advertisements you see and the suggestions you receive for new blogs to read, videos to watch, and products to buy. This is social saturation. In the digital age, you cannot escape it. Equipped with the tools of symbolic interactionism, however, you can understand its effects.

## Learning by Using the Symbolic Interactionist Perspective

In the excerpt below, a university student reconsiders her relationship with her phone and social networking sites. Which of the concepts from this chapter can you apply to her post? In light of what you've learned about social networking and the self, do you agree with what she says? What position do you take on your social media use?

---

**"Why I Refuse To Constantly Be Tied To My Phone"**

---

**Danielle Kopoian (2016)**

*In a world where it seems like everyone is constantly bound to their phones, I love putting my phone aside in order to truly live in the moment.*

Most people today have a love-hate relationship with their cell phones. Many people love being connected to their friends and enjoy going on social media. However, people tend to get aggravated when they have to constantly answer text messages and deal with demands from their jobs, even when they are not physically working. Personally, I used to always feel the need to stay up to date with my Twitter timeline, answer text messages within minutes of receiving them, and constantly update my Snapchat story. After being this way for years, I realized on a vacation during high school that checking social media that often just is not possible. Even though I was still afraid of not seeing something important on social media, I put that fear aside and realized that nothing that important really happens on social media anyways. Once I put down my phone more often during that trip, I enjoyed my life so much more. I realized that living in the moment and truly enjoying the time I had with my family was much more important than knowing everything that was going on on Twitter.

It has been several years since I had that revelation. Now, I never use my phone when I go out to eat with friends or when I am just doing something fun with loved ones unless I have to. I want to enjoy the time that I get to spend with the people I love having in my life. Avoiding using my phone allows me to connect with people so much more and makes me feel like I can talk to them about more important topics since I know I will not be distracted by my phone. I like giving people my full attention when we spend time together and I love it when people do the same for me. I wish more people would spend less time on their phones because it really does strengthen your relationships with others and allows you to appreciate the little things in life. …Of course, I still use my phone frequently and I love sharing things with my friends via social media, but I would much rather connect with my friends and family face to face than via text message anytime.

## Notes

1 Influencers often gain official sponsorship for product endorsements based on the number of likes and followers.
2 This has also been called the "mediated" (Meyrowitz 1997), "digital" (Chambers 2013) and "virtual" (Robinson 2007) generalized other.
3 The exception to this is the unfortunate example of online bullying.

**4** The existence of data doubles raises concerns about security, privacy, and surveillance. This topic is beyond the scope of the discussion of the self we engage in here, but interested readers can see Lyon (2007).

**5** See http://quantifiedself.com for a list of groups.

# References

Abidin, C. 2016. "'Aren't These Just Young, Rich Women Doing Vain Things Online?': Influencer Selfies as Subversive Frivolity." *Social Media + Society* 2:1–17.

Agger, B. 2004. *The Virtual Self: A Contemporary Sociology*. Malden, MA: Blackwell.

Agger, B. 2015. *Oversharing: Presentations of Self in the Internet Age*. New York: Routledge.

Altheide, D. 2000. "Identity and the Definition of the Situation in a Mass-Mediated Context." *Symbolic Interaction* 23:1–27.

Barcena, M., C. Wueest, and H. Lau. 2014. *Security Response: How Safe Is your Quantified Self?* Mountain View, CA: Symantech. Retrieved 18 June 2017. https://pdfs.semanticscholar.org/ac33/e020ac40e9f09b522fd518d425253e40bab2.pdf.

Batt-Rawden, K. and T. DeNora. 2005. "Music and Informal Learning in Everyday Life." *Music Education Research* 7:289–304.

Baumeister, R. 1986. *Identity: Cultural Change and the Struggle for Self*. New York: Oxford University Press.

Belk, R. 2014. "Digital Consumption and the Extended Self." *Journal of Marketing Management* 30:1101–1118.

Benzecry, C. 2011. *The Opera Fanatic: Ethnography of an Obsession*. Chicago, IL: University of Chicago Press.

Bergh, A., T. DeNora, and M. Bergh. 2014. "Forever and Ever: Mobile Music in the Life of Young Teens." Pp. 317–334 in *The Oxford Handbook of Mobile Music Studies*, Vol. 1, edited by S. Gopinath and J. Stanyek. New York: Oxford University Press.

Boesel, W. 2013. "What is the Quantified Self now?" *Cyborgology*, May 22. Retrieved June 20, 2017. https://thesocietypages.org/cyborgology/2013/05/22/what-is-the-quantified-self-now.

Bragazzi, N. and G. Del Puente. 2014. "A Proposal for Including Nomophobia in the New DSM-V." *Psychology Research and Behavior Management* 7:155–160.

Bull, M. 2000. *Sounding Out the City. Personal Stereos and the Management of Everyday Life*. Oxford: Berg.

Bull, M. 2001. "The World According to Sound: Investigating the World of Walkman Users." *New Media & Society* 3:179–197.

Bull, M. 2005. "No Dead Air! The iPod and the Culture of Mobile Listening." *Leisure Studies* 24:343–355.

Bull, M. 2006. "Investigating the Culture of Mobile Listening: From Walkman to iPod." Pp. 131–149 in *Consuming Music Together: Social and Collaborative Aspects of Music*, edited by K. O'Hara and B. Brown. Dordrecht: Springer.

Catalano, L. 2014. "How to Use #Selfies as Sociological Exercises." *The Society Pages*, June 30. Retrieved May 29, 2017. https://thesocietypages.org/teaching/2014/07/30/selfies.

Cerulo, K. 1997. "Reframing Sociological Concepts for a Brave New (Virtual?) World." *Sociological Inquiry* 67:48–58.

Chambers, D. 2013. *Social Media and Personal Relationships: Online Intimacies and Networked Friendships*. New York: Palgrave Macmillan.

Cooley, C. H. 1902. *Human Nature and the Social Order*. New York: Scribner.

De Nora, T. 1999. "Music as a Technology of the Self." *Poetics* 27:31–56.

De Nora, T. 2000. *Music in Everyday Life*. Cambridge: Cambridge University Press.

De Nora, T. and S. Belcher. 2000. "'When You're Trying Something on You Picture Yourself in a Place Where They Are Playing This Kind of Music' – Musically Sponsored Agency in the British Clothing Retail Sector." *The Sociological Review* 48:80–101.

Ellison, N., R. Heino, and J. Gibbs. 2006. "Managing Impressions Online: Self-Presentation Processes in the Online Dating Environment." *Journal of Computer-Mediated Communication* 11:415–441.

Franklin, B. 1916. *The Autobiography of Benjamin Franklin*. New York: Henry Holt.

Frith, S. 1996. "Music and Identity." Pp. 108–127 in *Questions of Cultural Identity*, edited by S. Hall and P. Du Gay. London: SAGE.

Gagnon, J. 1992. "The Self, Its Voices, and Their Discord." Pp. 221–243 in *Investigating Subjectivity: Research on Lived Experience*, edited by C. Ellis and M. Flaherty. Newbury Park, CA: SAGE.

Gardner, R. 2004. "The Portable Community: Mobility and Modernization in Bluegrass Festival Life." *Symbolic Interaction* 27:155–178.

Gergen, K. 1991. *The Saturated Self: Dilemmas of Identity in Contemporary Life*. New York: Basic Books.

Gould, E. 2008. "Exposed." *The New York Times Magazine*, May 25. Retrieved June 17, 2017. http://www.nytimes.com/2008/05/25/magazine/25internet-t.html.

Haenfler, R. 2006. *Straight Edge: Hardcore Punk, Clean Living Youth, and Social Change*. New Brunswick, NJ: Rutgers University Press.

Haggerty, K. and R. Ericson. 2000. "The Surveillant Assemblage." *British Journal of Sociology* 51:605–622.

Holdsworth, C. and D. Morgan. 2007. "Revisiting the Generalized Other: An Exploration." *Sociology* 41:401–417.

Holmquist, L. 2005. "Ubiquitous Music." *Interactions* 12:71, 78.

Jennings, S. 2000. "Becoming a Deadhead." Pp. 203–213 in *Deadhead Social Science: You Ain't Gonna Learn What You Don't Want to Know*, edited by R. Adams and R. Sardiello. Lanham, MD: Rowman & Littlefield.

Kassabian, A. 2013. *Ubiquitous Listening: Affect, Attention, and Distributed Subjectivity*. Berkeley, CA: University of California Press.

Katz, M. 2010. *Capturing Sound: How Technology Has Changed Music*, Rev. ed. Berkeley, CA: University of California Press.

Kaufman, P. 2014. "A Sociological Snapshot of Selfies." *Everyday Sociology*, January 13. Retrieved May 29, 2017. http://www.everydaysociologyblog.com/2014/01/a-sociological-snapshot-of-selfies.html.

Kopoian, D. 2016. "Why I Refuse To Constantly Be Tied To My Phone." *Odyssey*, October 10. Retrieved June 16, 2017. https://www.theodysseyonline.com/refuse-constantly-tied-phone.

Kotarba, J. 2002. "Rock 'n' Roll Music as a Timepiece." *Symbolic interaction* 25:397–404.

Lanius, C. 2015. "The Hidden Anxieties of the Quantified Self Movement." *Cyborgology*, May 5. Retrieved June 19, 2017. https://thesocietypages.org/cyborgology/2015/05/05/the-hidden-anxieties-of-the-quantified-self-movement.

Lupton, D. 2012. "M-Health and Health Promotion: The Digital Cyborg and Surveillance Society." *Social Theory & Health* 10:229–244.

Lupton, D. 2013a. "Understanding the Human Machine." *Institute of Electrical and Electronics Engineers Technology & Society Magazine* 32:25–30.

Lupton, D. 2013b. "Quantifying the Body: Monitoring and Measuring Health in the Age of mHealth Technologies." *Critical Public Health* 23:393–403.

Lupton, D. 2014a. "Self-Tracking Modes: Reflexive Self-Monitoring and Data Practices." Social Science Research Network. Retrieved June 18, 2017. http://ssrn.com/abstract=2483549.

Lupton, D. 2014b. "Self-Tracking Cultures: Towards a Sociology of Personal Analytics." Pp. 77–86 in *Proceedings of the 26th Australian Computer-Human Interaction Conference on Designing Futures: The Future of Design*. New York: ACM.

Lupton, D. 2015. "Personal Data Practices in the Age of Lively Data." *Social Science Research Network* Retrieved June 18, 2017. http://papers.ssrn.com/sol3/papers.cfm?abstract_id=2636709.

Lupton, D. 2016. "You are Your Data: Self-Tracking Practices and Concepts of Data." Pp. 61–80 in *Lifelogging*, edited by S. Selke. Weisbaden: Springer VS.

Lyon, D. 2007. *Surveillance Studies: An Overview*. Cambridge: Polity.

Marwick, A. 2015. "Instafame: Luxury Selfies in the Attention Economy." *Public Culture* 27:137–160.

McGuigan, J. 2005. "Towards a Sociology of the Mobile Phone." *Human Technology* 1:45–57.

Mead, G. [1934] 1962. *Mind, Self and Society: From the Standpoint of a Social Behaviorist*. Chicago, IL: University of Chicago Press.

Mehta, R. 2012. "Toolmaker Talk: Ross Larter (MoodPanda)." Quantified Self, February 1. Retrieved June 19, 2017. http://quantifiedself.com/2012/02/toolmaker-talk-ross-larter-moodpanda.

Meyrowitz, J. 1997. "Shifting Worlds of Strangers: Medium Theory and Changes in 'Them' versus 'Us.'" *Sociological Inquiry* 67:59–71.

Milkie, M. 1999. "Social Comparisons, Reflected Appraisals, and Mass Media: The Impact of Pervasive Beauty Images on Black And White Girls' Self-Concepts." *Social Psychology Quarterly* 62:190–210.

Morozov, E. 2013. *To Save Everything Click Here*. London: Allen Lane.

Murphy, S. 2014. "Meet the 'Most Connected Man' in the World." *Mashable*, March 13. Retrieved June 18, 2017. http://mashable.com/2014/03/13/most-connected-man-in-world-chris-dancy/#h.hDOy2N9qqW.

Nafus, D. and J. Sherman. 2014. "Big Data, Big Questions | This One Does Not Go Up To 11: The Quantified Self Movement as an Alternative Big Data Practice." *International Journal Of Communication* 8:1784–1794.

Parrish, A. 2012. "Gamification keeps me going (aka I'm the self-tracking type)." *Bikestyle*. Retrieved June 18, 2017. http://bikestylespokane.com/2012/06/09/gamificationkeeps-me-going-aka-im-the-self-tracking-type-an-andreapost.

Plant, S. 2001. "On the Mobile: The Effects of Mobile Telephones on Social and Individual Life." Motorola Report. Retrieved June 6, 2017. http://www.momentarium.org/experiments/7a10me/sadie_plant.pdf.

Radano, R. 1989. "Interpreting Muzak: Speculations on Musical Experience in Everyday Life." *American Music* 7:448–460.

Rettberg, J. 2014. *Seeing Ourselves through Technology: How We Use Selfies, Blogs and Wearable Devices to See and Shape Ourselves*. New York: Palgrave Macmillan.

Rippin, H. 2005. "The Mobile Phone in Everyday Life." *Fast Capitalism*. Retrieved June 6, 2017. http://www.uta.edu/huma/agger/fastcapitalism/1_1/rippin.html.

Robinson, L. 2007. "The Cyberself: The Self-ing Project goes Online, Symbolic Interaction in the Digital Age." *New Media & Society* 9:93–110.

Ruckenstein, M. 2014. "Visualized and Interacted Life: Personal Analytics and Engagements with Data Doubles." *Societies* 4:68–84.

Samuels, G. L. 2015. "How to use Instagram: A Guide for Male Latecomers." *The Telegraph*, May 7. Retrieved June 4, 2017. http://www.telegraph.co.uk/men/the-filter/11586053/How-to-use-Instagram-a-guide-for-male-latecomers.html.

Selke, S., ed. 2016. *Lifelogging*. Weisbaden: Springer VS.

Senft, T. 2008. *Camgirls: Celebrity & Community in the Age of Social Networks*. New York: Peter Lang.

Senft, T. 2013. "Microcelebrity and the Branded Self." Pp. 346–354 in *Blackwell Companion to New Media Dynamics* edited by J. Hartley, J. Burgess, and A. Bruns. Malden, MA: Wiley-Blackwell.

Senft, T. and N. Baym. 2015. "What Does the Selfie Say? Investigating a Global Phenomenon." *International Journal of Communication* 9:1588–1606.

Stavans, I. 2017. "I Love my Selfie: An Essay." *Los Angeles Review of Books*, April 14. Retrieved June 11, 2017. https://lareviewofbooks.org/article/love-selfie-essay.

Sterne, J. 2013. "The Non-Aggressive Music Deterrent." Pp. 121–138 in *Ubiquitous Music: The Everyday Sounds That We Don't Always Notice*, edited by M. Quiñones, A. Kassabian, and E. Boschi. London: Routledge.

Tenner, E. 2004. *Our Own Devices: How Technology Remakes Humanity*. New York: Vintage.

Turkle, S. 2008. "Always-On/Always-On-You: The Tethered Self." Pp. 121–137 in *Handbook of Mobile Communication Studies*, edited by J. Katz. Cambridge, MA: The MIT Press.

Turkle, S. 2011. *Alone Together: Why We Expect More from Technology and Less from Each Other*. New York: Basic Books.

Turkle, S. 2013. "The Documented Life." *The New York Times*, December 15. Retrieved June 3, 2017. http://www.nytimes.com/2013/12/16/opinion/the-documented-life.html.

Valenti, L. 2016. "The Kim Kardashian Guide to Taking the Perfect Selfie." *Marie Claire*, September 26. Retrieved May 31, 2017. http://www.marieclaire.com/celebrity/news/a15688/kim-kardashian-selfie-tips.

Wells, A. 1990. "Popular Music: Emotional Use and Management." *Journal of Popular Culture* 24:105–117.

Whitman, W. 2005. *Walt Whitman's Leaves of Grass: The First (1855) Edition*. New York: Penguin Books.

Willis, P. [1978] 2014. *Profane Culture*. Princeton, NJ: Princeton University Press.

Wolf, G. 2010. "The Data Driven Life." *The New York Times Magazine*, April 28. Retrieved June 20, 2017. http://www.nytimes.com/2010/05/02/magazine/02self-measurement-t.html?pagewanted=all&_r=0.

Woolgar, S. 1990. "Configuring the User: The Case of Usability Trials." *The Sociological Review* 38:58–99.

Zhao, S. 2005. "The Digital Self: Through the Looking Glass of Telecopresent Others." *Symbolic Interaction* 28:387–405.

# 9

# Amplifying Social Problems

Claimsmakers and Their Contexts

"A few days ago I called up a beekeeper inviting him to an environmental conference planned for June 2015. He declined because, he said, there would be no honeybees left in another year or two. I was stunned. I asked him to explain. 'Scientific evidence mounts almost daily confirming the decades-long observations of beekeepers that pesticides are playing a major role in the dramatic decline of honeybees and other pollinators,' he said to me. ...A world without honeybees would be unpleasant and sterile. ...The tragedy of my beekeeper friend is American tragedy written large. Time has come to say no to the poisoning of our world. In a civilized society there should be no chemical warfare anywhere, particularly in raising food." ("Honeybees on the Verge of Extinction"; Vallianatos 2014)

"When Internet addiction was first proposed as a psychological disorder in the 1990[s], it wasn't taken too seriously. These days however, very few people would try to argue that there is no such thing as problematic or excessive Internet use. Hundreds of research studies have found evidence showing that between 1–10% of individuals experience problems controlling their Internet use and they display similar physiological, neurological, and behavioral profiles of substance and gambling addicts. In 2014, the DSM (the psychologist's handbook that details all the known psychological disorders) was updated, which proposed Internet addiction as a potential disorder that required further investigation. ...What could be addictive about aimlessly using the Internet, to no specific end? Surfing the Internet could arguably be considered a form of information seeking, whether the question at hand is formed before we hit the Internet or whether it develops along the way. As we navigate the Internet, new information we weren't even looking for pops up, and before we long we can be ten pages deep into Wikipedia, absorbed in reading about a new topic without even planning to be there. Finding new information, whether it is intentionally searched for or simply

*The Social Self and Everyday Life: Understanding the World Through Symbolic Interactionism*, First Edition. Kathy Charmaz, Scott R. Harris, and Leslie Irvine.

discovered, is a pleasurable experience for our brains. Alternatively, perhaps Internet use is simply and more generally a different type of existence, to that offered by the three dimensional, less compliant real world: above all, it is a world where whatever you do will elicit an instant response – unlike real life. And perhaps instant feedback is not just reassuring, but becomes a prerequisite for well-being." ("Is Surfing the Internet Addictive? New Research Suggests Non-Specific Internet Use Can Be an Addictive Experience"; Greenfield 2015)

"Millions and millions of Americans …feel that Christmas is under attack in such a sustained and strategized manner that there is, no doubt, a *war* on Christmas. It's no longer permissible to wish anyone Merry Christmas. That's too exclusive, too insensitive. What if they're not Christian? What if they're an atheist? …All across America the battle is being joined. …Wannabe constitutional lawyers in local government offices all over the country are declaring unconstitutional normal and traditional Christmas representations such as Christmas trees, Santa Claus, treetop stars, wreaths, the singing of and listening to Christmas carols or Christmas instrumental music, attending a performance of Dickens's *A Christmas Carol*, the publication of the word 'Christmas' itself, and even the colors red and green! …The same phenomenon is afoot in Great Britain, Australia, and most of Europe as well. …Often the first shots of the battle are fired in schools. Many schools have changed Christmas trees into friendship trees or giving trees or holiday trees, [limited the] carols kids can sing and hear, [and] disinvited Santa or are giving him sidelong glances of suspicion…. There is a war on Christmas [and] it's much worse than you dreamed." (*The War on Christmas: How the Liberal Plot to Ban the Sacred Christian Holiday Is Worse than You Thought*; Gibson 2005:xv–xix)

Do you watch the news on television? Comment about social issues on Twitter or Facebook? Talk to friends and relatives about the weak job market or the high cost of higher education? Peruse online articles or blog posts about bullying, climate change, droughts, gun violence, homelessness, immigration, or sexual harassment? Listen to activists and politicians talking about crime, immigration, poverty, police shootings, or terrorism?

On any given day, the odds are good that you will be exposed to information and assertions about social problems. You have probably spent many hours of your life thinking and talking about them, as well. Nonetheless, it's likely you have considered these problems in isolation, one-at-a-time.

In this chapter, you'll learn to develop a systematic and consistent approach for thinking about and evaluating social problems. Symbolic interactionists are perhaps the only social scientists[1] who can offer a framework capable of analyzing the full spectrum of social ills that concern people – from the destruction of bee colonies, Internet addiction, and the "war on Christmas" to child abuse, gun violence, and other social ills (Best 2017; Blumer 1971). This perspective can be extremely useful whenever you decide which problems deserve your time, effort, or financial support.

## Objectivist and Interactionist Approaches to Social Problems

What are social problems? From an objective point of view, the answer seems clear: social problems are conditions or behaviors that cause harm to large numbers of people. The extinction of the honeybee could threaten the diversity and security of the food available to human beings, as bees are crucial pollinators of many fruits, vegetables, and nuts. Internet addiction also poses large-scale threats. It might impair millions of people's ability to navigate the "real" world – communicating face to face, maintaining close relationships, focusing on school and work tasks. News reports have even linked Internet addiction to mortal danger from strangers met online as well as from prolonged sitting (Schweingruber and Horstmeier 2013:200–201). A "war on Christmas" might undermine widely-cherished religious traditions.

The objectivist definition of social problems has much allure. It fits our common sense expectations, and seems workable. However, take a second look. Consider further the phrase "large numbers of people." Vallianatos (2014) implies that the loss of bees will impact virtually everyone. Greenfield (2015) suggests that 1–10% of individuals with internet access become addicted to the web. Gibson (2005) claims that "millions and millions" of Americans feel slighted by attacks on Christmas, and many more remain unaware of the damage being done.

These numbers seem large, but they do not settle the question. Exactly how many people must be affected, for an issue to rise to the level of a social problem? One hundred? One thousand? Ten thousand? A million? Or, instead of absolute numbers, we might choose to focus on percentages. Does 1% of the population need to be affected? Or 5%? In the U.S., a problem that affects 1% of the population would involve well over three million individuals. It's not necessarily easy to determine whether a troubling situation is "widespread enough" to merit our concern. Drawing the line between issues that are "small and insignificant" as opposed "big and consequential" is a subjective act. Often, the number of people affected by a problem may be small, yet the issue will attract significant attention and resources. Consider terrorism: Between 1970 and 2010, terrorist attacks killed fewer than 500 Americans, if we exclude the 9/11 attacks on the World Trade Center and the Pentagon (START 2011). Despite that relatively small number, terrorism has been and remains a matter of utmost concern to Americans and policy-makers.

The notion of "harm" also is more complicated than it appears at first glance. A negative situation or behavior can hurt people's health (physical and mental), finances, relationships, opportunities, and so on. Which types of harm can constitute a social problem? And how much harm? Who gets to measure the harm, or has the right to decide something is harmful in the first place? Often, many people disagree about the extent or even the existence of harm. For example, some suggest that legalizing marijuana and same-sex marriage is detrimental to society, but others argue exactly the opposite. Some people avow that helmet-free motorcycle riding is a social problem because riders who have accidents incur a substantial number of brain injuries and pass their healthcare costs onto society. Avid riders, in contrast, may assert that the real problem is governmental regulations (e.g. helmet laws) restricting individual freedom (Best 2017:37). And, of course, a supposed "war on Christmas" may instead be described as a positive and peaceful movement towards inclusivity.

An objectivist definition seems workable enough, until we start digging a bit deeper, and find an abundance of interpretive complexities. To an interactionist, these dilemmas provide fodder and justification for an alternative approach – one that highlights meaning-making and subjectivity.

From an interactionist point of view, social problems are interpretations. People create or **construct** social problems when they define situations as troubling. Any circumstance can be understood in many different ways, assuming people even notice it. A problem owes not only its existence but its contours – its perceived causes, effects, and solutions – to the human beings who observe and tell others about it (Blumer 1971).

*Interactionists define social problems as interpretations (rather than objective conditions). Any troublesome situation can be ignored, treated as normal, or described as problematic for various reasons and in various ways.*

*"Claims" are assertions that people make about problems. An interactionist collects and compares claims, and studies their origins and consequences.*

*Claimsmakers "construct" or "frame" issues by portraying them a particular sort of problem (e.g. as a disease, sin, crime, and so on).*

The act of "noticing" is an essential first step. In any given week or year, many potential problems fail to attract attention. We're busy. Our time and resources are limited. Of the potentially thousands of social problems we might consider, we have to choose a smaller number on which to focus our concerns. Individuals, news organizations, and even the federal government cannot pay attention to every troubling condition – far from it. Try this experiment: the next time you watch your local news, count how many social problems receive coverage. After subtracting commercials, routine weather temperatures and sports scores, and daily crime reports, very little space remains for discussing the huge range of issues that might negatively affect the region – pollution, corruption, decaying infrastructure, obesity, depression, bullying, elder abuse, and on and on.

Even if we have the time, there is no guarantee we will notice a potential problem. We may lack the intelligence or socialization needed to make sense of things. If you haven't been informed about climate change, or if your local community scoffs at the concept, then you might not observe or care about its possible manifestations. If you have been socialized to think of women as sub-servient, perhaps even the property of men, then it's unlikely that you will notice or be concerned about sexist language, sexual harassment, domestic violence, or women's right to vote. Before being warned about a coming "bee-pocalypse" or a "war on Christmas," you might have ignored a dead bee on the sidewalk or a "Happy holidays!" greeting, rather than wondering if they were small signs of undesirable trends.

Once noticed, a circumstance must be interpreted as troublesome to become a problem. Any situation can be "spun" in one or more directions. For example, various claimsmakers may cast frequent public intoxication as a sin, a crime, or an illness, or as completely normal and unremarkable. Divergent meanings can lead to divergent remedies and policies – such as Bible study, prayer, fines, imprisonment, medication, therapy, or indifference. Depending on the culture or subculture, a single interpretation may dominate, leading to a particular group or institution to have sole jurisdiction (e.g. the church), or multiple viewpoints and treatment plans may mingle collaboratively or competitively. A judge may reduce penalties for offenders who promise to enroll in religiously-based counseling and treatments, while medical professionals lobby for more science-based prevention and treatment strategies.

---

Drapetomania is an historical example that starkly illustrates the construction of social problems. In 1851, Samuel Cartwright, a doctor and "Professor of Diseases of the Negro" at the University of Louisiana, published an article in a medical journal that portrayed run-away slaves as suffering from a disease of the mind (Myers 2014). For Cartwright, the troublesome situation was not slavery itself, but slaves fleeing (what he saw as) their natural, God-given role. Today, almost everybody would agree that Cartwright's diagnosis is very far from a simple statement of facts. Supposed cases of drapetomania can be easily reframed as outcomes of a natural desire to escape exploitation and live freely.

**"Drapetomania, or The Disease Causing Negroes to Run Away"**
*Samuel A. Cartwright (1851:707–709)*

In noticing a disease not heretofore classed among the long list of maladies that man is subject to, it was necessary to have a new term to express it. The cause, in the most of cases, that induces the negro to run away from service, is as much a disease of the mind as any other species of mental alienation, and much more curable, as a general rule. With the advantages of proper medical advice, strictly followed, this troublesome practice that many negroes have of running away, can be almost entirely prevented, although the slaves be located on the borders of a free state, within a stone's throw of the abolitionists.

...Before the negroes run away, unless they are frightened or panic-struck, they become sulky and dissatisfied. The cause of this sulkiness and dissatisfaction should be inquired into and removed, or they are apt to run away or fall into the negro consumption. When sulky and dissatisfied without cause, the experience of those on the line and elsewhere, was decidedly in favor of whipping them out of it, as a preventive measure against absconding or other bad conduct. It was called whipping the devil out of them.

If treated kindly, well fed and clothed, with fuel enough to keep a small fire burning all night, separated into families, each family having its own house – not permitted to run about at night, or to visit their neighbors, or to receive visits, or to use intoxicating liquors, and not overworked or exposed too much to the weather, they are very easily governed – more so than any other people in the world. When all this is done, if any one or more of them, at any time, are inclined to raise their heads to a level with their master or overseer, humanity, and their own good require that they should be punished until they fall into that submissive state which it was intended for them to occupy in all after-time, when their progenitor received the name of Canaan, or "submissive knee-bender." They have only to be kept in that state, and treated like children, with care, kindness, attention, and humanity, to prevent and cure them from running away.

Complete consensus is rarely achieved. People disagree on the name of a problem, as well as its size, effects, causes, and remedies. Nevertheless, the more people who agree that a given circumstance is bad, the more **legitimate** the problem becomes in minds, policies, and institutions. Few people in the U.S. today worry about witchcraft and demonic possession. Almost no activists, politicians, journalists, teachers, or everyday citizens call attention to these once-feared threats.[2] Conversely, most North Americans would now agree that beating children is intolerable and harmful. However, prior to the 1960s, maltreatment was not so consistently recognized or widely condemned. Children were property of their guardians. For centuries, "The purposeful beating of the young ...found legitimacy in beliefs of its necessity for achieving disciplinary, educational or religious obedience" (Pfohl 1977:310–311).

The extent of a problem's legitimacy depends on the perceived quality of its advocates, not just quantity. The denunciation of marijuana by a president or senator carries more weight than similar comments by a small-time blogger.

Such individuals also command a better position to institute laws and programs that aim to reduce drug consumption, further legitimizing and institutionalizing the meaning of the behavior. Fame, prestige, wealth, and other resources can make some claimsmakers more influential than others. Celebrities, church leaders, CEOs, successful authors, and other prominent individuals can raise alarm bells and lobby for policy changes. For example, celebrity Jenny McCarthy has widely promoted the idea that vaccines cause autism in children, even though medical researchers strongly deny any connection.

> *Social problems are legitimated when audiences endorse the way claimsmakers have framed a troublesome situation. Legitimacy is a matter of degree and may only exist among particular communities. Full consensus is rarely possible. Powerful and famous individuals can help legitimate a problem, as can the creation of laws, policies, and institutions designed to prevent or reduce the problem.*

## Amplifying Social Problems

In order to attract attention to a problem, and convince others that something needs to be done, claimsmakers appeal to our emotions – such as our sympathies, fears, and moral outrage. Most of us feel badly when we hear of diseased trees, abandoned pets, or homeless people sleeping on sidewalks. Our empathy for other living things, may compel us to listen and want to help. Alternatively, we may be scared into action. If someone tells us that we (or those we care about) are in danger, then we may become highly concerned and motivated. Our sense of morality can also prove instrumental. If we learn that some individuals willfully commit deplorable acts – such as bullying, humiliating, torturing, raping – then our outrage may propel us to take action against the injustice.

To elicit strong reactions from us, claimsmakers tend to **amplify** social problems – they portray social issues as larger and more consequential than they may actually be. Precision can be boring. Accuracy may be laudable but less compelling. A variety of rhetorical strategies can be employed to inflate the seriousness of social problems and thereby raise our sense of alarm.

**Basic hyperbole** occurs when claimsmakers characterize situations in the most extreme terms. Politicians, pundits, and everyday folk can choose to describe public education, healthcare, or the economy as "terrible," "in the toilet," "could not be worse," or "completely dysfunctional," even when scores of countries are worse off. Compare the statement "Our healthcare system is a total disaster!" with "Our healthcare system is relatively strong but could be more affordable. Next year, rates are expected to rise 20 percent in some states, although subsidies will offset some of those costs." Even if the latter description were more accurate or reasonable, it would probably be less captivating. A politician who hyperbolically decries "A total disaster!" may influence a large audience, as the sound bite is replayed and quoted repeatedly on television, online, and in print. The less melodramatic official who attempts to offer a more lengthy and nuanced discussion of the issue may receive less coverage.

Consider the hyperbolic claim that someone is "living in hell." Hell is a scary place. The word conjures images of intense and unending torture, with no hope of reprieve. However, if you Google the phrase "living in hell," you'll find that claimsmakers make prolific use of the descriptor for all sorts of conditions. People say they are "living in hell" when they are dealing with Addison's disease, AIDS, air pollution, Alzheimer's, anorexia, anxiety, arthritis, asthma, and the aftermath of abortion. Those who define themselves as suffering an addiction – to alcohol, drugs, food, gambling, pornography, sex – also sometimes claim to be living in hell. Likely, some if not all of these claims are hyperbolic. (Readers should note that we only explored "living in hell" claims focused on problems starting with the letter "A." You can find many more claims.)

Another way to amplify social problems is to treat rare **incidents as trends** (Glassner 2004). Two or three occurrences of a phenomenon can suffice for claimsmakers to declare that a dangerous pattern is emerging and growing exponentially – perhaps "spreading like wildfire." Two school shootings, in different states, can be described as an "epidemic" of violence sweeping the country. A few muggings may be characterized as a "crime wave." A few overdoses may be enough to raise alarm bells over the "plague," "outbreak," or "crisis" of heroin addiction. In all these cases, real, and serious issues may exist. However, claimsmakers invoke language that characterize the issue in a melodramatic fashion rather than with cautious precision. Claims about explosive growth often do not cite rigorous, multi-year data that puts the trend in perspective (Best 2001).

A third way claimsmakers can amplify social problems is by framing or interpreting them in a **universalizing** manner. A universalizing assertion states or implies that a dangerous situation can happen to anyone, anywhere, at any time; it emphasizes *what is possible* rather than *what is likely*. For example, it is true that obesity and homicide may "know no boundaries" and can be found in virtually all sectors of society. However, obesity and homicide rates vary by class, race, gender, age, region, and other variables. Not everyone has an equal chance of being afflicted; some individuals have a much lower chance than others. A young black male who lives in Chicago runs a greater risk of dying from gun violence than an elderly white female who lives in the suburbs. Portraying a problem as "random" or "crosses all lines" usually overstates its impact, but has the benefit of attracting attention, generating alarm, and mobilizing others to act.

In July 1985, the cover of *Life* magazine announced, in all-caps and bright-red font, that "NOW NO ONE IS SAFE FROM AIDS" (Best 2004:65–66). Quite possibly, this universalizing headline sought to attract attention and create alarm by making the problem seem bigger than it was. Consider President Donald Trump's universalizing assertions about gun violence.[3] During his 2016 campaign, he promised African Americans and many Hispanics "We'll get rid of the crime. You'll be able to walk down the street without getting shot. Right now, you walk down the street, you get shot." Such language portrays an improbability as a likely event, regardless of whether a person is a young or old, a gang member or an attorney, a man or a woman, and so on.

A fourth way to amplify social problems is to invoke the **war metaphor** – to portray undesirable conditions or actors as enemies of the state. Along with other politicians and pundits, many presidents have declared war on social problems (Best 1999). In the 1930s, Franklin Roosevelt announced wars on the depression, farm surpluses, rural poverty, and crime. In the 1950s, Eisenhower called for "a new kind of war ...upon the brute forces of poverty and need" (Best 1999:143). In the 1960s, Lyndon Johnson declared war on poverty and crime. Next, Nixon renewed the war on crime and added cancer to the list. Then, Gerald Ford initiated an "all-out war against inflation," followed by Jimmy Carter, who called the energy crisis "the moral equivalent of war" (Best 1999:143). Ronald Reagan repeatedly declared war on drugs, and George W. Bush launched a war on terror.

By invoking the concept of war – and related terms like attack, defend, battle, fight, enemy – claimsmakers strengthen the sense of urgency with which a problem should be treated (Loseke 2009). Wars tend to involve existential threats from evildoers who must be stopped at all cost. Those who do not join the cause of war risk being seen as traitors; everyone should be on the side of good, not evil. "You're either with us or against us in the fight on terror" George W. Bush famously stated.[4] In wars, claimsmakers usually postpone the debate over the expense until the conflict is over. Compare the melodrama of the war metaphor to the boring, circumspect language of science: "Research indicates that, by enacting policies X, Y, and Z, we might reduce poverty by 2.9% within five years, assuming the economy continues to grow at least 1.5% annually."

Wars can be declared on social problems, or problems themselves can be characterized as wars. For example, conservative pundits have raised alarms over a putative war on Christmas (as this chapter's opening excerpt demonstrates). Examples of "attacks" include substituting greetings of "Happy holidays!" for "Merry Christmas!" and replacing nativity scenes with non-denominational decorations in business and government settings. Gibson (2005) and others portrayed this movement towards secularization and religious inclusivity as the equivalent of war. Leftist commentators, meanwhile, have condemned a "war on women" whenever Republicans speak of limiting abortion rights or defunding Planned Parenthood clinics. In both cases, the war metaphor significantly magnifies an issue as claimsmakers interpret problems in accordance with their own perspectives and agendas.

> *Claimsmakers amplify social problems – or make them seem bigger and more consequential – through a variety of rhetorical strategies, such as hyperbole, treating incidents as trends, universalization, the war metaphor, domain expansion, scary numbers, and typifying examples.*

A somewhat subtler way to amplify social problems is through the practice of **domain expansion** (Best 1990). Claimsmakers who want to attract concern to a new issue often find it advantageous to place the phenomenon under the umbrella of an already-legitimated social problem. Essentially, the argument is "This too is an example of that thing we all agree is bad!" For example, exposing one's children to second-hand smoke can be described as unhealthy and ill-advised. However, if the issue is framed as a form of child abuse – a behavior widely condemned – then the practice seems even more outrageous and deplorable. Or, consider sexual harassment. Early cases involved the use of threats or bribes to extort sex from one's employees. Over the decades, claimsmakers expanded the domain to include other forms of conduct, such as making lewd jokes or posting swimsuit calendars (Best 1999:104–105).

Domain expansion makes an existing problem bigger by increasing the range of issues it covers; simultaneously, the newer issues benefit by "piggybacking" onto the legitimacy and seriousness of the established social problem (Loseke 2003:61). Yet we can identify drawbacks to this form of amplification: an established problem may become "watered down." As claimsmakers expand the domain in new directions, a social problem may grow increasingly controversial and new claims greeted more skeptically. For example, child abuse began as a problem of severe bodily harm inflicted upon very young children (Best 1990). Later, claimsmakers advocated for the inclusion of sexual abuse, emotional abuse, and neglect, as well as spanking, penile circumcision, religious indoctrination, and traditional gender role socialization, all under the umbrella of child abuse. Clearly, what started as a relatively nonpartisan issue grew less so over time.

A sixth strategy for amplifying social problems is to employ **scary numbers**, by reporting figures in a way that magnifies a problem's apparent size or impact. Statistics are used and misused by all sorts of claimsmakers – journalists, activists, politicians, and bloggers, in addition to scientific experts (Best 2001; Robinson and Scherlen 2007). When a phenomenon is too new or extremely difficult to measure, claimsmakers offer speculative estimates that tend to overstate the problem's potential size. Such guestimates take the form of "big round numbers," as when an architecture professor claimed that one billion birds died each year in the U.S., from collisions with windows (Best 2008:31). Other claimsmakers put such bird deaths as low as 3.5 million, but all the figures were based on highly speculative measures (Best 2008:32). By choosing the biggest guesstimate, claimsmakers attempt to elicit more sympathy or outrage for their cause – in this case, pushing for building practices and warning systems that might protect birds from harm.

Advocates who want to amplify an issue might choose to use percentages instead of absolute numbers. Imagine that two commercial airplanes crashed in one year, followed by three crashes in the next year. "An increase from two to three crashes" sounds less alarming than "There was a 50 percent increase in plane crashes this year!" Claimsmakers may opt for the latter description, if they seek to gain attention or mobilize resources (cf. Glassner 1999:5). Conversely, they can avoid percentages that sound low. "A million Americans suffer from X" sounds more compelling than "0.3% of the population suffer from X," even though both figures are roughly equivalent (Best 2008:65). So, claimsmakers might choose whichever description makes a problem seem bigger – one that employs absolute numbers or one that uses percentages.

Citing statistics sounds authoritative but can be dry. Colorful anecdotes can augment or replace quantitative evidence. Claimsmakers can use carefully chosen **typifying examples** of a phenomenon in order to generate maximum concern. These incidents rarely represent the average or most common case, yet claimsmakers may imply (or allow audiences to infer) that the anecdote is typical. For example, consider the opening comments of Senator Walter Mondale, during the 1973 hearings for the Child Abuse Prevention Act:

> Only 10 days ago the stepmother of 9-year-old Donna Stern of Cedar Grove, Md. was found guilty of the premeditated murder and torture of the child. The child had been beaten, burned, and whipped by the stepmother. Ugly as it sounds, this is not an isolated case. Each year some 60,000 children in this country are reported to have been abused. (Best 1990:68)

Beating, burning, whipping, and killing a child is a particularly extreme form of child abuse. Yet Mondale suggests Donna Stern's case exemplifies many others, and provides a fitting story from which to begin discussing what to do about abuse more generally. A less severe example – such as a parent who spanks or grabs a misbehaving child so hard it leaves a bruise – would not be as compelling. Such atrocity tales, especially when framed as typical, can amplify a problem much more than stories of routine or commonplace acts.

Horrific acts can be committed against non-human entities too; just think of animal abuse or the pollution and destruction of the environment. Consider this discussion of an atrocious bird-killing building in Chicago:

> At first glance, it looks like an insanely prolific morning of birding: 4,136 Song Sparrows, 3,632 Dark-eyed Juncos, 3,362 Swamp Sparrows, 2,532

White-throated Sparrows, and 1,417 Hermit Thrushes. But the numbers don't represent living birds. They tally the birds that died after colliding with one Chicago building from the fall of 1978 to 2004. And a frightening number of birds of other species were also killed. In all, 31,705 individuals from 141 species were found dead at the building. The story is similar across the country. Collision with manmade structures ranks second among causes of death among migratory birds in North America.[5]

The author suggests that the story of this one horrific building is played out similarly across the country. Notice the author's use of strategic use of statistics, as well: a 26-year tally is given, rather than an annual average. Together the typifying example and use of scary numbers serves to amplify the problem and plays to our sympathies. A more representative example, such as a single-family home with significantly fewer bird deaths, might be more representative but less compelling.

## The Contexts of Claimsmaking

Our discussion so far has emphasized the interpretive options we have when considering social issues. We can ignore potentially troublesome situations, or regard them as normal and acceptable, or portray them as problematic in various ways. Claimsmakers can use a range of rhetorical strategies – from basic hyperbole to domain expansion and atrocity tales – to persuade others that something needs to be done. We have many alternatives, when formulating our thoughts and arguments about social issues. The choices we make give meaning to things and shape our subsequent actions.

Interpretations and claims do not occur in a vacuum, however; social contexts enable and limit them. Various social factors may encourage or discourage claimsmakers' amplification of social problems. Fearmongering, sympathy-mongering, and outrage-mongering may occur more or less often, and achieve more or less success, depending on the conditions under which claimsmaking occurs.

First, consider how human beings' opportunities for communicating about social problems have increased over the past one hundred years. Even a remote island dweller or a rural farmer can readily make and hear hundreds of social problems claims on any given day. The twentieth century saw the invention and popularization of radio, television, and the Internet. Each started small but grew rapidly. We went from a few radio stations, to dozens in any major city, to hundreds of satellite channels and thousands of podcasts; from just a few major television networks, to hundreds of channels on cable and satellite, to a nearly infinite array of viewing choices via online streaming; from a small number of primitive Internet news sites and blogs, to millions of them; from typewriters and expensive printing presses to cheap personal printers, photocopying, and digital documents.

To be sure, we can also communicate about social problems face-to-face, as we talk with family, friends, neighbors, community leaders, and others. Human beings have almost always had such possibilities. What has changed is the massive proliferation of **claimsmaking venues and technologies.** In a single day, you can skim through dozens of tweets decrying illegal immigration; watch a medical talk show about how sugar is killing us; listen to a podcast about the underfunding of pensions; peruse a "neighborhood watch" crime flier that appeared in your mailbox; receive a scary email from your mom, warning about the dangers of identity theft; read a news story about the loss of jobs to automation.

The evidence is clear: Our opportunities for communicating about social problems have expanded tremendously. So, claimsmaking has a historical dimension. Our capacity to produce and consume claims depends on the forms and amount of interaction we can have with others. Currently, that capacity is immense. At the same time, claimsmaking venues and technologies can impose constraints on our conduct. Sometimes these constraints require or encourage us to express ourselves in brief snippets of thought. One example is Twitter's current limit of 280 characters. In another instance, consider how politicians speak in soundbites to ensure that newspapers and news broadcasters capture and repeat or replay their core message. Internet surfers have little patience for longwinded arguments, thus encouraging bloggers to compose catchy "click-bait" titles and relatively succinct articles. Striking visual evidence can also help claimsmakers publicize their concerns or hinder them in its absence. News broadcasters may prefer to cover claimsmakers when their stories can be combined with compelling video or photographic content, rather than relying on simple, plainspoken, verbal argument. In addition, claimsmakers who can connect their issues to a recent catastrophe or scandal may stand a better chance of receiving coverage than those who can't. The press tends to favor "moral dramas" that (like a soap opera) allow for much repetition of the basic story as new developments slowly unfold over weeks or months (Monahan 2010).

*Contexts affect claimsmaking. Cultural settings may promote, guide, or limit the number and kinds of assertions that can be made about troublesome situations. Claimsmaking is shaped by the current technologies and venues for communicating about problems, by existing institutions and careers that support advocates, by shared cultural beliefs and traditions, and by the level of audience gullibility.*

The sheer number of options we have for disseminating claims thus empowers claimsmakers while exerting pressure on them. In a sense, claimsmakers must compete in a **social-problems marketplace** (Best 2017:46). Consider this analogy. Just as numerous brands of cereal and soda vie for consumers' attention and resources (via advertisement campaigns, packaging, and other efforts), so too do activists who want to raise awareness and prompt action about troublesome situations. Claimsmakers can be seen as **moral entrepreneurs** who wish to improve the world by "selling" others on their view of it, alongside numerous rivals all attempting to do the same (Becker 1963). Such intense competition likely encourages claimsmakers to adopt hyperbole, the war metaphor, scary numbers, atrocity tales, and other techniques, in an all-out effort to be seen and heard. Thus, the proliferation of venues and technologies for claimsmaking contributes to the existence of a competitive marketplace of ideas, creating a set of enabling as well as constraining conditions.

In a further elaboration of the marketplace analogy, Best (1999) has argued that a **victim industry** arises in tandem with claimsmaking. A victim-industry interweaves a collection of institutions and careers promoting the creation and labeling of social-problems victims in the U.S. The fields of law, medicine, and education, for example, have grown to offer a wide range of positions and specialties. Within each realm, various actors may stand to benefit by creating and advocating for new kinds of victims. Activists lobby for new laws to protect victims, while attorneys file suits on behalf of victims. Legislators can improve their standing with voters by supporting victims (of cyber bullying, stalking, etc.). In the U.S., Republicans can benefit by demonstrating that they are "tough on crime," while Democrats can display their concern for women, children, and marginalized communities (Best 1999:122). Police Chiefs can portray illicit drug users as victims of "domestic terrorists" (i.e. drug traffickers) to attract attention and mobilize support for policing, while simultaneously bolstering their profiles and careers.[6]

Medicine and education operate similarly. Doctors and therapists can identify new kinds of victims (e.g. PTSD, Internet addiction), which potentially raises the status of their profession, advances claimsmakers' careers, and generates business. Academic researchers can accomplish parallel goals, by writing articles, books, and grant applications on the plight of victims (Best 1999).

In short, the existence of problem-identifying institutions and careers shapes claimsmaking about social problems. The victim industry may be smaller in some countries or eras, thereby limiting opportunities for claimsmaking. Well-developed institutions and career paths can do the opposite – encouraging the identification and condemnation of more and more troublesome situations. Of course, this observation does not necessarily undermine any particular issue or claim. Individuals and professions have incentives to notice and decry problems, but it does not follow that those issues aren't significant or that the claimsmakers aren't sincere. Remember, our overall goal in this section is merely to demonstrate how social contexts shape the extent, form, and effectiveness of claimsmaking.

**Cultural resources** are a fourth contextual factor that shapes claimsmaking. As we suggested earlier, claimsmakers' perspectives are products of prior socialization. That's an important reason why some troubling conditions are ignored or interpreted in one way rather than another. The same is true of claimsmakers' audiences. To successfully raise alarm about troublesome conditions, claimsmakers must take into account the prevailing values, concepts, and symbols. For example, Dr. Martin Luther King famously drew on the Declaration of Independence as he led a social movement against racial discrimination. Although not a governing document, the Declaration did assert that "all men are created equal." King successfully cited that well-known and revered language to bolster his argument that the U.S. was not living up to its founding principles in its treatment of African Americans.

Another type of cultural resource consists of **vocabularies of motive** (Mills 1940). People absorb and then affirm the "logic" of certain kinds of explanations for behavior. They can link troublesome conduct to a number of potential causes. Consider alcoholism, bullying, or marital infidelity. For any of these behaviors, we could invoke our childhood upbringing as the reason for our actions, suggesting that our parents provided poor models of responsible consumption, polite conduct, or committed partnering. Instead, we might blame genetics, claiming an innate tendency towards addiction, aggression, or procreation. Alternatively, we could cite external factors, by claiming that peer pressure, work stress, or abundant temptations pushed us to behave badly. Or, we could argue that a spell or a mystical agent is responsible – as in "The devil made me do it." Lastly, we could merely attribute the conduct to freewill or bad decision-making.

These vocabularies of motive may be acceptable in varying degrees – or not at all – depending on the cultural context. Claimsmakers who want to raise attention to an issue must be mindful of the sorts of claims that will sound convincing to their audiences. A secular or scientifically literate society will likely scoff at mystical explanations, except in some subcultural communities. Similarly, the argument that genetic drives or inborn personality traits cause alcoholism, bullying, or infidelity might be seen as incomprehensible in premodern times, or as merely an excuse or "cop-out" in today's settings where people cherish the notion of personal responsibility.

The topic of skepticism overlaps with a fifth contextual factor that shapes claimsmaking: the general **gullibility of audiences** (Best 2001). If claimsmakers address relatively *naïve* listeners – trusting and uneducated – then their assertions will likely encounter little resistance. Claimsmakers can make hyperbolic arguments ("We're in an epidemic!" "It can happen to anyone!") with almost no questioning or opposition. People who adopt a *cynical* mindset make tougher audiences. Cynics doubt the honesty and accuracy of any assertions. However, they tend to do so inconsistently: it's difficult to live in an information-free world, where nothing is true. As a result, cynics tend to discount claims that contradict their preconceptions, while agreeing with claimsmakers who adopt the same ideological persuasion (whether liberal, conservative, and so on). *Critical thinkers*, on the other hand, try to weigh the pros and cons of all arguments about social problems. They seek specifics, evaluate evidence, and compare competing perspectives. Critical thinkers do not want any claimsmakers to dupe them – even those whose ideology they share. Critical audiences tend to put more constraints on claimsmakers, followed by cynics. (In fact, a key objective of this chapter is to promote the critical mindset – as you might have noticed.)

## Conclusion

The dominant approach to social problems – in sociology and in everyday life – is to treat problems as harmful conditions affecting large numbers of people. In this chapter, we have explained the interactionist alternative: to approach social problems as interpretations. Unlike theoretical perspectives tailored to study issues of class, gender, the environment, or other topics, symbolic interactionists have a point of view that you can apply to any and all potentially problematic situations. By focusing on claimsmakers, their rhetorical strategies, and the enabling–constraining effects of social contexts, interactionists offer an array of concepts useful for anyone who wants to evaluate – or make – claims about virtually any troublesome condition in society. Consumers and producers of social problems claims can both benefit from a better understanding of the way claimsmakers must compete to persuade their audiences in a crowded marketplace of ideas.

The interactionist approach rests on the premise that all problems are socially constructed. No issue has inherent meaning; all troublesome conditions, once noticed, must be understood and described through human language (Best 2017; Blumer 1971).

However, this tenet does not imply that we must, in practice, consider all interpretations as equal. We are free to decide – in fact, we must decide – which problems are most real and pressing. Claimsmakers may use similar strategies – such as hyperbole, treating incidents as trends, scary statistics, atrocity tales – to decry witchcraft and demonic possession as they do to raise alarm about gun violence and climate change. Perhaps, like us, you agree that the latter issues are more significant than the former. Yet, no matter how "real" gun violence and climate change may be, these problems will always be depicted in different ways by different claimsmakers. An interactionist perspective helps us better navigate the cacophony of claims that surround troublesome situations, from the most fanciful to the most severe.

## Learning by Using the Symbolic Interactionist Perspective

Let's examine an excerpt from a blogger who, in 2016, had almost a million Twitter followers. Can you use any ideas from this chapter to analyze this author? What is Nelson's main claim? Can you summarize or critique his article, using concepts such as constructing/framing, amplifying, hyperbole, scary numbers, claimsmaking venues and technologies, victim industry, vocabularies of motive, and moral entrepreneur? Can you briefly compare a naïve, cynical, and critical reading of this essay? Hypothetically, if Nelson had employed a typifying example (or perhaps an atrocity tale), what would that have looked like?

---

### "Helicopter Parents Share the Blame for Millennials' Alcoholism"

**Jerry Nelson (2016)**

Millennials consumed almost half of all the wine in 2015, drinking about 160 million cases of wine – even more than baby boomers. Is there a reason behind all this?

…Helicopter parents raised Millennials to believe they were somehow "special" and unique little snowflakes. Thanks helicopter parents. Every Millennial who played tee-ball or little league won a trophy – merely for showing up. The Millennial's life wrapped around the era of the Self-Esteem Movement of their parents and their helicopter parents taught them they were able to be anything they wanted when they grew up – nothing would stand in their way.

Reality hit soon enough. College tuitions became more expensive, and the housing market collapsed. The small amount of help their parents offered couldn't be found.

…When the Millennials started to come of age, depression was the mental illness of the day. Prozac Nation sealed the zeitgeist and now, anxiety zoomed by depression as the leading mental health concern. And depression can easily lead to alcoholism. Millennials, used to having their egos stroked and self-esteem boosted, are finding reality crashing in on them now as they reach "adulthood."

Jean Twenge, a researcher who has examined the data on generational studies, says, "Today's young people face a competitive workplace squeezed by sky-high housing prices and inflating health care costs."

…Anxiety is feeding self-medication among Millennials. Self-medication, the use of mood-altering substances, including alcohol and drugs, assuages the symptoms of anxiety and depression. When self-medication is at the root of addictions, the underlying issue of stress is overlooked.

Millennial's lives are different from the Baby Boomers who raised them. When Boomers look at Millennials, they tend to feel they are looking at a group of people bent on staying forever young. Millennials are often called "adultescents" for their penchant for video games, their unwillingness to marry or even start saving for the down payment on a house.

Although this generation appears to have an extended adolescence, it might not be – strictly – their fault. The adults that raised them convinced the kids they deserved this freedom – yet failed to prepare them: the world wouldn't hand it to them.

The Millennials may be unique snowflakes, but there are 7 billion unique snowflakes. It is important the uniqueness of increased anxiety disorders and the related capacity for addiction is realized and the real adults step up to meet them where they are.

## Notes

1 For example, feminist and Marxist theories tend to be tailored towards problems centered on gender or class. This does not mean that such perspectives are not valuable in their own right, or that their concerns cannot be combined (cautiously) with an interactionist or constructionist framework.

2 With some exceptions. Search YouTube.com for "exorcisms," and add the key words "Sean Hannity" or "ABC 20/20."

3 Downloaded November 10, 2016 from https://www.washingtonpost.com/news/post-politics/wp/2016/08/22/donald-trump-to-african-american-and-hispanic-voters-what-do-you-have-to-lose

4 Downloaded 10 November 2016 from http://edition.cnn.com/2001/US/11/06/gen.attack.on.terror

5 http://www.birdwatchingdaily.com/featured-stories/15-products-that-prevent-windows-strikes Downloaded 7 November 2016. Article by Jennifer Horton, originally in *Birdwatching* magazine, 23 April 2013.

6 Downloaded on November 11, 2016 from http://www.nytimes.com/1988/05/19/us/reagan-and-bush-place-new-stress-on-the-drug-issue.html

## References

Becker, H. 1963. *Outsiders: Studies in the Sociology of Deviance*. New York: Free Press.

Best, J. 1990. *Threatened Children: Rhetoric and Concern about Child-Victims*. Chicago, IL: University of Chicago.

Best, J. 1999. *Random Violence: How We Talk About New Crimes and New Victims*. Berkeley, CA: University of California.

Best, J. 2001. *Damned Lies and Statistics: Untangling Numbers from the Media, Politicians, and Activists*. Berkeley, CA: University of California.

Best, J. 2004. *More Damned Lies and Statistics*. Berkeley, CA: University of California.

Best, J. 2008. *Stat-spotting: A Field Guide to Identifying Dubious Data*. Berkeley: University of California.

Best, J. 2017. *Social Problems*, 3rd ed. New York: Norton.

Blumer, H. 1971. "Social Problems as Collective Behavior." *Social Problems* 18:298–306.

Cartwright, S. A. 1851. "Report on the Diseases and Physical Peculiarities of the Negro Race." *New Orleans Medical and Surgical Journal* 8:691–715.

Gibson, J. 2005. *The War on Christmas: How the Liberal Plot to Ban the Sacred Christian Holiday Is Worse than You Thought*. New York: Sentinel.

Glassner, B. 1999. *The Culture of Fear: Why Americans Are Afraid of the Wrong Things*. New York: Basic Books.

Glassner, B. 2004. "Narrative Techniques of Fearmongering." *Social Research* 74(4):819–826.

Greenfield, S. 2015. "Is Surfing the Internet Addictive? New Research Suggests Non-Specific Internet Use Can Be an Addictive Experience." Posted April 30, 2015. Retrieved on October 24, 2016 https://www.psychologytoday.com/blog/mind-change/201504/is-surfing-the-internet-addictive.

Loseke, D. R. 2003. *Thinking about Social Problems*. New York: Aldine de Gruyter.

Loseke, D. R. 2009. "Examining Emotion as Discourse: Emotion Codes and Presidential Speeches Justifying War." *Sociological Quarterly* 50:497–524.

Mills, C. W. 1940. "Situated Actions and Vocabularies of Motives." *American Sociological Review* 5(6):904–913.

Monahan, B. A. 2010. *The Shock of the News: Media Coverage and the Making of 9/11*. New York: NYU Press.

Myers, B. E. 2014. "'Drapetomania': Rebellion, Defiance and Free Black Insanity in the Antebellum United States." UCLA Dissertation. Downloaded on November 14, 2016 from http://escholarship.org/uc/item/9dc055h5.

Nelson, J. 2016. "Helicopter Parents Share the Blame for Millennials' Alcoholism." *Psych Central*. Retrieved November 5, 2016 http://blogs.psychcentral.com/sober-life/2016/07/helicopter-parents-share-the-blame-for-millennials-alcoholism.

Pfohl, S. J. 1977. "The Discovery of Child Abuse." *Social Problems* 24(3):310–323.

Robinson, M. B. and R. G. Scherlen 2007. *Lies, Damned Lies, and Drug War Statistics: A Critical Analysis of Claims Made by the Office of National Drug Control Policy*. Albany, NY: SUNY Press.

Schweingruber, D. and M. Horstmeier. 2013. "The Evolution of Internet Addiction." Pp. 195–207 in *Making Sense of Social Problems: New Images, New Issues*. Boulder, CO: Lynne Rienner.

START. 2011. "Background Report: 9/11, Ten Years Later." National Consortium for the Study of Terrorism and Responses to Terrorism. Downloaded December 10, 2012 from http://www.start.umd.edu/start/announcements/BackgroundReport_10YearsSince9_11.pdf.

Vallianatos, E. 2014. "Honeybees on the Verge of Extinction." Updated January 25 2014. Downloaded October 24, 2016 from http://www.huffingtonpost.com/evaggelos-vallianatos/honeybees-on-the-verge-of_b_4326226.html.

# 10

# Individuals and Institutions

> "Once I was out of work three or four months, employment agencies, and companies would get very suspicious. [They'd think] 'You're in this hot field and you haven't been able to get a job for four months? There must really be something wrong with you,' and they wouldn't touch you with a ten-foot pole." (unemployed professional; Newman 1988:66)
>
> "You really have to get in touch with where you are in this whole process and realize that job you just lost is not you. That didn't define your net worth. It may have defined your financial worth, but it didn't define you, your worth as a person... I've never been out of work before, and I've always looked at my job as who I am. When you... lose your job it's like, 'Okay, who am I? If I don't have to work anymore, who am I now?'" (former corporate executive; Garrett-Peters 2009:552)
>
> "I think the one thing I would like to emphasize is how devastating the layoff was.... It was just the most eye-opening, *humiliating, humbling* experience I have ever been through. It took away almost my whole sense of being and doing and existing." (former programmer/business analyst: Garrett-Peters 2008:552; emphasis original)

These excerpts from studies of involuntary job loss suggest the considerable impact the experience can have. At the heart of any experience of change, whether positive or negative, is this question: "who will I be, now that this has happened?" People's responses to this question may seem highly individual, stemming from character or personality. Without dismissing individual factors, symbolic interactionists use a different lens to examine the experience. Unlike psychology, which might study the individual traits that make someone respond to job loss in a particular way, symbolic interactionism examines the social factors involved in his or her response. Specifically, interactionists

*The Social Self and Everyday Life: Understanding the World Through Symbolic Interactionism,*
First Edition. Kathy Charmaz, Scott R. Harris, and Leslie Irvine.
© 2019 John Wiley & Sons, Inc. Published 2019 by John Wiley & Sons, Inc.

emphasize that individuals exist within **institutions**, which shape their actions and ideas.

In everyday language, people use the word "institutions" in so many different ways that it can be difficult to figure out exactly what the term means. If you Google "institutions," you will see (at least) two uses of the word. First, it can refer to corporations and organizations of various sorts. Universities are often called institutions, and fans of Harry Potter will know that the fictional "Durmstrang Institute" is a wizarding academy. This use of the word can also refer to facilities that provide care for people with special needs. Examples of this use of the word include "psychiatric institutions" and "residential institutions" for senior citizens and the disabled. In this sense, placing a person in the care of such a facility involves institutionalizing them. Second, the word "institutions" can also refer to established customs or practices, such as "the institution of marriage." People use this meaning of the word to describe a long association with a person or place. For example, one might describe a group of friends who meet for coffee every Friday as "something of an institution" at the café.

Although the concept of "institutions" is essential to sociology, sociologists also use the term to refer to a diverse – some might say baffling – array of phenomena. To offer just a short list, they have applied the labeled to the family, marriage and courtship, religion, the economy, schools, sports, mental hospitals, political systems, taxation, and handshakes (see Martin 2004). This variety of practices, rules, procedures, customs, and entities might initially seem to have little in common. Once you gain a sense of what "institutions" means, you'll be able to examine the relationship of individuals and institutions. When you reach the end of this chapter, you will understand the importance of institutions in shaping people's beliefs, actions, ideas, and feelings.

To understand institutions, it would help to have a definition. We could begin by looking at the list above. Unfortunately, nothing on this list has any inherent quality that makes it an institution. Creating a list of institutions and working backward to a definition overlooks an important point: *human beings created institutions.* We constructed the meaning of religion, sports, handshakes, and the other things on the list in the first place. As Peter Berger and Thomas Luckmann wrote in *The Social Construction of Reality*, institutions emerge because we human beings tend to do things in habitual ways, even when no one else is around. For example, Berger and Luckmann write:

> Even the solitary individual on the proverbial desert island habitualizes his activity. When he wakes up in the morning and resumes his attempts to construct a canoe out of matchsticks, he may mumble to himself, "There I go again," as he starts on step one of an operating procedure consisting of, say, ten steps. In other words, even solitary man has at least the company of his operating procedures. (1966:52).

Repeated, or habitualized, actions become patterned into conventional ways of doing things. Habitualization frees people from the burden of having to decide how to get things done every time they face a task. Although there can be many ways of building canoes and many ideas about who should build them, habitualization narrows the options so that people no longer have to think about how to do it. Having decided how to build canoes and who should build them, they can devote their energy to matters other than figuring out the building of canoes. Through habitualization, people understand that doing the same task the same way they did it last time will yield the same result.

Once people habitualize tasks and actions, and establish who performs them, they develop **typifications**. Recall that in creating typifications, people say, "these things belong together. They are of the same type." As people share typifications of habitualized tasks and actions and those who perform them, the shared typifications become **institutions**. As Berger and Luckmann put it:

> The institution posits that actions of type X will be performed by actors of type X. For example, the institution of the law posits that heads shall be chopped off in specific ways under specific circumstances, and that specific types of individuals shall do the chopping (executioners, say, or members of an impure caste, or virgins under a certain age, or those who have been designated by an oracle). (1966:53)

With this background, we can begin to define institutions as *collectively recognized beliefs and ways of doing things*. Once established, institutions endure for two closely related reasons. First, institutions endure because people experience them as *objective* reality. Instead of seeing the social world as the result of human action, we see it as external to human beings. It is easy to see why this would be the case. We were born into social arrangements that existed long before we arrived and will continue to exist long after we've departed. We were born into ideologies and other sets of beliefs, as well as hierarchies based on race, ethnicity, gender, and class. We had no hand in inventing institutions; we learn about them through socialization and experience them as "reality," just "how things are done." This is the paradox of institutions: that human beings are "capable of producing a world that [they] then experience as something other than a human product" (Berger and Luckmann 1966:61).

Second, institutions endure because people *internalize* them through socialization. Internalization involves the formation of a generalized other, as discussed in Chapter 3. We take the information about "how things are done," what is appropriate, and what is meaningful very personally. We don't simply learn *about* the social world, passively acquiring facts and rules. The process of learning shapes our subjective experience of who we are. We don't simply learn about the building of canoes; we come to understand why we must build canoes in a particular way.

We learn about institutions through the process of socialization, but socialization also takes place within institutions. The identities we acquire reflect the institutions in which we find ourselves embedded, for a "socialized person is a society in miniature" (Shibutani 1955:564). In important ways, then, institutions provide anchors for our sense of who we are, securing us to relationships, actions, and beliefs from which we derive meaning and purpose (Irvine 1999).

Institutions have tremendous power over people. They shape our actions and beliefs, present us with opportunities, and put some possibilities out of our reach. Institutions "control human conduct by setting up predefined patterns of conduct, which channel it in one direction as against the many other directions that would theoretically be possible" (Berger and Luckmann 1966:52). However, people sometimes have opportunities to challenge and even transform institutions. Charles Horton Cooley (1909:314) wrote, "the individual is always cause as well as effect of the institution." Institutions may constrain us, but they do not immobilize us. We can often exercise **agency**, or the ability to "act otherwise" (Giddens 1979:75). For example, during the 1960s, feminists and civil rights activists "acted otherwise" by challenging the institutions of gender and race.

One of the advantages of symbolic interactionism is its ability to address both constraint and agency. Interactionism recognizes that although individuals make choices, institutions influence the choices available to them. For interactionists, people are not simply pushed around by the power of institutions, but they cannot escape their influence, either.

> *Institutions consist of collectively recognized beliefs and ways of doing things. Constraint refers to the way institutions limit human actions and beliefs. Agency refers to the ability to influence and change institutions.*

As collective endeavors, institutions are created, maintained, and reproduced by people interacting regularly and over time. Although institutions shape individual behavior, an individual, acting alone, cannot create an institution. Therefore, the concept of the **group** links institutions and individuals. In sociology, "group" refers to continuing interaction that involves more than one person. "Interaction" is important because, sociologically speaking, a "group" does not refer simply to a number of people. Two or three people waiting to cross a street or catch a bus do not make up a group. Rather, the term "group" suggests that the members identify with one another and have some collective purpose or interest. And "continuing" is important because groups are defined by sustained interaction, rather than the spontaneous conversation that might occur among strangers at a baseball game.

Groups differ in many ways, including by size and the amount of influence they have on members. **Primary groups,** such as families, tend to be small. The face-to-face interactions and relatively permanent, intimate ties that exist in primary groups make them highly influential (Cooley 1956). As discussed in Chapter 5, families can take various forms, but in general, the members share close relationships and provide support in times of need. A great deal of socialization takes place in families. It is here that we first become aware of others and interested in winning their approval. In our families, we learn language, including the meaning of objects and the names for the people around us. We learn how to be members of society. In addition, our families provide us with a sense of identity. Our closest friends are a primary group, too. Because of the intimacy of friendship, combined with the time we spend together, our close friends have a profound influence on what we believe and what we do.

**Secondary groups** influence their members, too, although not nearly to the same extent as primary groups do (Cooley 1956). Secondary groups lack the emotional closeness found in primary groups. They are larger and less personal than primary groups, and they do not usually last as long. A college class is an example of a secondary group. The collective purpose of learning the subject matter brings the students together. Secondary groups also socialize their members. Think about the interaction in the classes you have taken. Perhaps some classes involved discussion, and you quickly learned whether it would be free-flowing or highly structured, and whether certain students would speak more than others. Students in a class learn the expectations for conduct; in other words, they are socialized. But as much as we might enjoy our classmates, learn from them, and value their opinions, they do not shape our thoughts and actions in the ways that our families and close friends do. They don't have much lasting influence on our sense of identity, either. Once the class ends, we stop considering ourselves members of that particular group.

People are also influenced by **reference groups.** A **reference group** is "that group, real or imaginary, whose standpoint is being used as the frame of reference by the actor" (Shibutani 1961:258; see also Shibutani 1955). A reference group consists of people whose perspective we use to interpret our experiences. We identify with reference groups, seeing how well our behaviors, attitudes, and appearances measure up to theirs. Reference groups have influence over us because we strive to be like them. They support the values we use to assess our own conduct. For example, suppose you have not yet decided how to vote in an upcoming election. Suppose, too, that you have become interested in climate change and environmental protection. You see that the campus environmental group is passing out flyers supporting a particular candidate. Because you respect the group's views, you decide to vote for that candidate in the election. Alternatively, imagine that you need to buy a new computer. As you are sitting in class, you look around and notice what brands the other students are using. You decide to buy a particular brand of computer using your classmates as a reference group.

Reference groups can consist of people you will never encounter, imaginary people, and those not yet born (Shibutani 1961). For example, consider how many people measure themselves by the standards set by celebrities, such as the Kardashians. Those who yearn for "the good old days" conjure up a long-gone reference group, often one highly enhanced by imagination. A desire to save the planet for "future generations" could motivate interest in climate change and environmental activism. As you think about getting a job after graduation, you might filter what you post on social media, knowing that employers you have not yet encountered will do a search when they consider hiring you.

We can have several reference groups, depending on the context. As Shibutani explains, "Each time a man [sic] enters a new communication channel – subscribes to a new periodical, joins a new circle of friends ...or begins to listen regularly to some radio program – he is introduced into a new social world. People who communicate develop an appreciation of one another's tastes, interests, and outlook upon life.... Each man's outlook is both shaped and limited by the communication networks in which he becomes involved" (1961:258). Whereas your classmates might influence what you do in the classroom setting, they have far less influence, if any, on your conduct when you are at work or when you go out with friends on the weekend. Even within a specific setting, we engage in **selective sensitivity** when it comes to reference groups (Shibutani 1961:257). The opinions of some matter more than others do. The voices of the friends urging you to stay out just a little later might be overruled by the parental voices telling you to get home to bed.

> *Groups refer to interactions involving more than one person. Group members usually identify with one another and have some collective purpose or interest.*
>
> *Primary groups tend to be small. The face-to-face interactions and relatively permanent, intimate ties that exist in primary groups make them highly influential.*
>
> *Secondary groups are less influential than primary groups. They are larger and less personal, lacking the emotional closeness of primary groups, and they usually do not last as long.*
>
> *Reference groups are real or imaginary groups whose standpoint we use as a frame of reference for our own actions.*

## How Institutions Shape Individuals

In the rest of this chapter, we'll examine the relationship between individuals and institutions using examples from one setting; work. Work is just one of the many institutions that make up our social world. Others include education, criminal justice, language, retirement, the media, gender, and popular music.

Work illustrates the significance of institutions in people's lives in several ways. A considerable amount of adult life involves making a living. Only a very fortunate few can get by without working. Along with an income, jobs provide a sense of identity and a way to learn and use skills. Jobs structure people's time and create connections to social groups. People often think of work in individual terms, such as "my" job interview, "my" performance evaluation, "my" promotion, and "my" pay raise or bonus. "Yet, without denying the importance of our own efforts," sociologist Rudi Volti writes, "we also have to recognize that *work is a highly social activity*" (2012:ix; emphasis added). As he explains:

> Success or failure at work reflects individual performance, but it also is influenced by the performance of coworkers. The formal and informal social interaction that takes place in the workplace imparts a set of skills, values, and attitudes that heavily influences how the work is done. On a larger scale, the way a society is structured will go a long way toward determining the kind of work that is done, who does it, how they go about doing it, and what they will get for their efforts. (Volti 2012:ix)

The last part of that quote, about "determining the kind of work that is done, who does it, how they go about doing it, and what they will get for their efforts," should sound familiar. Think back to our matchstick canoe builder. As you read earlier in this chapter, these sorts of decisions represent typifications. Shared typifications become institutions. Therefore, workplaces offer ideal settings in which to examine the relationship between institutions and individuals. In what follows, we will use the context of work to consider how institutions shape people's actions and opportunities. We'll begin with an example that might seem, at least initially, extreme. Later, we'll examine how people exercise agency and resist the constraints of institutions.

In 1908, Henry Ford, the founder of the Ford Motor Company, introduced the Model T. With a price tag of $850, many Americans could purchase cars for the first time. The Model T became so popular that Ford could not keep up with production. At the time, a group of highly skilled workers made each car entirely by hand. Each one was a work of craftsmanship, and workers could complete only a few cars per day. Because machine shops in other companies produced the parts, they did not come in standard sizes. Workers had to shape each part on site to fit each car. The job required advanced metalworking skills in addition to mechanical knowledge, and workers exercised a considerable amount of judgment and decision-making in the course of building a single car (Meyer 1981).

To meet the growing demand for the Model T, Ford implemented the techniques of mass production, including the use of standardized, interchangeable parts, and a moving assembly line. Workers no longer built an entire car together. Instead, each man performed only a few routine movements on each car while a line of cars moved by. Within a few years, mass production had greatly reduced the time it took to build a car, which in turn reduced costs.

The new production methods also transformed the character of the Ford work force. The job no longer required metalworking or mechanical skills, and the production process was simplified so that workers no longer used their own judgment. The work became **deskilled** (Braverman 1974), meaning that the proverbial "man off the street" could learn the tasks in a few days (Meyer 1981:52).

The deskilling of jobs constitutes an initiative to maximize profit by reducing human error and coordinating the work force. Under deskilling, management – whether Ford or any other manufacturer – controls the production process and workers simply execute tasks that require no conceptual effort. Deskilling represents part of what Max Weber ([1922] 1968, 2011) described as ongoing "rationalization," or concern with efficiency, that characterizes modern societies. It has evolved into what sociologist George Ritzer (2008) calls "McDonaldization," whereby the principles of the fast food restaurant come to dominate numerous sectors of society. McDonald's has succeeded, Ritzer (2008:13) claims, "because it offers consumers, workers, and managers efficiency, calculability, predictability, and control." Customers who order a Big Mac – or a Starbucks coffee – get the same product regardless of who makes it.

In terms of profit, deskilling has tremendous potential. For workers, however, deskilling makes the work repetitive and boring. The workers at Ford grew alienated, estranged from the products they made and having little control over the process of production (Marx 1972). Workers became little more than cogs in the industrial machine. The mind-numbing nature of the work, combined with the non-stop assembly line and the pressure to produce more cars at a faster pace made the job dangerous. The accident rate increased with the rate of production. Men working on the line commonly lost fingers, for example, but even those who managed to avoid injury suffered from the intense heat and poor air quality in the plant.

Although *any* job seems better than being unemployed, the company could not attract sufficient numbers of workers who had the discipline of the original skilled workforce. At the time, Ford employed large numbers of immigrants. Because many of them had been peasants or farmers in their home countries, they had an orientation to work that did not suit mass production. They had no stake in their work, and they expressed their dissatisfaction with the monotony and the increased pressure through frequent absences or by simply quitting. Many walked off the job, causing the assembly line to come to a stop.

Ford needed reliable workers to keep the cars rolling off the line. To encourage employees "to alter their attitudes and habits to meet the rigorous requirements of mass production," Ford revolutionized American industry in 1914 by increasing wages and reducing the length of the workday and week (Meyer 1980:69). Workers would earn $5 a day for an eight-hour day, up from $2.34 for nine hours, five days a week. Most employers required workers to work six days.

The "Five Dollar Day" had the explicit goal of encouraging workers to adopt the "attitudes and habits" required for producing Model Ts. In addition, the higher wage would increase sales because workers on the production line could buy a Model T with about four months' pay.

Together, the practices of reorganizing production using assembly lines, standardizing parts, and deskilling labor, along with paying wages that transformed workers into consumers became known as "Fordism." Because of the success of Ford Motor Company – it became one of the most profitable companies in the world – these practices were *institutionalized*, becoming the dominant paradigm not only for building cars, but for all types of large-scale industrial production. Manufacturers all over the world followed Ford's example of industrial efficiency.

## Creating "Good Ford Men"

There is a saying that "there's no such thing as a free lunch." In a classic illustration of this, Ford's "Five Dollar Day" came with a catch. Ford considered half of the $5 – about what the workers had previously made – wages, to which all workers were entitled. The other half was considered "profits," which only "good Ford men" would share (Hooker 1997:48). "Good Ford men" were those who conformed to the expectations associated with Fordism. However, the effort the company put into selecting and creating "good Ford men" illustrates the long reach of institutions.

To determine eligibility for the profit-sharing plan, Ford Motor Company established the unfortunately named "Sociological Department." Teams of investigators from the Department went to employees' homes to determine whether they demonstrated the "thrift, good habits, and good home conditions" that characterized "good Ford men" (Hooker 1997:48). Any employees who did not measure up had six months to change their ways. Those unwilling to become the preferred type of Ford employees would lose their jobs. Through an "Americanization Campaign," immigrant employees were enrolled in the Ford English School. Immigrants also had lessons in topics that included table manners, personal hygiene, and using a bank.

In his autobiography, Henry Ford (1922:80, 111) explained, "We expect the men to do what they are told.... The organization is so highly specialized and one part is so dependent upon another that we could not for a moment consider allowing men to have their own way." In short, Ford Motor Company used the white, American middle class as its **reference group**. Ford socialized its workers so that they internalized American middle-class norms and values, in the service of increased production. Socialization reproduced "good Ford men," or workers who were compatible with Fordism.

Although Ford's methods, especially the use of "morality police" in the form of the Sociological Department, seem harsh by today's standards, organizations continue to socialize their employees. Along with employee orientation sessions, online training videos, and handbooks, they use the practice called "onboarding," to assimilate new employees into the organization the accepted ways of doing things. For example, contemporary advice for training new employees asks managers to consider this:

> Does your organization email a packet of intimidating forms to complete? Maybe herd everyone into a room to complete the forms? Send them around the building to get signatures from department heads? Is that really the way you want to welcome the people that you hope will buy into your culture, become committed, engaged long-term employees? Probably not. (Silberman, Beich, and Auerbach 2015:362)

As an alternative, managers are advised to put new employees into teams and send them on a scavenger hunt to find the human resources office, the best sandwich in the cafeteria, and the copy machine. According to this plan:

> Along the way they meet people, find their way around the building, and learn much about the organization. Of course there are prizes involved, and the best part is that they become a part of two teams – the small team of new employees and the corporate team. (Silberman, Beich, and Auerbach 2015:362)

In Chapter 6, you saw how socialization extends even to the emotional lives of workers, particularly in jobs that involve emotional labor. Hiring practices give preference to applicants who already possess the traits, such as sociability, enthusiasm, and graciousness, associated with the company's image. Training and orientation programs introduce new hires to appropriate ways to interact with customers or clients. Managers and supervisors evaluate and support or reprimand employees' ability to present the desired image.

In sum, socialization allows organizations to run smoothly. Moreover, by going beyond the requirements of the workplace and transforming the hearts and minds of employees, organizational socialization also constitutes one of the ways institutions shape and constrain individuals. Socialization never produces absolute conformity, however. If it did, we would all act like robots, simply doing what we were programmed to do, and nothing would ever change. As you read earlier in this chapter, even within the constraints of institutions, individuals have the freedom to think and to "act otherwise" (Giddens 1979:75). In other words, they can resist constraint by exercising agency. Let's look now at some examples of agency in the workplace.

## Responses to Constraint

Even in tightly controlled environments, workers find ways to resist the constraint of workplace policies and practices. As you saw above, many Ford workers found the job so intolerable that they simply walked away. Although the Five Dollar Day improved conditions, the stock market crash of 1929 and the Great Depression that followed meant that fewer people could afford to buy cars. In response to declining sales, Ford cut wages and laid off two-thirds of its work force, but required the remaining workers to maintain levels of production. On 7 March 1932, 300 current and unemployed workers marched in the bitter cold to the main factory with a list of demands (Grevatt 2009). When they arrived, police and Ford's security force began to shoot at the unarmed crowd, killing four marchers and injuring over 60 others. What began as "The Hunger March" became the "Ford Massacre" (see Baskin 1972).

Although this tragedy did not lead to immediate changes in Ford's employee relations policies, it inspired solidarity among workers, enhancing their sense of themselves as a group. Years later, autoworkers eventually gained the right to unionize and bargain collectively for fair wages and better working conditions (see Greer 2009).

The Ford Hunger March illustrates how workers engage in *formal* resistance to institutional constraint by going on strike or refusing to work, filing grievances, or taking legal action. Formal acts of resistance require collective action and a significant amount of planning. More often, workers engage in *informal* acts of resistance. Informal resistance occurs so often in workplaces that researchers refer to it as "routine" resistance (Prasad and Prasad 1998; see also Scott 1985).

Examples of informal resistance include joking on the job, which can reduce boredom and break up routine (Collinson 1988; Fine and Wood 2010). In a classic study of factory work, Donald Roy (1959:158) described "how one group of machine operators kept from 'going nuts' in a situation of monotonous work activity." The men in Roy's work group structured their day around rituals and jokes. For instance, one man brought peaches to share with the others every day. At a point in mid-morning, he would announce, "Peach time!" and the work group would break for a snack. About an hour later, one worker stole the banana another brought for lunch. The thief would announce that it was "Banana time," and proceed to help himself. Although the worker who brought the banana never actually ate it, he continued bringing one for the thief every day. Roy (1959:159) noted, "At first this daily theft startled and amazed me. Then I grew to look forward to the daily seizure and the verbal interaction which followed." Later came "Window time" and routine, playful interaction about the blast of cold air. After lunch, "Coke time" marked the afternoon break. These rituals, Roy argued, made the long day in a job with no creative outlet easier to endure.

As "banana time" also shows, humor has a social function by creating solidarity among those who engage in it. Within the constraints of the job, workers invented their own ways to have fun. Jokes differentiate members of the "joking culture" from others, particularly those in management, who are often the target of the jokes (Fine and de Soucey 2005). To be sure, not every joke told or prank pulled in the work place represents resistance. Moreover, some jokes can create a hostile work environment. Overall, however, humor can act as an outlet "for hostilities and for discontent ordinarily suppressed by the group" (Coser 1959:180).

Employees can also engage in informal resistance through expressing cynicism and taking an ironic stance toward corporate culture initiatives that include slogans, jargon, and the bestowing of certificates (Fleming and Spicer 2003; Kunda 1992). These acts of resistance take place "offstage," out of the direct view of managers and others in authority (Scott 1990). For example, in a study of a communications firm, two workers told the researcher about the employee handbook, which included fill-in-the-blank exercises on policies known as "the 3Fs":

> KIM:  Yeah, you get a handbook and it says [in a childish tone]
> "What are the 3Fs?"
> and you think [in the same sarcastic tone]
> "Oh, gee, would they be the 3Fs I saw on the other page?"
> It's very much an adult/child relationship they are trying to instigate here.
> MARK:  [in a sarcastically immature voice] I keep mine with me on my desk all the time. I might just forget the 3Fs so I can never be without it.
> KIM:  [in a fatherly voice] What about your recognition certificate, son – have you got that?
> MARK:  Of course!
> KIM:  [back to her own voice] I don't. I lost mine [laughs]. (Fleming 2005:296)

By remaining at a cynical distance, Kim and Mark informed the researcher that they did not "buy into" the institutionalized aspects of their jobs.

Other types of informal resistance include wasting time and reducing effort, a practice known as "goldbricking" (Ackroyd and Thompson 1999; Burawoy 1979). Workers can also falsify time records and steal money and property (Shigihara 2013). In jobs with high standards for customer service, such as food serving and bartending, employees can resist management's conceptions of the ideal service encounter. For example, a bartender in one study reported, "We've got more rules and regulations than the United Nations! As long as you're confident that the customer doesn't know and nobody else is looking, most of the time, you can just do your own thing. I know it's not 'customer focused,' but who'll ever know?" (Harris and Ogbanna 2002:169).

When workers engage in routine or informal resistance, they temporarily loosen some of the constraints their jobs place on them. They also establish themselves as autonomous individuals in charge of their own lives (Prasad and Prasad 1998, 2000). Acts of informal resistance involve no open aggression and pose no direct challenge to institutionalized ways of doing things. Nevertheless, these acts set limits on the influence of institutions. Informal resistance may not challenge or overturn institutionalized practices in the ways that union organizing and formal resistance make possible, but it can allow employees to construct a sense of self that contrasts with the one expected in – and even provided by – the workplace (Fleming and Spicer 2003; Goffman 1959).

## The Loss of Institutional Anchors

Although we live our lives embedded in institutions, we can also become *un*embedded in various ways. We have examined how work shapes identity and how people assert identities within the constraints of work, but what happens when people lose their jobs? This chapter began with excerpts of interviews with three people living that experience. One described the difficulty of looking for a job while unemployed. Another asked, "who am I now, without a job?" The third described job loss as "devastating," "humbling," and "humiliating." We'll use the experience of job loss to investigate what happens when people lose these institutional anchors.

In current economic conditions, job loss and long-term unemployment are commonplace. Changes in the global economic structure mean that many blue-collar jobs, especially those involving unskilled manual labor, no longer exist or don't exist in the same large numbers as in the past. Many white-collar jobs have been "outsourced" to save labor costs, either to companies that employ low-wage temporary workers or to workers located in other countries. Corporate mergers, bankruptcy, and restructuring often lead to "downsizing," permanent layoffs of hundreds or thousands of workers at once (Scott and Davis 2007). Consider just a few examples:

> In 2011, Borders, the largest bookseller in the United States, went bankrupt. It closed its stores and laid off 10,700 workers.
>
> In 2015, computer manufacturer Hewlett-Packard eliminated 30,000 jobs.
>
> In 2016, big technology companies laid off massive numbers of workers. Microsoft cut 4,700 jobs, IBM cut 5,000, and Intel cut 12,000 jobs.
>
> In 2017, department store closures meant the loss of tens of thousands of jobs. JCPenney closed 168 stores, Macy's closed 68 stores, and Sears/Kmart closed 150 stores.

Jobs provide people with several kinds of resources. At the tangible level, they provide income. Many jobs have provided benefits such as health insurance and profit sharing. Jobs provide intangible resources, too. Many are associated with **occupational prestige**, which refers to the status and esteem afforded by others. Physicians and lawyers, for example, consistently rank as the most prestigious occupations, with food servers among the lowest.

Jobs provide social connections, too, as even "banana time" reveals. Coworkers often become friends, and some can feel like family (see Kondo 2009). Add to this the finding that the number of office workers who report having a "work spouse," or a close, platonic friend of the opposite sex, may be as high as 65% (Erwin 2009), and it becomes clear that jobs deeply influence people's lives. In addition, going to work, along with the routines on the job, provide structure that organizes time. Jobs give people a reason to get up in the morning, and work routines break the day into segments. Finally, jobs also create opportunities to experience **self-efficacy**, or the sense that one can accomplish tasks and make things happen (Gecas and Schwalbe 1983).

The loss of a job constitutes "a well-documented threat to both economic and psychological well-being" (Garrett-Peters 2009:548; see also Brand 2015). Job loss brings material concerns, such as paying rent or mortgage, buying food, and meeting medical expenses. But the loss of a job can cause people to blame themselves, questioning their worth and even their sense of who they are (Cohn 1978). To be sure, the impact of the loss on depends on whether the worker had a role in bringing about the unemployment. Workers who voluntarily leave a job, and even prepare for doing so, see the experience differently (Ezzy 2000). The impact also depends on whether the worker considered the job central to the conception of him or herself. And the loss of a temporary job requiring few skills would have less of an impact than would the loss of a career one found meaningful and rewarding, in a profession for which one had studied long and hard.

## "Who am I Now?"

To gain a sense of the impact of this latter kind of loss, look again at the quotes that open this chapter. The first person imagined employment agencies looking at him and thinking, "'There must really be something wrong with you'" (Newman 1988:66). Another struggled to understand who he was without a job. He said, "I've always looked at my job as who I am." As a result, when he lost his job, he asked himself, "Who am I now?"

Questions of "what's wrong with me" and "who am I" indicate a damaged or threatened concept of oneself. As discussed in Chapter 4, Erving Goffman (1963) used the concept of **stigma** to describe spoiled identities. Goffman

(1963:3) defined stigma as an "attribute that is deeply discrediting," which reduces the bearer "from a whole and usual person to a tainted, discounted one." In short, a stigmatized person has, or is believed by others to have, some characteristic that devalues him or her (see Link and Phelan 2001). Goffman enumerated types of stigmas. Along with "tribal stigmas" that accompany race or religion (Hordge-Freeman 2015) and "abominations of the body" in the form of physical disabilities or deformities (Cahill and Eggleston 1995), unemployment constitutes a "blemish of character."

Unemployed workers cope with the associated stigma in various ways. Some engage in what Goffman (1963) called "in-group" stigma management by associating with other unemployed people in support groups for job seekers. Some redefine the meaning of unemployment as being "employed full-time to find a job" (Garrett-Peters 2009:555). Treating unemployment as a job in itself provides a goal and helps displaced workers "preserve a sense of competence" (Garrett-Peters 2009:555). As part of this, they often structured their time around job-search activities. Having free time sounds appealing at first, but, as one unemployed worker said, it is "very overrated." "You can have too much time to yourself," he said, "and when you do, when you start watching the daytime soaps and getting involved in them... then you start climbing the walls looking for jobs because you've been unemployed too long" (Ezzy 2000:129). Faced with undirected time, many unemployed workers nevertheless got up every day, Monday through Friday, as they would have done for a job. Research indicated that dedicating time to the job search helped in "restoring damaged feelings of efficacy" (Garrett-Peters 2009:562).

In sum, once shaped by the institutionalized practices of work, people who lost those institutional anchors that secured a sense of self found the need to replace them.[1] They attempt to restore the structure and consistency that work brought to their days and weeks. Some seek out affiliation with others to substitute for interaction with co-workers. Overall, jobs, and job loss, highlight the powerful influence institutions have on individuals.

## The Role of Place

Symbolic interactionist research reminds us that we experience institutions in particular places (Milligan 1998). Quite simply, a **place** is "a unique spot in the universe" (Gieryn 2000:464). Wherever you are while reading this chapter, you are in a place. It might be a library, your home, your room, a coffee shop, or a bus. That place might also be the town where your university is located, or your hometown, or somewhere you happen to be visiting. Place also has material form, or physicality. "Whether built or just come upon, artificial or natural, streets and doors or rocks and trees, place is stuff. It is a compilation of things or objects at some particular spot in the universe" (Gieryn 2000:645).

Place is not merely a setting for social interaction. Place *influences* interaction. For example, growing up is one experience in a small, rural town, and another one altogether in a large city. Watching a movie in a theater differs from watching it at home. Everything happens somewhere, and *what* happens depends on *where* it happens.

We invest places with meaning and value. A particular spot in the universe, with whatever material form we find or build there, only becomes a place because of how we interpret it, imagine it, perceive it, and talk about it. What we might first experience "as undifferentiated space becomes *place* as we get to know it better and endow it with value" Tuan (1977:6; emphasis added). For example, recall the neighborhood where you live, or perhaps the one in which you grew up. Before it became "your" neighborhood, it was just another street and set of buildings. It might not be particularly distinct or impressive in any way, but it becomes special because you know it as "yours." Anthropologist Dorinne Kondo describes this experience:

> A jumble of unfamiliar buildings when I moved in, the Tokyo neighborhood where I lived began to take on increasing familiarity and significance as impersonal facades gave way to homes populated by friends and acquaintances.... The gray house down the street was not just any gray house; it was Tanoue-san's home, where I might be invited to have a cup of tea and have a chat, if I happened by at the right time. (2009:7)

As we endow places with value, we develop emotional and symbolic bonds with them (Debenedetti, Oppewal, and Arsel 2014; Milligan 1998). The affection you feel for your house, your neighborhood, your room, or another place is known as **place attachment**. It is defined as the emotional connection between an individual and "a physical site that has been given meaning through interaction" (Milligan 1998:2; see also Altman and Low 1992; Hidalgo and Hernandez 2001). Similar to attachments to other people, place attachment "can provide feelings of security, belonging and stability" (Hay 1998:25). Place attachment involves an *interactional past*, or "the memories of interactions associated with a site" (Milligan 1998:2). In this way, memories are "placed," rather than free-floating. Place attachment also involves *interactional potential*, or "the future experiences perceived as likely or possible to occur in a site" (Milligan 1998:2). Advertising aimed at young homeowners often plays on interactional potential to sell insurance, furniture, even paint. The ads portray children taking their first steps in the home, growing up, and sharing family dinners, suggesting that the product can improve or safeguard the home's interactional potential.

Place attachment accounts not only for the connections people feel to their homes and communities. It also explains why people feel anger, distress, and even grief over the loss of these places, whether through natural disasters

(Chamlee-Wright and Storr 2009; Erikson 1976; Katovich and Hintz 1997), "urban renewal" (Fried 1963; Gans 1962; Weaver 1966), forced migration (Eastmond 2007), eviction (Desmond 2016), or other reasons. Attachment builds up slowly, over time, and disruption often happens quickly. Because place attachment links the past with the future through interactional potential, it provides a sense of continuity (Milligan 1998). Disruption through the loss of place breaks that continuity by closing off the past and leaving the future uncertain.

As we give places meaning and become attached to them, they help to create and anchor our identities. **Place identity** is situated in or symbolized by an environment (Cuba and Hummon 1993). Alongside the question of "*who* am I?" place identity responds to questions of "*where* am I?" and "where do I belong?" (Cuba and Hummon 1993:112).

Although it is easy to understand place attachment in the context of home, people also become attached to workplaces. Offices, shops, and other settings acquire meaning for those who work there every day, sometimes for years or even decades. Interactions at work establish memories and link identities to those places. The relocation of a workplace or the failure of a business can arouse strong emotions. The loss transforms the collective identity of co-workers from "who we *are*" to "who we *were*."

> A *"place"* is a unique spot in the universe.
> Place attachment is the emotional link formed to a physical site that has been given meaning through interaction.
> Place identity is an interpretation of self that situated in or symbolized by that unique spot

## Conclusion

From the symbolic interactionist perspective, understanding individuals requires understanding institutions. Institutions emerge because people repeat, or habitualize, their actions so that they become routine. People develop typifications of those actions, and of who does them. As they share typifications, the typifications become institutions. People experience institutions through interactions within groups. Their interactions occur in places endowed with meaning and significance.

In this chapter, we have examined how institutions influence people's actions and ideas. It's important to recognize that, by emphasizing the importance of institutions, symbolic interactionists do not see people as passively following the crowd, going along with what everyone else does. Interactionists leave room for agency, or the ability to "act otherwise." Thus, we have also seen examples of how people resist the influence of institutions. Symbolic interactionism has sometimes been criticized for focusing *too much* on agency and not enough on how agency is determined by social structure.

Interactionists understand the relationship between individuals and institutions as reciprocal. Social institutions shape people's actions, ideas, attitudes, and beliefs, but people influence institutions, too. Events and exposure to different groups can challenge what we take for granted. We can "color outside of the lines," as the saying goes. Doing so does not mean rejecting group membership altogether, however. Rather, when we color – or step – outside the lines of one group, we find ourselves within the lines of another. We can change groups, but we cannot escape group life altogether.

## Learning by Using the Symbolic Interactionist Perspective

Below are a few excerpts from a study Melinda Milligan (2003) conducted of a student-run coffee house that moved to a new location. Can you use any of the concepts from this chapter, such as – institutions, identity, groups, and especially the concepts related to place – to analyze the experience of the employees?

---

**The Coffee House and Employee Identity**

**Melinda Milligan (2003:385–386, 397)**

The Coffee House is a nonprofit, student-controlled restaurant located on a university campus.... It was founded in 1967 by students who wanted to create an alternative eating and socializing establishment on campus.... By the early 1990s, when this study was conducted, the organization employed approximately 200 part-time undergraduate students and two full-time managers. It required that Coffee House employees, with the exception of full-time managers, be undergraduate students at the university. The Coffee House had a reputation for serving healthy, inexpensive food that was prepared from "scratch," encouraging employee involvement in decision making, and promoting environmental awareness.

In 1991, the Coffee House relocated to a new building. Most employees opposed the move and were distraught when it took place. As noted above, at the new site those who had worked at the old location became known as "old" employees, and those who were hired after the move became known as "new" employees.

---

It was great. It was fun. It wasn't a job. You got to be loud. It was more than a place to work, it was a place to hang out with your friends and, you know, meet people who you would hang out with on the weekend. The people. The people. That's what sticks out, you know. It was just the greatest time. It wasn't working. It was fun. (Kimberly, kitchen worker)

I felt pretty negative there [after the move]. I mean I didn't enjoy it. While the old Coffee House felt like home and I was happy to go there, the new Coffee House, I was like, 'Oh, hey, I'm here to work a shift.' It was more businesslike. Yeah, it didn't have the character or the trust or the uniqueness of the old one at all. (Ricardo, kitchen worker)

The whole idea that there were traditions, there were knowns, that this is the way that stuff is done, and it kind of helps you. So the problem, I think what happened with identities when the Coffee House moved [was] that it was an unknown. It was just a huge unknown. It generated anxiety because no one knew what was going to happen and there was sort of like anger about, how could you change to something that hadn't been there before? (Anne, kitchen worker)

## Note

1 Although we focus on unemployment, the same effort is involved when other forms of loss occur, such as divorce and break-ups (Irvine 1999).

## References

Ackroyd, S. and P. Thompson. 1999. *Organizational Misbehaviour*. London: SAGE.

Altman, I. and S. M. Low, eds. 1992. *Place Attachment*. New York: Plenum Press.

Baskin, A. 1972. "The Ford Hunger March – 1932." *Labor History* 13(3):331–360.

Berger, P. and T. Luckmann. 1966. *The Social Construction of Reality: A Treatise on the Sociology of Knowledge*. Garden City, NJ: Anchor Books.

Brand, J. 2015. "The Far-Reaching Impact of Unemployment and Job Loss." *Annual Review of Sociology* 41:359–375.

Braverman, H. 1974. *Labor and Monopoly Capital. The Degradation of Work in the Twentieth Century*. New York: Monthly Review Press.

Burawoy, M. 1979. *Manufacturing Consent: Changes in the Labor Process under Monopoly Capitalism*. Chicago, IL: University of Chicago Press.

Cahill, S. E. and R. Eggleston. 1995. "Reconsidering the Stigma of Physical Disability." *The Sociological Quarterly* 36(4):681–698.

Chamlee-Wright, E. and V. H. Storr. 2009. "'There's No Place like New Orleans': Sense of Place and Community Recovery in the Ninth Ward after Hurricane Katrina." *Journal of Urban Affairs* 31(5):615–634.

Cohn, R. M. 1978. "The Effect of Employment Status Change on Self-Attitudes." *Social Psychology* 41(2):81–93.

Collinson, D. L. 1988. "'Engineering Humor': Masculinity, Joking and Conflict in Shop-Floor Relations." *Organizational Studies* 9(2):181–199.

Cooley, C. H. 1909. *Social Organization*. New Brunswick, NJ: Transaction Publishers.

Cooley, C. H. 1956. *Social Organization: A Study of the Larger Mind*. New Brunswick NJ: Transaction Publishers.

Coser, R. L. 1959. "Some Social Functions of Laughter: A Study of Humor in a Hospital Setting." *Human Relations* 12(2):171–182.

Cuba, L. and D. M. Hummon. 1993. "A Place to Call Home: Identification with Dwelling, Community, and Region." *Sociological Quarterly* 34(1):111–131.

Debenedetti, A., H. Oppewal and Z. Arsel. 2014. "Place Attachment in Commercial Settings: A Gift Economy Perspective." *Journal of Consumer Research* 40(5):904–923.

Desmond, M. 2016. *Evicted: Poverty and Profit in the American City*. New York: Penguin Random House.

Eastmond, M. 2007. "Stories as Lived Experience: Narratives in Forced Migration Research." *Journal of Refugee Studies* 20(2): 248–264.

Erikson, K. T. 1976. *Everything in Its Path: Destruction of Community in the Buffalo Creek Flood*. New York: Touchstone.

Erwin, P. 2009. "7 Signs You Have a Work Spouse." CNN.com. Retrieved January 8, 2017. http://www.cnn.com/2008/LIVING/worklife/11/10/cb.seven.signs. work.spouse/index.html?eref=rss_us.

Ezzy, D. 2000. "Fate and Agency in Job Loss Narratives." *Qualitative Sociology* 23(1):121–134.

Fine, G. A. and M. de Soucey. 2005. "Joking Cultures: Humor Themes as Social Regulation in Group Life." *Humor: International Journal of Humor Research* 18(1):1–22.

Fine, G. A. and C. Wood. 2010. "Accounting for Jokes: Jocular Performance in a Critical Age." *Western Folklore* 69(3/4):299–321.

Fleming, P. 2005. "Workers' Playtime? Boundaries and Cynicism in a 'Culture of Fun' Program." *The Journal of Applied Behavioral Science* 41(3):285–303.

Fleming, P. and A. Spicer. 2003. "Working at a Cynical Distance: Implications for Power, Subjectivity and Resistance." *Organization* 10(1):157–179.

Ford, H. and S. Crowther. 1922. *My Life and Work*. New York: Cornstalk Publishing Company.

Fried, M. 1963. "Grieving for a Lost Home." Pp. 151–171 in *The Urban Condition*, edited by L. J. Duhl. New York: Simon and Schuster.

Gans, H. J. 1962. *The Urban Villagers*. New York: Free Press.

Garrett-Peters, R. 2009. "'If I Don't Have to Work Anymore, Who Am I?': Job Loss and Collaborative Self-Concept Repair." *Journal of Contemporary Ethnography* 38(5):547–583.

Gecas, V. and M. L. Schwalbe. 1983. "Beyond the Looking-Glass Self: Social Structure and Efficacy-Based Self-Esteem." *Social Psychology Quarterly* 46(2):77–88.

Giddens, A. 1979. *Central Problems in Social Theory: Action, Structure and Contradiction in Social Analysis*. Berkeley, CA: University of California Press.

Gieryn, T. F. 2000. "A Space for Place in Sociology." *Annual Review of Sociology* 26(1):463–496.

Goffman, E. 1959. *The Presentation of Self in Everyday Life*. New York: Doubleday Anchor.

Goffman, E. 1963. *Stigma: Notes on the Management of Spoiled Identity*. Englewood Cliffs, NJ: Prentice Hall.

Greer, I. 2009. "Automobile Workers' Strikes." Pp. 389–397 in *The Encyclopedia of Strikes in American History*, edited by A. Brenner, B. Day and I. Ness. Armonk, NY: Routledge.

Grevatt, M. 2009. "The Ford Hunger March of 1932." *Workers World*. 25 March. Retrieved March 7, 2017. http://www.workers.org/2009/us/ford_hunger_march_0402.

Harris, L. C. and E. Ogbanna. 2002. "Exploring Service Sabotage: The Antecedents, Types and Consequences of Frontline, Deviant, Antiservice Behaviors." *Journal of Service Research* 4(3):163–183.

Hay, R. 1998. "Sense of Place in a Developmental Context." *Journal of Environmental Psychology* 18(1):5–29.

Hidalgo, M. C. and B. Hernandez. 2001. "Place Attachment: Conceptual and Empirical Questions." *Journal of Environmental Psychology* 21(3):273–281.

Hooker, C. 1997. "Ford's Sociology Department and the Americanization Campaign and the Manufacture of Popular Culture Among Assembly Line Workers c. 1910–1917." *Journal of American Culture* 20(1):47–53.

Hordge-Freeman, E. 2015. *The Color of Love: Racial Features, Stigma, and Socialization in Black Brazilian Families*. Austin, TX: University of Texas Press.

Irvine, L. 1999. *Codependent Forevermore: The Invention of Self in a Twelve Step Group*. Chicago, IL: University of Chicago Press.

Katovich, M. A. and R. A. Hintz Jr. 1997. "Responding to a Traumatic Event: Restoring Shared Pasts within a Small Community." *Symbolic Interaction* 20:275–290.

Kondo, D. K. 2009. *Crafting Selves: Power, Gender, and Discourses of Identity in a Japanese Workplace*. Chicago, IL: University of Chicago Press.

Kunda, G. 1992. *Engineering Culture: Control and Commitment in a High-Tech Corporation*. Philadelphia, PA: Temple University Press.

Link, B. G. and J. C. Phelan. 2001. "Conceptualizing Stigma." *Annual Review of Sociology* 27:363–385.

Martin, P. Y. 2004. "Gender as Social Institution." *Social Forces* 82(4):1249–1273.

Marx, K., trans. (1972) "Economic and Philosophic Manuscripts of 1844: Selections." Pp. 133–145 in *The Marx-Engels Reader*, edited by R. Tucker. New York: W. W. Norton.

Meyer, S., III. 1980. "Adapting the Immigrant to the Line: Americanization in the Ford Factory, 1914–1921." *Journal of Social History* 14(1):67–82.

Meyer, S., III 1981. *The Five Dollar Day: Labor Management and Social Control in the Ford Motor Company, 1908–1921*. Albany, NY: SUNY Press.

Milligan, M. J. 1998. "Interactional Past and Potential: The Social Construction of Place Attachment." *Symbolic Interaction* 21(1):1–33.

Milligan, M. J. 2003. "Displacement and Identity Discontinuity: The Role of Nostalgia in Establishing New Identity Categories." *Symbolic Interaction* 26(3):381–403.

Newman, K. S. 1988. *Falling from Grace: Downward Mobility in the Age of Affluence*. Berkeley, CA: University of California Press.

Prasad, A. and P. Prasad. 1998. "Everyday Struggles at the Workplace: The Nature and Implications of Routine Resistance in Contemporary Organizations." Pp. 225–257 in *Research in the Sociology of Organizations*, edited by P. Bamberger and W. Sonnenstuhl. Stamford, CT: JAI.

Prasad, P. and A. Prasad. 2000. "Stretching the Iron Cage: The Constitution and Implications of Routine Workplace Resistance." *Organization Science* 11(4):387–403.

Ritzer, G. 2008. *The McDonaldization of Society 5*. Thousand Oaks, CA: Pine Forge Press.

Roy, D. F. 1959. "'Banana Time': Job Satisfaction and Informal Interaction." *Human Organization* 18(4):158–168.

Scott, J. C. 1985. *Weapons of the Weak: Everyday Forms of Peasant Resistance*. New Haven, CT: Yale University Press.

Scott, J. C. 1990. *Domination and the Arts of Resistance: Hidden Transcripts*. New Haven, CT: Yale University Press.

Scott, W. R. and G. F. Davis. 2007. *Organizations and Organizing: Rational, Natural, and Open Systems Perspectives*. New York: Taylor and Francis.

Shibutani, T. 1955. "Reference Groups as Perspectives." *American Journal of Sociology* 60:562–569.

Shibutani, T.1961. *Society and Personality: An Interactionist Approach to Social Psychology*. New Brunswick, NJ: Transaction Publishers.

Shigihara, A. M. 2013. "It's Only Stealing a Little a Lot: Techniques of Neutralization for Theft Among Restaurant Workers." *Deviant Behavior* 34(6):494–512.

Silberman, M., E. Biech and C. Auerbach. 2015. *Active Training: A Handbook of Techniques, Designs, Case Examples, and Tips*, 2nd ed. Hoboken, NJ: Wiley.

Tuan, Y. 1977. *Space and Place: The Perspective of Experience*. Minneapolis, MN: University of Minnesota Press.

Volti, R. 2012. *An Introduction to the Sociology of Work and Occupations*. Thousand Oaks, CA: SAGE.

Weaver, R. C. 1966. *Dilemmas of Urban America*. Cambridge, MA: Harvard University Press.

Weber, M. [1922] 1968. *Economy and Society: An Outline of Interpretive Sociology*. New York: Bedminster Press.

Weber, M. 2011. *The Protestant Ethic and the Spirit of Capitalism: The Revised 1920 Edition*, translated by S. Kalberg. New York: Oxford University Press.

# 11

# Inequality in Interaction

"I am surrounded by black and Latino boys.

As I looked around the common room of my new dorm this was all I could think about. It was September 1993, and I was a rather young 14-year-old leaving home for the first time. My parents, who had helped me unpack my room and were about to say good-bye, noticed as well. We didn't say anything to one another. But the surprise on their faces mirrored my own. This was not what I expected, enrolling at a place like St. Paul's School. I thought I would be unlike everyone else. I thought my name and just-darker-than-olive skin would make me the most extreme outlier among the students. But though my parents grew up in small rural villages in Pakistan and Ireland and my father was not white, they had become wealthy. My father was a successful surgeon; my mother was a nurse. I had been at private school since seventh grade, and being partly from the Indian subcontinent hardly afforded one oppressed minority status. For the other boys around me, those from poor neighborhoods in America's urban centers, St. Paul's was a much more jarring experience.

I quickly realized that St. Paul's was far from racially diverse. That sea of dark skin only existed because we all lived in the same place: the minority student dorm. There was one for girls and one for boys. The other 18 houses on campus were overwhelmingly filled with those whom you would expect to be at a school that educates families like the Rockefellers and Vanderbilts. This sequestering was not an intentionally racist practice of the school. In fact the school was very self-conscious about it and a few years prior tried to distribute students of color across all houses on campus. But the non-white students complained. Though their neighborhoods of Harlem and the Upper East Side might border each other, a fairly large chasm separated the non-elite and elite students. They had difficulty living with one another. Within a year the minority student dorm returned. Non-white students were sequestered in their own space, just like most of them were in their ethnic neighborhoods back home." (Khan 2011:1–2)

*The Social Self and Everyday Life: Understanding the World Through Symbolic Interactionism*, First Edition. Kathy Charmaz, Scott R. Harris, and Leslie Irvine.
© 2019 John Wiley & Sons, Inc. Published 2019 by John Wiley & Sons, Inc.

The excerpt above comes from a book entitled, *Privilege,* by sociologist Shamus Khan (2011). The book draws on Khan's study of St. Paul's School, an elite boarding school in the northeastern United States. Khan graduated from St. Paul's in 1996 and later returned as a teacher while he also conducted research. The school enrolls only around 550 students. Describing St. Paul's as "a place where most of our nation doesn't belong" (Khan 2011:43), Khan's research focuses on the role of such schools in reproducing inequality.

The brief recollection above raises intriguing points about equality and inequality. At one level, Khan's acceptance into St. Paul's represents the fulfillment of the promise the United States has long held for immigrants: even the son of a Pakistani father and an Irish mother can attend one of the most prestigious schools in the country. One might easily see this as evidence that the United States is a level playing field, and anyone who works hard can "make it" here. Khan's experience also seemingly epitomizes the image of the United States as a "melting pot." Dark-skinned students received the same education as those who defined themselves as "WASPS," or White Anglo-Saxon Protestants. Yet, on arriving at St. Paul's, Khan found himself sequestered in minority student housing. Although this arrangement would strike most people as a clear example of discrimination, Khan points out that the students of color claimed they preferred it to living among white students.

What thoughts occurred to you as you read this excerpt from *Privilege*? Did the housing arrangement seem unequal? Does the students' perception matter for whether it constitutes discrimination? Your responses to these questions might lead you to consider broader issues. For example, does inequality exist apart from those who perceive it? Does it matter if those who are affected by a situation perceive it as unproblematic? What if those people claim to *enjoy* the situation?

These are some of the questions we'll address in this chapter. To begin, we'll examine different ways of approaching the topic of inequality.

## Studying Inequality

Many sociologists take the existence of inequality for granted. They assume that it exists "out there," objectively, as an "inherent aspect of the social landscape" (Harris 2001:463, 456). Some consider inequality "a universal feature of all human societies" (Turner 1986:77). In treating inequality as an unfortunate but pervasive fact of society, sociologists have typically focused on three main dimensions: class or economic issues, such as one's income or wealth; power, or the amount of influence and control one can exert over others; and status, or the respect, honor, or esteem one receives.

This perspective on inequality has a long history in sociology, dating back to the work of the founding fathers, Karl Marx and Max Weber. Although their ideas about stratification differed, both Marx and Weber emphasized the pervasiveness and importance of disparities in these areas. Over the past several decades, sociologists have followed their lead. Inequality has become not just one of many topics studied by sociologists, but a central focus of the field (Best 2018; Cancian 1995). Using quantitative methods such as survey research, sociologists often analyze large-scale economic data on wages and employment or poverty rates. They map trends in income and wealth, tracing the comparative rise or fall of the working, middle, and upper classes. Starting in the 1970s, sociologists added race and gender to the mix. They have since studied the impact of discrimination on opportunities to earn high salaries and obtain positions of authority and respect.

This approach has its merits. For instance, if one defines inequality in terms of income disparities, then one can document that, among full-time workers in the United States, women made 80% of every dollar earned by men in 2015 (Hegewisch and DuMonthier 2016). This approach can also tell us that 43.1 million Americans lived in poverty in 2015 (Proctor, Semega, and Kollar 2016).

Symbolic interactionism can enrich the understanding of inequality by paying attention to the *meaning* of situations considered unequal. Situations that people consider "equal" or "unequal" are usually open to multiple interpretations. Any claims people make about inequality will always depend on the purposes and perspectives of those making them (Harris 2000). Here's an example of how this works.

Consider one person's $50000 annual household income and another's $100000 income. One person makes twice as much as the other; doesn't that constitute inequality? Well, it all depends. To a homeless person struggling to scrape together a few dollars to buy a meal, the question might seem absurd. When you have nothing at all, a debate over tens of thousands of dollars makes little sense. Both individuals may seem "rich." Moreover, someone who holds the perspective that money can't buy happiness would consider differences in income irrelevant.

Suppose the two people in this example work at the same job. Suppose, too, that the person with the $50000 a year income had just graduated from college, and the person with the $100000 income had the same level of education plus 10 years of experience. Would the difference seem unfair? Suppose, however, that they have the *same* level of education and experience, but the person making $100000 is a man and the one making $50000 is a woman. In that situation, does it represent inequality? What if they both made $50000 a year at their jobs, but the one with the $100000 income had purchased a winning lottery ticket? Does inequality exist in *that* situation?

No objective indicators *require* labeling a situation in which an individual or group has more wealth than another does as "unequal." We could call it fairness based on merit, or attribute it to karma. Descriptions of situations as equal or unequal are **interpretive accomplishments.** Inequality is not inherent in income or class differences; rather, people attach the label of "inequality" to such situations (Harris 2000, 2001). Unequal annual incomes or unequal treatment *might* represent inequality, or they might not. Recall that, in Khan's study of St. Paul's School, the students of color reportedly *preferred* separate housing. Simply put, context matters. Different individuals and groups may have different interpretations of the contexts surrounding potential inequalities, including whether or how much those contexts matter.

> **Inequality primarily relies on definitions of unjust disparities between people and provides ways to understand their situations and relationships.**

To grasp how characterizing difference as inequality represents an interpretive act, let's consider some examples. The first comes from a study of children's conduct in public. An approximately four-year-old boy is holding on to a pant leg of a man in a checkout queue at a discount department store. While they wait, the woman immediately behind the man in the queue makes faces at the boy. He calmly looks up at her for a few moments and then pointedly sticks out his tongue. At that very moment, the man turns his head and sharply inquires: "What are you doing?" The boy replies: "Daddy, she's making faces at me." The man informs the boy that "she was only joking around" and instructs him to "tell the lady you're sorry." The boy furrows his brow and purses his lips but complies (Cahill 1987:397).

In this scenario, the father reminds the boy that children must **defer** to adults by respecting their requests (Goffman 1956). As anyone who has been a child knows, children cannot expect adults to reciprocate by showing deference to *them*. A hierarchy gives adults greater social power, relative to children. The boy's reaction to his father's request – note that he apologized but scowled while doing so – suggests that he resented being held to a different standard, compared to the (adult) woman. At one level, the father was simply "teaching the uninitiated what morally responsible public actors must know and do" (Cahill 1987:396). However, as Cahill writes, "there is also a more immediate lesson. When in public places, the young always must be mindful of the overwhelming dominance and dictates of their ever watchful elders" (Cahill 1987:396).

Would you describe the interaction between father and son as unequal? One could easily see a situation involving "overwhelming dominance" that way. Certainly, the relationship between children and adults, and between parents and children, is asymmetrical. Few people would see it as a case of *inequality*, however, in the sense of an injustice that should end immediately. Typically, people do not interpret the unequal relationships that exist between adults and children as "inequality," in the sense of unfairness or oppression. Instead, we consider the authority adults have over children as normal. Guiding a child in polite conduct exemplifies good parenting, not oppression.

In this example, you can see that "inequality" takes on meaning through our perceptions of situations. In other words, in every situation, "some interpretive assembly is required" (Harris 2001:457). People "assemble" inequality when they notice ambiguous actions, such as a parent scolding a child and ignoring the parallel actions of a nearby adult, and define them as injustice, rather than good parenting. Let's examine other ways that people interpret ambiguous situations differently.

Much of the traditional research on marriage assumes that "equality is simply an objective characteristic that relationships possess to varying degrees" (Harris 2009:214; Hochschild and Machung 1989; Schwartz 1994). Sociologists then attempt to measure how much equality exists in a marriage. They ask couples who controls the finances, for example, or who does which household tasks, whose sexual needs have priority, or who has the power to make major decisions (Deutsch 1999; Shelton and John 1996; Straus and Yodanis 1995). They assign numerical values to the responses. They eventually produce "a quantitative representation of the level of equality" that exists within a marriage (Harris 2009:216). This allows researchers to correlate marital inequality scores with other variables, such as race and ethnicity, marital satisfaction, level of education, or income.

Interactionist research on marriage suggests another approach. Rather than setting out to determine the causes and extent of inequality, Scott Harris (2001) asked couples to decide for themselves whether their marriages were equal or unequal, as well as how so. When Harris interviewed participants, he didn't ask which partner did more of the housework or had more influence on decisions. He allowed people to talk about what mattered to them, and how they understood equality and inequality.

Harris found that the particulars of couples' situations could be interpreted in various ways, including, but not limited to, inequality. For example, he interviewed a man he called Wayne,[1] who described his marriage as unequal mainly because his wife, Tonya, had become increasingly domineering. She dictated what he could and could not do. The couple owned a small hotel and ran it together. Both Wayne and Tonya had children from previous marriages, and Wayne felt particularly frustrated because Tonya made it difficult for him to visit his children. He regularly worked the front desk at the hotel while Tonya visited *her* children, but when he wanted a day off to visit *his* children, he found that she had already made her own plans and could not cover the desk for him. Wayne interpreted his situation as unequal, but the examples he used could just as easily have illustrated poor planning or a lack of communication about schedules.

Similarly, a woman named Deborah told Harris her marriage was *completely* unequal. She described her husband, Bill, as "old fashioned," a "'control freak' who enjoyed making the rules and feeling like 'the man of the house'" (2006:79). To make her point, she said that she frequently went into the bathroom while

Bill was using it. She saw nothing wrong with this. Bill became angry, however, and told Deborah that he wanted privacy. She described Bill's reaction as unfair, and it counted as evidence that he was on a "power trip." Yet from another perspective, Deborah's behavior may have seemed rude for not respecting Bill's privacy.

*Because situations and conditions have many possible meanings, people must notice and interpret them as unequal to understand them as such.*

Further evidence that inequality is an interpretive act comes in the way people sometimes revise their interpretations in retrospect. They come to interpret a situation or relationship they once considered acceptable as unequal or exploitive. A poignant example comes from the memoir of a noted Austrian woman named Adelheid Popp. Born in 1869, Popp rose from the poorest ranks of the working class to become a noted socialist activist (Kelly 1987; Maynes 1995). Popp's abusive father died when she was six years old, forcing her to work part time to help support her family. By age 10, she left school to work full time. Her memoir includes this recollection:

> When I'd rush to work at six o'clock in the morning, other children of my age were still sleeping. And when I hurried home at eight o'clock at night, then the others were going to bed, fed and cared for. While I sat bent over my work, lining up stitch after stitch, they played, went walking or sat in school. (Maynes 1995:63–64)

Popp recalls that, apart from occasionally hoping "just once to sleep in," she accepted her situation (Maynes 1995:64). She described herself as "thoroughly imbued with the feeling that my destiny was to work" (Kelly 1987:129). Much later, Popp saw the economic inequality that forced her into relentless work as a child. This understanding left her "overcome by a feeling of boundless bitterness because I had never enjoyed childhood pleasures or youthful happiness" (Maynes 1995:64). Of course, Popp's was not the only interpretation that changed. Society's view of child labor also changed. Today, advanced nations have outlawed the labor that Popp, and millions of other children, considered her "destiny."

Another example of retrospective reinterpretation comes from recollections of two sociologists who attended Harvard University 20 years apart. Beth Hess (1999:1) recounts that, during her time on the Harvard campus in the mid-1940s, "a rather large library was built, but without toilet facilities for women students, a potential problem that was solved by simply barring us from the building."

Some history will clarify the impact of this recollection. Before the Internet made articles and hard-to-obtain books widely available to students, professors placed books and hard copies of the readings they assigned in their courses "on reserve" at the library. Students could then obtain the materials for two-hour periods, and sometimes overnight. Libraries also used this arrangement before photocopying made it easy to reproduce print materials. Students devoted considerable time to taking notes from the readings before returning them to the library. By barring women from the library, Harvard University also prevented women from obtaining the resources required for their courses.

Reflecting on how she and her female classmates reacted, Hess recalls that they "thought it quite stupid, but then so were most of the other ways in which women were treated on a campus that would rather not have had us there, and so grateful were we simply to be permitted into the sacred precincts that it never occurred to us to protest" (Hess 1999:1–2; see also Ulrich 2004). Today, no university library in the United States could legally bar women from entering. Title IX of the Education Amendments of 1972 prohibits discrimination based on sex. In the 1940s, however, laws, norms, and attitudes differed.

The "rather large library" that Hess described is Harvard's Lamont Library. Recalling her experience in the 1960s, sociologist Evelyn Nakano Glenn, writes, "the readings for our courses were reserved in two places, the Social Relations and Lamont libraries. The latter permitted entry only to men and was the only one open on Sundays" (Glenn 1997:73). Because of this arrangement, "the men students had twice as much opportunity during the week and an extra day on the weekend to do the reserve reading" (Glenn 1997:73). To keep up with her courses, Glenn had to ask her husband, who was not a student, to obtain the required readings for her from Lamont Library.

Just as "it never occurred" to Hess and the women students of the 1940s to protest, Glenn, too, recalls that, without a name for sexist practices, "none of the women students, myself included, directly challenged this arrangement" (Glenn 1997:74). After the 1970s, however, "gender inequality" became relevant as a concept for making sense of social life. Women attending Harvard today have full access to Lamont Library, and any effort to ban them, or to give men double the opportunity to learn, would surely generate protests.

Although equal library access for both sexes seems assured today, other issues will become relevant over time. Interpretations of inequality do not always take the same familiar forms. Its meaning is always subject to interpretation.

> *People act based on their perceptions of inequality, if and when the issue becomes relevant to them.*

## Reproducing Inequality through Interaction

Once people interpret a situation as unequal, their interpretations influence their subsequent interaction. In other words, once you see a situation in a particular way, as unfair, it can be difficult to see it any other way. Your perception will shape how you think about and behave within that situation. If you see a situation as unfair, for example, you might harbor some resentment toward others. You might behave differently toward them than you would if you felt as if you were treated fairly. In this section, we'll consider some of the interactional strategies that often appear in situations of inequality. Examining these strategies will illustrate how inequality is maintained and reproduced through common, everyday interaction (Schwalbe et al. 2000).

## Boundary Maintenance

The persistence of inequality requires boundaries between dominant and subordinate groups. In this context, the term "boundaries" refers to the various ways social groups differentiate themselves by including some people, beliefs, and ways of doing things and excluding others (Epstein 1992; Lamont 2001). Boundaries of this sort exist symbolically, rather than physically or objectively, as in walls or fences. These boundaries are "conceptual distinctions" (Lamont and Molnár 2002:168). We make these sorts of distinctions throughout everyday life. We rather arbitrarily lump some things together based on similarity (Zerubavel 1996). We consider both a pen and a pencil writing instruments, and we count both carrots and cheese as food. We also split things we arbitrarily consider to be different. We distinguish writing instruments from food, for example. And although both carrots and cheese are food, they also differ; we put carrots and cheese in their respective categories of vegetables and dairy products.

We also make distinctions about people and groups of people (see Wilkins, Mollborn, and Bó 2014). These, too, are arbitrary, rather than objective or logical. We distinguish the working class from the middle and upper class. We distinguish people by gender, race, ethnicity, and religion, and we distinguish "us" from "them." Boundary maintenance is one of the interactional mechanisms through which people perpetuate difference.

When Shamus Khan returned to St. Paul's as a teacher and researcher, he witnessed a powerful example of how interaction maintains boundaries between groups of people. He realized that many members of the cleaning staff had worked there since his student days. On encountering one staff member, Khan (Khan 2011:53) wrote, "I was embarrassed that I did not remember her." In retrospect, he regretted that generations of St. Paul's students "interact with most staff by ignoring them" (2011:54). Students seldom know the names of people who clean the buildings, maintain the grounds, or prepare and serve their meals. For example, students have long known one cafeteria staff member only as the "Milk Gnome," because of his short stature and his responsibility for restocking the milk (Khan 2011:72).

One day, Khan asked a cleaner named Suzanne why he didn't know her name and why they had never interacted. She responded:

> Because you don't have to, *Shamus*; and we know not to." As she said my name, she pointed forcefully to the upper left-hand area of her

shirt. Suzanne wears a nametag. The message was clear: she knows and is expected to know my name; no such expectation exists for me. I am provided a tag to look at when needed. (Khan 2011:67; emphasis original)

Although ignoring people might seem like normal adolescent self-absorption, something deeper is at work in this example. When those who hold positions of privilege disregard members of marginalized groups, they reinforce a symbolic boundary. At St. Paul's, status and power differences allow the students to ignore the staff, rendering them socially irrelevant. Staff members become what Goffman (1963:83–84) called "nonpersons," or "objects not worthy of a glance." Many African American scholars have noted how not having one's presence acknowledged by white people preserves the "color line" (DuBois [1903] 1989), or the boundary that defines races (e.g. Collins 1990; Cooper 1892; Rollins 1985). Research on the homeless, another marginalized group, reveals that they are routinely "ignored or avoided" by passers-by, except when they receive "negative attention," such as taunting (Snow and Anderson 1993:199; see also Irvine, Kahl, and Smith 2012). Through interaction, this preserves the boundary between the "haves" and the "have-nots."

By ignoring the staff members and failing to learn their names, the students at St. Paul's maintain the boundary that sets the elite apart from everyone else. Granted, few students openly *intended* to define themselves as superior to the staff. Nevertheless, their conduct illustrates how boundary maintenance reproduces inequality.

> *Through creating and maintaining boundaries, social groups differentiate themselves by including some people, beliefs, and ways of doing things, and excluding others.*

## Othering

Boundaries delineate differences between groups, but inequality requires designating some groups as not only different, but also as inferior and undeserving of a share of the resources, whatever those might be. For example, in *Harry Potter and the Philosopher's Stone*, Draco Malfoy and Harry meet while being fitted for school robes at Madam Malkin's. Malfoy asks Harry whether his parents were "our kind," meaning a "pure-blood" wizard, and the only kind Malfoy sees as deserving of an education in magic and wizardry. Not realizing that the orphaned Harry is himself a half-blood wizard, Malfoy says, "I really don't think they should let the other sort in, do you? They're just not the same, they've never been brought up to know our ways" (Rowling 1997:61). The "other sort" refers to the "Muggles," the children of non-magical parents and the victims of discrimination and prejudice by those who value blood lineage.

By distinguishing "our kind" from the "Muggles," Malfoy engages in the process known as **Othering** (Fine 1994). His interaction with Harry illustrates how the production of inequality begins with defining oneself or one's own group as superior, or as an "in-group." Thus defined, the in-group then sets the standards against which it measures the "out-group." Through Othering, the in-group constructs the out-group as not only different, but also inferior in some sense, such as economically, morally, intellectually, or, in Malfoy's example, genetically (Fine 1994; Schwalbe et al. 2000).

In the "real" world, as in the world of Harry Potter, Othering reproduces inequality by marking those considered "different" from oneself or from the mainstream. In a study of elementary-school-aged children in the U.S., Barrie Thorne (1993) observed Othering in classrooms and on playgrounds. Consider, for example, the common cultural ritual known as "cooties." This involves designating an individual as symbolically capable of contaminating other children through touch or even through presence. In children's culture, girls typically possess a unique ability to give boys cooties, while boys cannot contaminate girls or other boys. Therefore, the ritual of cooties makes girls, but not boys, into Others.

Although cooties might seem like harmless play, perceiving someone as a source of contamination constitutes "a powerful statement of social distance and claimed superiority" (Thorne 1993:75; see also Thorne and Luria 1986). Through the ritual of cooties, children learn, and communicate a hierarchy that positions boys above girls. This "harmless" element of children's culture thus reproduces existing gender inequalities. Male superiority keeps boys free of cooties. It also prescribes the appropriate standards of behavior that keep boys in the dominant group. Thorne found that most boys upheld the gendered standards; few played with girls, for instance. Notably, one boy who occasionally played with girls endured teasing from classmates of both sexes (Pascoe 2005; Thorne 1992:117). Thus, girls, too, participated in Othering and the reproduction of gender inequality.

On or off the school playground, inequality, and Othering exist as reciprocal processes (Schwalbe et al. 2000). Inequality occurs when a person or group gains some advantage, such as money or social status, at the expense of another person or group. Othering establishes categories of people as inferior and undeserving, and therefore as exploitable, from the viewpoint of the dominant group. The power of the dominant group ensures that its viewpoint becomes "reality." The existence of allegedly inferior, undeserving Others justifies their continued exploitation by the dominant group.

*Differences between groups translate into the inferiority of out-groups through the interactional process known as Othering.*

## Microaggressions

An Asian American student's classmates tell her that she speaks English very well. A biracial student is continually asked, "What are you?" A Mexican-American student's white friends tell him they think of him as white. A white student tells her African American friend, "I don't see color. I only see people."[2]

Although overt forms of racial discrimination have become less acceptable in the post-civil-rights era, discrimination continues to manifest itself in face-to-face interaction through **microaggressions**. These include remarks, such as the examples above, that "communicate hostile, derogatory, or negative racial slights and insults to the target person or group" (Sue 2010:5; see also Pierce 1970). Microaggressions also include nonverbal behaviors or gestures, such as eye-rolling, ignoring, or scrutinizing. Together, they represent an important means of reproducing inequality. They reflect attitudes of inclusion and exclusion seen in Othering.

Microaggressions have a powerful impact on their targets (Bonilla-Silva 2010). They can make a classroom, workplace, or campus feel unwelcome and even hostile (Solórzano, Ceja, and Yosso 2000). Members of targeted groups can feel invisible, isolated, and afraid. A speaker's denial of racist meaning or intention (e.g. "I didn't mean it that way" or "I was just kidding") and the strategy of blaming the victim ("You're too sensitive") may exacerbate the consequences of microaggressions. The ambiguity of microaggressions places people of color in the position of discerning the meaning of the interaction and determining whether the slight was intentional. The stress of continually coping with microaggressions and determining appropriate responses can impair academic or job performance (Sue, Capodilupo, and Holder 2008).

From the perspective of the speaker (or perpetrator; Sue et al. 2008), microaggressions can seem trivial. Moreover, speakers are often unaware that they have engaged in an offensive act. Consequently, microaggressions pit the views of whites, who hold the power to define the interaction in nonracial terms, against the racial experiences of people of color. For a white person who sees him or herself as bias-free and non-racist, the realization that one is not free of prejudices challenges the perception of oneself as a good person. The claim of colorblindness, as in "I don't see color," denies responsibility for perpetuating racial inequality. Only those in positions of power have the luxury of not seeing race. People of color and members of disadvantaged groups face constant reminders of difference. For members of the dominant group, being aware of biases, rather than claiming they don't exist, opens up possibilities for addressing discrimination and prejudice.

*Microaggressions communicate hostile, derogatory, or negative racial slights, and insults to the target person or group.*

## Subordinate Adaptation

Whereas Othering and microaggressions reproduce inequality, additional interactional strategies help members of subordinate groups adapt to inequality. They can even help people in disadvantaged groups wrest some power from the system that has disadvantaged them. These strategies entail accepting existing hierarchical arrangements but finding ways to make existence within the hierarchy less problematic. As Harris (1997:4) writes, "many types of relationships can be quite satisfying despite being characterized by status inequality." Here, for instance, an undergraduate student describes accepting unequal status to preserve a friendship:

> In [my friend's] mind, I will always be inferior. I can't be nearly as smart; I'm still in school and, at that, it is only a state school, not a university. Many view this friendship as nothing short of pathetic, but to me it has made me a stronger person, for I have learned tolerance, not to take myself too seriously, and if I can't like myself how are others supposed to? (Harris 1997:8)

The rewards for this unequal friendship came through lessons in tolerance and personal strength. Other relationships, such as those between teachers and students or mentors and protégés, while unequal, can also bring mutual rewards. However, adapting to inequality reproduces larger systems of disadvantage. Members of lower status groups can accept arrangements that demean or devalue them but still gain from associating with the dominant group. This is known as "trading power for patronage" (Schwalbe et al. 2000:427).

Studies of "little sister" groups on college campuses illustrate this well (Stombler 1994; Stombler and Martin 1994). Little sisters are women who serve as mascots at fraternities. In choosing little sisters, fraternity men seek women they deem attractive, who like to "attend parties, smile and laugh, flirt, and who were agreeable" (Stombler and Martin 1994:156). Fraternities use little sisters to recruit new members; the promise of access to desirable young women gives a fraternity a competitive edge over others (Martin and Hummer 1989). Little sisters do not attain full membership in the fraternities, however. Their role is to make the fraternity house a "nice place to be," and "'take care' of the guys" (Martin and Hummer 1989:467). In return for their service, little sisters gain the approval and companionship of men who "often dominate the top positions of student government, service organizations, and intramural sports" (Stombler 1994:298).

The example of little sisters reveals how young women accept and adapt to inequality on college campuses by winning the favor of men, who hold higher status. Little sisters accept the rules that disadvantage women in exchange for whatever power the men will grant them. One might easily dismiss this example as outdated. After all, aren't men and women equal today? What's the problem if attractive young women want to use their looks to gain the attention of fraternity brothers?

It's true that men and women have equal access to higher education today. Universities can no longer prohibit women from entering libraries, as you saw in the recollections of Beth Hess and Evelyn Nakano Glenn. Moreover, women are now more likely than men to obtain four-year degrees (Snyder, Dillow, and Hoffman 2008).[3] But equal access, and the numerical success of women, does not translate into equality of experience. On American college campuses in the twenty-first century, women's *social* status continues to come mainly from their *"erotic* status," or their "sexual appeal to powerful men on campus" (Hamilton 2014:250). In an extensive study of college fraternities and sororities, DeSantis (2007) found that "at virtually every institution of higher education in the United States, fraternities sponsor activities, usually under the guise of a fundraiser, aimed at getting women to perform for them" (DeSantis 2007:69). Examples include beauty pageants, talent shows, cheerleading competitions, and dance contests.

Why is this a problem? If the little sisters enjoy the fraternity brothers' attention, what's wrong with using their sexuality to win it? Research responds to these questions by asking who ultimately benefits from arrangements such as these (Giuffre and Williams 1994; Wilkins 2004). Clearly, little sister organizations and fraternities benefit men. Regardless of whether the young women enjoy the attention they receive, the fraternity subculture leaves women no option *but* to trade on their desirability. Although the women who participate usually recognize the subordinate position in which these activities place them, they also understand "that there is no substitute for inviting sexuality" for winning "positive attention from men" (DeSantis 2007:71).

The pressure to be nice, to flirt, and to defer to men creates vulnerability on the part of women. Some men exploit this vulnerability to extract nonconsensual sex. According to reliable estimates, between one in four and one in five women experience attempted or completed rape while enrolled in college (Boyle 2015; Fisher, Cullen, and Turner 2000). A higher proportion of rapes are perpetrated by fraternity members, in fraternity houses, or after fraternity events (Armstrong, Hamilton, and Sweeney 2006; Murnen and Kohlman 2007). This fact does not condemn all fraternities, or all fraternity members. Rather, it reveals that the fraternity subculture means one experience for men and another one entirely for women. A system that places women at greater risk of sexual victimization is one that reproduces gender inequality.

Little sisters and other college women might well enjoy the attention they receive from fraternity brothers. Their attention is part of the "reward" for adapting to subordination. But enjoyment does not preclude the possibility that inequality is at work. Rather, it masks the gender inequalities of a system that values women only for their desirability.

It is essential to understand that the fraternity system also reproduces racial inequality. Fraternities on American college campuses are segregated not only by gender, but also by race. Although their constitutions officially prohibit racial discrimination, white fraternities continue to exclude nonwhite candidates for membership (Hughey 2007, 2010; Ray 2013). Moreover, white fraternity brothers seldom consider women of color as little sisters (Stombler and Martin 1994).

> *Members of subordinate groups sometimes cope with inequality by accepting hierarchical arrangements but finding ways to make existence within the hierarchy less problematic.*
>
> *Trading power for patronage involves accepting subordinate status while deriving benefits from association with the dominant group.*

## Emotion Management

Inequality has emotional consequences. Reflect for a moment on the children's ritual of cooties. How do you imagine the target – the girl designated as having cooties – felt in being singled out? How did the other children feel in singling her out? Recall that the little sisters of a fraternity often enjoy the attention of a group of young men. How do you imagine it makes them feel? What do the fraternity brothers feel in the company of attractive, sociable young women?

As you now recognize, people reproduce inequality in interaction through Othering, boundary maintenance, and subordinate adaptation. To be effective, these interactional strategies must have emotional impact. The children instigating the ritual of cooties must generate collective enthusiasm about targeting a "carrier." They must also lack sympathy for the pain of the child designated as Other. The Other would likely feel anger and resentment about not being given the respect the other children take for granted. And fear of embarrassment might prevent her from telling teachers and parents about the "game" and thereby ending it. Thus, maintaining a system of inequality, even on the playground, depends on generating some emotions and managing others (Fields, Copp, and Kleinman 2006).

In Chapter 6, we introduced **emotion management,** which occurs when people attempt to shape their own, or others' emotional experiences and displays. We don't just "have" emotions. We actively "work" on them to conform to norms about what we should feel in a situation (Hochschild 1979). Emotion management plays an important role in reproducing inequality. People hold beliefs that justify hierarchies, such as race, class, gender. These beliefs are most "effective" when people feel strongly about them (Fields et al. 2006). Consequently, emotions sustain the beliefs that reproduce inequality. Some examples will illustrate how this works.

Jennifer Pierce (1995) studied the emotional labor that occurs within law firms. Recall that emotional labor is emotion management that is required, implicitly or explicitly, in one's paid work. Pierce compared the emotional labor done by trial lawyers, most of whom are men, with the emotional labor of paralegals, who are mostly women. She found that beliefs about emotion and gender combined to reproduce gender inequality in the firm.

The male lawyers often relied on aggression and intimidation, generally considered acceptable masculine forms of behavior because of their association with domination and control. The male lawyers also engaged in "highly emotional, dramatic, flamboyant, shocking presentations" intended to "evoke sympathy, distrust, or outrage" in the courtroom (Pierce 1995:53). Even their acts of friendliness were "strategic." The paralegals' job, in contrast, involved reassuring clients and witnesses and deferring to attorneys. Their gender and their lower status in the firm brought expectations to be pleasant, understanding, and supportive, behaviors typically associated with women, and even with mothering. The caretaking emotional labor served to justify the lower status of the paralegals, while the adversarial emotional labor of the male lawyers justified their greater power – and salaries. Thus, emotion management reproduced the hierarchies of gender and occupation in the law firm.

Research has also examined the role of emotions in maintaining racial inequality. Amy Wilkins (2012) studied emotion management among African American men in predominantly white universities. To participate successfully in the university setting, African American men must avoid being stereotyped as "the angry black man," described as one who "perceives racial discrimination everywhere and consequently is always enraged" (Wingfield 2007:12). Although anger is culturally associated with masculinity, upwardly mobile *black* men must defy masculine emotional expectations by controlling their anger and appearing non-threatening (Collins 2004; Wingfield 2010; see also Hughey 2008). In addition, the image of the "angry black man" restricts the expression of feelings of race-based discrimination.

To succeed in a setting dominated by the white middle class, many African American university men adopt an emotion management strategy Wilkins calls "moderate blackness." This connotes "emotionally restrained, politically temperate black people who get along well with whites" (Wilkins 2012:36). Moderate blackness helps individual men establish identities as "easygoing black people who aren't 'out to start a revolution'" (Wilkins 2012:36). This tactic allows them to avoid racial conflict and fit in among white peers.

Moderate blackness makes the black university men's lives less problematic by making racial subordination tolerable at the individual level. However, precisely because it makes subordination tolerable, it also perpetuates inequality. Because it relies on the stereotype of "the angry black man" as a contrast, the emotion management involved in moderate blackness inhibits black men's ability to express anger, even when appropriate and legitimate. They must manage their emotions to express "calm resignation or perhaps shame at their lowly position, but not hostility or outrage" (Harris 2015:27). Moreover, the need to distance themselves from the stereotype diminishes the likelihood that the men will challenge race-related discrimination.

> *Sustaining a system of inequality requires the management of emotions associated with advantages and disadvantages.*

## Resisting and Challenging Inequality

As you have seen, people create and maintain inequality through face-to-face interaction. They face emotional risks by violating boundaries or not conforming to expectations. Nevertheless, research indicates that people *do* step out of their comfort zones and resist or challenge inequality.

In the study of marriage discussed above, Harris found that both Wayne and Deborah found ways to stand up to their spouses. For example, after giving in to Tonya for "years and years," Wayne had started to say, "I don't like the way you're treating me" (Harris 2001:468, 469). Deborah began to confront Bill for his manipulating and controlling ways. Whereas Bill's harsh responses and yelling once made her feel that she had done something wrong, Deborah said, "now I just put it to him like, 'Stop playing head trips because I'm not doing anything wrong and I'm not gonna deal with it'" (Harris 2001:470).

Other research offers examples of how people resist inequality in face-to-face interaction. For example, when a passerby shouts to a homeless person, "Get a job, you lazy bum," the person might respond by declaring, "I ain't no bum" (Snow and Anderson 1993:214). By distancing him or herself from the slur, the homeless person also copes with the individual consequences of inequality, namely, the stigma of homelessness.

Face-to-face interaction offers ongoing opportunities for people to challenge and resist inequalities. Taking such opportunities might involve confronting the person who tells a joke about race, class, gender, or sexual preference (Bonilla-Silva and Forman 2000; Ronai, Zsembik, and Feagin 2014). Another opportunity might arise for questioning the absence of non-dominant groups' history, culture, and perspectives in school curricula, the political arena, and countless other social contexts (Collins 1990; Epstein 1996). Undoing inequality also involves challenging dominant understandings to "de-other" identity groups such as ethnic and religious minorities and people with disabilities (Davis 2006). It might also lead to engagement in social movements or efforts to change policies (Gould 2009). Whatever form it takes, it will involve emotional risk on the part of those who resist (Goodwin, Jasper, and Polletta 2009). Although the outcome of these efforts cannot be known in advance, one thing is clear: nothing will change without them.

## Conclusion

Some sociologists who study inequality take its existence as an objective fact. In other words, they take inequality for granted and focus on the distribution of resources within a society. They then measure how much inequality exists by studying disparities in income or wealth, power, or status. Another perspective on inequality approaches it as an interpretation of a situation. This perspective assumes that situations are usually open to multiple interpretations, including those that people consider "equal" and "unequal." The purposes and perspectives of those making the interpretations influence the perceptions of situations as equal or unequal situations.

Symbolic interactionism can enrich the understanding of the experience of inequality whether approached as a fact or as an interpretation. In this chapter, we have focused on interactionism's insights into how people interpret situations as unequal. We have also considered how they reproduce, adapt to, and challenge inequality in face-to-face interaction.

## Learning by Using the Symbolic Interactionist Perspective

The series of excerpts below comes from a famous essay by Brent Staples, an editorial writer for *The New York Times*. Staples holds a Ph.D. in psychology from the University of Chicago. His essay appeared in 1986, first in *Ms* magazine and later in *Harper's*. It has been widely reprinted over the years. See which of the ideas from this chapter you can apply to his experience.

---

**Black Men and Public Space**

---

**Staples (1986)**

My first victim was a woman – white, well dressed, probably in her early twenties. I came upon her late one evening on a deserted street in Hyde Park, a relatively affluent neighborhood in an otherwise mean, impoverished section of Chicago. As I swung onto the avenue behind her, there seemed to be a discreet, uninflammatory distance between us. Not so. She cast back a worried glance. To her, the youngish black man – a broad six feet two inches with a beard and billowing hair, both hands shoved into the pockets of a bulky military jacket-seemed menacingly close. After a few more quick glimpses, she picked up her pace and was soon running in earnest. Within seconds she disappeared into a cross street.

That was more than a decade ago, I was twenty-two years old, a graduate student newly arrived at the University of Chicago. It was in the echo of that terrified woman's footfalls that I first began to know the unwieldy inheritance I'd come into – the ability to alter public space in ugly ways. It was clear that she thought herself the quarry of a mugger, a rapist, or worse. Suffering a bout of insomnia, however, I was stalking sleep, not defenseless wayfarers.

The fearsomeness mistakenly attributed to me in public places often has a perilous flavor. The most frightening of these confusions occurred in the late 1970s and early 1980s, when I worked as a journalist in Chicago. One day, rushing into the office of a magazine I was writing for with a deadline story in hand, I was mistaken for a burglar. The office manager called security and, with an ad hoc posse, pursued me through the labyrinthine halls, nearly to my editor's door. I had no way of proving who I was. I could only move briskly toward the company of someone who knew me.

Over the years, I learned to smother the rage I felt at so often being taken for a criminal. Not to do so would surely have led to madness. I now take precautions to make myself less threatening. I move about with care, particularly late in the evening. I give a wide berth to nervous people on subway platforms during the wee hours, particularly when I have exchanged business clothes for jeans. If I happen to be entering a building behind some people who appear skittish, I may walk by, letting them clear the lobby before I return, so as not to seem to be following them. I have been calm and extremely congenial on those rare occasions when I've been pulled over by the police.

And on late-evening constitutionals I employ what has proved to be an excellent tension-reducing measure: I whistle melodies from Beethoven and Vivaldi and the more popular classical composers. Even steely New Yorkers hunching toward nighttime destinations seem to relax, and occasionally they even join in the tune. Virtually everybody seems to sense that a mugger wouldn't be warbling bright, sunny selections from Vivaldi's Four Seasons. It is my equivalent of the cowbell that hikers wear when they know they are in bear country.

## Notes

1  Consistent with the conventions of qualitative research, participants are identified through pseudonyms rather than their real names.
2  For more examples, see the website www.microaggressions.com, which allows people to post the microaggressions that have been directed at them.
3  In addition to the United States, higher proportions of females than males attain college degrees in most European countries, Australia, Canada, and New Zealand.

# References

Armstrong, E., L. Hamilton, and B. Sweeney. 2006. "Sexual Assault on Campus: A Multilevel, Integrative Approach to Party Rape." *Social Problems* 53:483–499.

Best, J. 2018. *American Nightmares: Social Problems in an Anxious World.* Berkeley, CA: UC Press.

Bonilla-Silva, E. 2010. *Racism without Racists: Color-Blind Racism and the Persistence of Racial Inequality in the United States.* Lanham, MD: Rowan and Littlefield.

Bonilla-Silva, E. and T. Forman. 2000. "'I am not a racist but...': Mapping White College Students Racial Ideology in the USA." *Discourse and Society* 11:50–85.

Boyle, K. 2015. "Social Psychological Processes that Facilitate Sexual Assault within the Fraternity Party Subculture." *Sociology Compass* 9:386–399.

Cahill, S. 1987. "Children and Civility: Ceremonial Deviance and the Acquisition of Ritual Competence." *Social Psychological Quarterly* 50:312–321.

Cancian, F. 1995. "Truth and Goodness: Does the Sociology of Inequality Promote Social Betterment?" *Sociological Perspectives* 38:339–366.

Collins, P. 1990. *Black Feminist Thought: Knowledge, Consciousness, and the Politics of Empowerment.* Boston: Unwin Hyman.

Collins, P. 2004. *Black Sexual Politics: African Americans, Gender, and the New Racism.* New York: Routledge.

Cooper, A. 1892. *A Voice from the South by a Black Woman from the South.* Xenia, OH: Aldine Press.

Davis, L., ed. 2006. *The Disability Studies Reader*, 2nd ed. New York: Routledge.

DeSantis, A. D. 2007. *Inside Greek U: Fraternities, Sororities, and the Pursuit of Pleasure, Power, and Prestige.* Lexington, KY: University Press of Kentucky.

Deutsch, F. 1999. *Halving It All: How Equally Shared Parenting Works.* Cambridge, MA: Harvard University Press.

DuBois, W. E. B. [1903] 1989. *The Souls of Black Folk.* New York: Bantam.

Epstein, C. 1992. "Tinkerbells and Pinups: The Construction and Reconstruction of Gender Boundaries at Work." Pp. 232–256 in *Cultivating Differences: Symbolic Boundaries and the Making of Inequality*, edited by M. Lamont and M. Fournier. Chicago, IL: University of Chicago Press.

Epstein, S. 1996. "A Queer Encounter: Sociology and the Study of Sexuality". Pp. 145–67 in *Queer Theory/Sociology*, edited by S. Seidman. Malden, MA: Blackwell Publishers.

Fields, J., M. Copp, and S. Kleinman. 2006. "Symbolic Interactionism, Inequality, and Emotions." Pp. 155–178 in *Handbook of the Sociology of Emotions*, edited by J. Stets and J. Turner. New York: Springer.

Fine, M. 1994. "Working the Hyphens: Reinventing Self and Other in Qualitative Research." Pp. 70–82 in *Handbook of Qualitative Research*, edited by N. K. Denzin and Y. Lincoln. Thousand Oaks CA: SAGE.

Fisher, B., F. Cullen, and M. Turner. 2000. *The Sexual Victimization of College Women: Research Report.* Washington, DC: U.S. Department of Justice, Bureau of Justice Statistics.

Giuffre, P. and C. Williams. 1994. "Boundary Lines: Labeling Sexual Harassment in Restaurants." *Gender & Society* 8:378–401.

Glenn, E. 1997. "Looking Back in Anger? Re-remembering my Sociological Career." Pp. 73–102 in *Feminist Sociology: Life Histories of a Movement*, edited by B. Laslett and B. Thorne. New Brunswick, NJ: Rutgers University Press.

Goffman, E. 1956. "The Nature of Deference and Demeanor." Pp. 47–95 in *Interaction Ritual*. New York: Random House.

Goffman, E. 1963. *Stigma: Notes on the Management of Spoiled Identity*. Englewood Cliffs, NJ: Prentice Hall.

Goodwin, J., J. Jasper, and F. Polletta, eds. 2009. *Passionate Politics: Emotions and Social Movements*. Chicago, IL: University of Chicago Press.

Gould, D. 2009. *Moving politics: Emotion and ACT UP's Fight against AIDS*. Chicago, IL: University of Chicago Press.

Hamilton, L. 2014. "The Revised MRS: Gender Complementarity at College." *Gender & Society* 28:236–264.

Harris, S. R. 1997. "Status Inequality and Close Relationships: An Integrative Typology of Bond-Saving Strategies." *Symbolic Interaction* 20:1–20.

Harris, S. R. 2000. "The Social Construction of Equality in Everyday Life." *Human Studies* 23:371–393.

Harris, S. R. 2001. "What can Interactionism Contribute to the Study of Inequality? The Case of Marriage and Beyond." *Symbolic Interaction* 24:455–480.

Harris, S. R. 2006. *The Meanings of Marital Equality*. Albany, NY: SUNY Press.

Harris, S. R. 2009. "Objective and Interpretive Approaches to Equality in Marriage." *Journal of Constructivist Psychology* 22(3):213–236.

Harris, S. R. 2015. *An Invitation to the Sociology of Emotions*. New York: Routledge.

Hegewisch, A. and A. DuMonthier. 2016. Fact Sheet: The Gender Wage Gap, *2015: Annual Earnings Differences by Gender, Race, and Ethnicity*. IWPR #C446. Washington DC: Institute for Women's Policy Research.

Hess, B. 1999. "Breaking and Entering the Establishment: Committing Social Change and Confronting the Backlash." *Social Problems* 46(1):1–12.

Hochschild, A. 1979. *The Managed Heart: Commercialization of Human Feeling*. Berkeley, CA: University of California Press.

Hochschild, A., with A. Machung. 1989. *The Second Shift*. New York: Avon Books.

Hughey, M. 2007. "Crossing the Sands, Crossing the Color Line: Non-Black Members of Black Greek Letter Organizations." *Journal of African American Studies* 11:55–75.

Hughey, M. 2008. "Virtual (Br)others and (Re)sisters: Authentic Black Fraternity and Sorority Identity on the Internet." *Journal of Contemporary Ethnography* 37:528–560.

Hughey, M. 2010. "A Paradox of Participation: Nonwhites in White Sororities and Fraternities." *Social Problems* 57:653–679.

Irvine, L., K. Kahl, and J. Smith. 2012. "Confrontations and Donations: Encounters Between Homeless Pet Owners and the Public." *The Sociological Quarterly* 53:25–43.

Kelly, A., ed. 1987. *The German Worker: Working Class Autobiographies from the Age of Industrialization.* Berkeley, CA: University of California Press.

Khan, S. 2011. *Privilege: The Making of an Adolescent Elite at St. Paul's School.* Princeton, NJ: Princeton University Press.

Lamont, M. 2001. "Symbolic Boundaries." *International Encyclopedia of the Social and Behavioral Sciences* 23:15341–15347.

Lamont, M. and V. Molnár. 2002. "The Study of Boundaries in the Social Sciences." *Annual Review of Sociology* 28:167–195.

Martin, P. and R. Hummer. 1989. "Fraternities and Rape on Campus." *Gender & Society* 3:457–473.

Maynes, M. 1995. *Taking the Hard Road: Life Course in French and German Workers' Autobiographies in the Era of Industrialization.* Chapel Hill, NC: University of North Carolina Press.

Murnen, S. and M. Kohlman. 2007. "Athletic Participation, Fraternity Membership, and Sexual Aggression among College Men: A Meta-analytic Review." *Sex Roles* 57:145–157.

Pascoe, C. J. 2005. "'Dude, You're a Fag': Adolescent Masculinity and the Fag Discourse." *Sexualities* 8:329–346.

Pierce, C. 1970. "Offensive Mechanisms." Pp. 265–281 in *The Black Seventies*, edited by F. Barbour. Boston, MA: Porter Sargent Publisher.

Pierce, J. 1995. *Gender Trials: Emotional Lives in Contemporary Law Firms.* Berkeley, CA: University of California Press.

Proctor, B., J. Semega, and M. Kollar. 2016. *Income and Poverty in the United States, 2015. U.S. Census Bureau, Current Population Reports*, P60-256(RV). Washington, DC: U.S. Government Printing Office.

Ray, R. 2013. "Fraternity Life at Predominantly White Universities in the U.S.: The Saliency of Race." *Ethnic and Racial Studies* 36:320–336.

Rollins, J. 1985. *Between Women: Domestics and Their Employers.* Philadelphia, PA: Temple University Press.

Ronai, C., B. Zsembik, and J. Feagin. 2014. *Everyday Sexism in the Third Millennium.* New York: Routledge.

Rowling, J. K. 1997. *Harry Potter and the Philosopher's Stone.* New York: Scholastic.

Schwalbe, M., D. Holden, D. Schrock, S. Godwin, S. Thompson, and M. Wolkomir. 2000. "Generic Processes in the Reproduction of Inequality: An Interactionist Analysis." *Social Forces* 79:419–452.

Schwartz, P. 1994. *Peer Marriage: How Love Between Equals Really Works.* New York: Free Press.

Shelton, B. and D. John. 1996. "The Division of Household Labor." *Annual Review of Sociology* 22:299–322.

Snow, D. and L. Anderson. 1993. *Down on Their Luck: A Study of Homeless Street People.* Berkeley: University of California Press.

Snyder, T., S. Dillow, and C. Hoffman. 2008. *Digest of Education Statistics 2007* (NCES 2008-022). National Center for Education Statistics, Institute of Education Sciences, U.S. Department of Education. Washington, DC.

Solórzano, D., M. Ceja, and T. Yosso. 2000. "Critical Race Theory, Racial Microaggressions, and Campus Racial Climate: The Experiences of African American College Students." *Journal of Negro Education* 69:60–73.

Staples, B. 1986. "Just Walk on By: A Black Man Ponders His Power to Alter Public Space." *Ms*, September, 54+.

Stombler, M. 1994. "'Buddies' or 'Slutties': The Collective Sexual Reputation of Fraternity Little Sisters." *Gender & Society* 8:297–283.

Stombler, M. and P. Martin. 1994. "Bringing Women In, Keeping Women Down: Fraternity 'Little Sister' Organizations." *Journal of Contemporary Ethnography* 23:150–184.

Straus, M. and C. Yodanis. 1995. "Marital Power." Pp. 437–442 in *The Encyclopedia of Marriage and the Family*, vol. 2, edited by D. Levinson. New York: Macmillan.

Sue, D. 2010. *Microaggressions in Everyday Life: Race, Class, Gender, and Sexual Orientation*. New York: Wiley.

Sue, D., C. Capodilupo, and A. Holder. 2008. "Racial Microaggressions in the Life Experience of Black Americans." *Professional Psychology: Research and Practice* 39:329–336.

Thorne, B. 1992. "Girls and Boys Together... but Mostly Apart: Gender Arrangements in Elementary Schools." Pp. 117–132 in *Education and Gender Equality*, edited by J. Wrigley. London: The Falmer Press.

Thorne, B. 1993. *Gender Play: Girls and Boys in School*. New Brunswick, NJ: Rutgers University Press.

Thorne, B. and Z. Luria. 1986. "Sexuality and Gender in Children's Daily Worlds." *Social Problems* 33(3):176–190.

Turner, B. 1986. *Equality*. New York: Tavistock.

Ulrich, L. T. 2004. *Yards and Gates: Gender in Harvard and Radcliffe History*. New York: Palgrave Macmillan.

Wilkins, A. 2004 "'So Full of Myself as a Chick': Goth Women, Sexual Independence, and Gender Egalitarianism." *Gender & Society* 18:328–349.

Wilkins, A. 2012. "'Not Out to Start a Revolution': Race, Gender, and Emotional Restraint among Black University Men." *Journal of Contemporary Ethnography* 41:34–65.

Wilkins, A., S. Mollborn, and B. Bó. 2014. "Constructing Difference." Pp. 125–154 in *Handbook of the Social Psychology of Inequality*, edited by J. McLeod, E. Lawler, and M. Schwalbe. New York: Springer.

Wingfield, A. 2007. "The Modern Mammy and the Angry Black Man: African American Professionals' Experiences with Gendered Racism in the Workplace." *Race, Gender, & Class* 14:196–212.

Wingfield, A. 2010. "Are Some Emotions Marked 'Whites Only'? Racialized Feeling Rules in Professional Workplaces." *Social Problems* 57:251–268.

Zerubavel, E. 1996. "Lumping and Splitting: Notes on Social Classification." *Sociological Forum* 11:421–433.

# 12

# Conclusion

The Benefits of Studying Symbolic Interaction

We've covered a lot of ground over the course of the previous eleven chapters. We hope you've come away with a better understanding of a wide range of phenomena – from the body and emotions to social problems and inequality. It's time to reflect on and integrate what we've learned.

Sometimes students are tempted to set aside or even forget course material, once they pass a final exam or write a term paper. Clearly, that's less than ideal – especially in this case. Symbolic interactionism (SI) aims to illuminate our everyday lives. Thus, it would be a shame if you did not try to connect with the material in a personal way and take away some positive impressions and lasting lessons.

We would not have written this book if we did not believe SI offered an interesting, enlightening, and useful perspective. On every page, we hope you can find ideas that fit those descriptions. Thus, we conclude this textbook in an optimistic and uplifting fashion, by highlighting why studying SI is valuable.

## The Value of Studying Symbolic Interactionism

### Social Interaction Is a Ubiquitous (and Enjoyable) Topic

As we've seen, symbolic interactionists study people's behavior in face-to-face and mediated interactions. Human beings are active and interpretive: we give meaning to the situations we encounter, and we act on those meanings (Chapter 2). People are embedded in larger contexts, and so are shaped and constrained in many ways. Yet interactionists emphasize how people acquire and employ social resources (e.g. identities, perspectives) as well as how they navigate, challenge, or circumvent constraints such as cultural norms or unequal distributions of power or privilege. Its focus on how people *do* things makes SI quite compelling.

*The Social Self and Everyday Life: Understanding the World Through Symbolic Interactionism,* First Edition. Kathy Charmaz, Scott R. Harris, and Leslie Irvine.
© 2019 John Wiley & Sons, Inc. Published 2019 by John Wiley & Sons, Inc.

With apologies to instructors who teach foreign languages, art, calculus, chemistry, history, or economics, few other subjects can offer a set of concepts to make sense of the full range of our daily experiences.

Most of us constantly interact with co-present others, from shortly after we wake up until the moment we fall asleep. Together we argue, joke, work, play, worship, and so on. Even when alone, social interaction is never far away. We may bathe and select an outfit to wear in complete privacy but do so while anticipating the dramaturgical effects our appearance (or "costume") will have on others. We may travel or work in isolation but listen to podcasts or ponder the stories we will tell our friends and family (cf. Schweingruber and Berns 2005). Our solitary prayers may consist of imagined interactions with a deity whose personality and responses we envision, just as we may imagine what a boss, spouse, or child might say to us upon learning about an accomplishment or mistake (Sharp 2010; Shibutani 1955). Our dreams, too, are social (Fine and Leighton 1993). Dreams may replay, rehearse, or invent relations with others. The way we interpret and share dreams can shape our thinking and conduct and influence our companions. In short, virtually all areas of our lives – even seemingly nonsocial endeavors – are amenable to interactionist analysis and insights.

Chapters 3–11 summarized interactionist research on the body, emotions, health, family, media, social problems, institutions, and inequality. This list is by no means comprehensive, nor is our treatment of each topic exhaustive. Far from it.

Rather, we have offered a selective discussion of interactionist concepts to demonstrate the utility and appeal of studying human beings as co-constructors of reality. People are constantly creating, applying, negotiating, and acting upon meanings. We are socialized into perspectives and identities (Chapter 3). We hide or transform or boldly flaunt the bodily traits our cultures define as stigmatizing (Chapters 4–5). We redefine situations to shape feelings, for ourselves and for our employers (Chapter 6). We promote and demote kin ("no son of mine" or "like a daughter to me") and so talk family relationships into and out of existence (Chapter 7). We measure ourselves against virtual others, such as Internet celebrities (Chapter 8). We are shaped by institutions and we also exercise agency to resist their influence (Chapter 10). And so on.

Usually, such material is easily applicable to one's own experiences and observations. At the least, interactionist research makes heretofore unexplored activities – whether gangs, prostitution, or chess clubs – much more intelligible and much less "foreign" (Fine 2015; Katz 1988; Prus and Grills 2003). Either way, most of our students find interactionist research to be compelling or even "fun."

## SI Provides a Useful Vocabulary for Understanding Social Life, Via Its Focus on Generic Social Processes

Symbolic interactionism gives us both a perspective on social life and a vocabulary for analyzing it. Many students have told us that our courses on SI have helped them see things they hadn't noticed before, even though the behaviors were occurring right before their eyes. Other students express their gratitude over learning about social worlds to which they had no prior exposure. Interactionist research can help us see routine matters in a new light, or it can help us forge comparisons between unfamiliar and familiar settings. Its concepts help us organize a multitude of scattered instances into a framework, so we can classify our observations, experiences, and ideas.

For example, recall how the interactionist notion "life as theater" helps us analyze and compare different situations (see Chapters 2 and 6). Dramaturgical interactionists give us the tools to examine the ways people enact strategic performances for their audiences. Restaurants and funeral homes both might contain *front stages* (kitchen and chapel) where positive impressions are made on customers, and out-of-view *back stages* where employees may drop the act and behave "out of character" (Turner and Edgley 1976). *Props* and *stage design* may be used by dentists (strategic placements of diplomas, medical posters, bright decor) as well as by strip clubs (dim lighting, darker colors, televisions showing sports but no cartoons) in order to set the mood for clientele (Lerum 2001). Formal or informal *costumes* may help project desired images, whether worn by gang members or police officers (Katz 1988). Or, different people may employ parallel strategies of *cognitive deep acting* – by changing thoughts about a situation in order to change how they or others feel (Harris 2015). We may tell ourselves "there are plenty of fish in the sea," in order to reduce depression after a break-up, or to increase confidence before a blind date. A doctor may refer to an illness as a "challenge" rather than a "tragedy," just as a flight attendant may refer to the remote likelihood of "a water landing" rather than "a crash into the ocean," in order to reduce despair or fear.

With concepts such as these, symbolic interactionists illuminate *generic social processes* (GSPs) – the "parallel sequences of activity" that cut across diverse situations (Prus 1987:251). For example, we can apply the identity hierarchy depicted in Chapter 5 to other situations such as job loss or rejected college applications in which people's hopes and dreams are disrupted or negated.

Let's revisit Chapter 9. There we learned about the various strategies that claimsmakers can use to amplify social problems. To make an issue sound more threatening, advocates may *treat isolated instances as trends*, use extreme examples to *typify* an issue, and *universalize* the problem by asserting it can happen to anyone. These and other rhetorical devices can be used to heighten concerns about crime, drugs, the environment, family, healthcare, poverty, and a multitude of other issues. As consumers and as producers of claims about social problems, it can be illuminating and even empowering to understand the generic moves that claimsmakers may make to persuade audiences to take a problem seriously. The right concept can enable us to identify parallels between seemingly distinct settings, and thereby act more intelligently and effectively. In this case, we might think more critically about a claim we hear, or we might craft a more convincing claim for audiences of our own.

## SI Can Assist in Self-Improvement

SI provides a perspective and vocabulary for analyzing social interaction, but its practical utility does not end there. Interactionism can do more for us than simply making us "smarter" and more perceptive. There are many other lessons and skills we can learn from interactionism and apply for our personal benefit.

For example, all of us have "minor bodily stigmas" (see Chapter 4). Whether a speech impediment, discolored skin, bad breath, a lack of height or excessive weight, none of us is perfect. Reading about interactionist work on how people live with stigmas makes them, potentially, more manageable. We find out that we're not alone, not by a long shot. We can learn how others hide, disguise, or modify their undesirable bodily traits, and how others muster the courage to challenge cultural norms. The interactionist premise "meaning is not inherent" can help us take our supposed faults less seriously, and empower us to "talk back" to those who would judge us harshly.

Interactionism's approach to family diversity can yield similar benefits. In Chapter 7, we discussed how family is socially constructed, in two broad ways. First, kinship practices vary by culture. No single model of family is universal: some societies have preferred polygamy to monogamy, arranged marriages to self-selection, extended-family households to nuclear ones, and so on. Second, we can describe or characterize any particular set of relationships in various ways. A teenager may describe her father as a "dysfunctional dictator" but his spouse may see him as "setting clear boundaries"; co-workers may refer to themselves as "family" rather than merely "colleagues." A deep understanding of such discrepant descriptions can serve many positive purposes. You may realize that your family is neither natural nor automatic – it takes interpretive and interactional work to sustain it. In addition, you might gain the confidence to question what your companions take as inevitable – such as marrying heterosexually, or marrying at all. If your ideal life involves putting activism, a career, or some other moral calling above creating offspring, then you should be better equipped to explain your choice to stay childfree – and even, occasionally, to remind yourself of the validity of your lifestyle. One can pursue many viable forms of kinship, as one attempts to carve out a meaningful life.

Like most subjects taught at universities, studying SI does not lead to a single specific job, in the way majoring in accounting sometimes leads to a position as an accountant. However, interactionism can provide useful skills – such as critical thinking and cultural sensitivity – as well as information that can be invaluable for many kinds of careers. Recall Chapter 6, where you learned about emotion management techniques and strategies. As you consider the occupation you'd like, interactionist research can help you assess the emotional labor involved in the path you are considering. For example, Patricia Martin

(2005) found that most doctors, nurses, police officers, attorneys, and victim advocates were unprepared for the challenges of working with victims of rape. By reading about those challenges, and the kinds of strategies some workers developed to overcome them, you might be able to provide more supportive care and avoid inflicting further damage on victims. You might also be able to minimize the distress the situation prompts in you and feel prouder of the work you do. Similarly, reading interactionist research about your future career would likely make you a much better interviewee and candidate for graduate school and/or employment – for example, in medicine (Erickson and Grove 2008; Smith and Kleinman 1989), financial advising (Delaney 2012), law (Pierce 1995), education (Bloch 2012), and other fields.

Interactionism can help you understand how you have been shaped by institutions, groups, and organizations. In Chapter 10, you saw how profoundly work influences people's lives. Although few readers of this book will find work in factories such as in our example of the Ford plant, workplaces of all kinds shape the people within them. But you also saw that people are not powerless in the face of institutions. They can also exercise agency, acting in self-willed ways to resist and challenge pressures to conform.

### Altruism

One question to ask is: What can interactionism do for me?

A somewhat separate and more laudable question is: How can I use interactionism to improve the world for others? It's possible and probably healthy to focus a good part of our thinking on how we can serve the well-being of those near to and far from us.

Socially-minded individuals can certainly put interactionist concepts and research towards positive purposes. The personal benefits of reading interactionist work on the body or family that we discussed above can also be put to altruistic purposes. For example, interactionist insights can make us more capable and confident as we challenge restrictive or oppressive definitions of beauty and family – not just for ourselves, but for our close companions, our communities, and the larger society. Or, by drawing on research such as Martin (2005), you might advocate on behalf of the downtrodden. In your place of employment or in realm of government, you could lobby for more training opportunities for those who work with rape victims.

Because symbolic interaction places so much emphasis on taking the roles of others, the perspective can help us have more empathy and sympathy for other people, especially those on the margins of society (cf., Ruiz-Junco 2017). An old saying reminds us, "You can't understand someone else until you've walked a mile in their shoes." By trying to understand other people's situations, you learn about their trials and troubles. You gain a greater appreciation of what they struggle with and you are less likely to judge them harshly.

Thus, SI can help you develop the "muscles" for reflecting on other people's situations and experiences, and then working on their behalf. Interactionists tend to be acutely aware of the importance of language for creating consequential meanings in everyday life. Thus, reading their work may equip one to challenge the "othering" (Chapter 11) that may occur in routine conversation or in political discourse. We reproduce inequality when we create symbolic boundaries between "them" and "us." We do this through small interactional moves, such as not learning the names of the people who clean our schools and workplaces, as well as through the creation of laws and policies. Interactionist work on inequality can prompt you to see the situation through the eyes of those we take for granted, and work on their behalf.

## Final Thoughts

In keeping with the premises of SI, we must admit that "interesting, enlightening, and useful" are matters of interpretation. Many but not all students appreciate SI, and that's okay. You are free to adopt any parts of interactionist that seem valuable and discard the rest.

Interactionist concepts do not lend themselves to simple or formulaic applications. Instead, they must be wielded creatively by people – thinking and feeling individuals who employ their own culturally-acquired yet idiosyncratic perspectives as they pursue objectives within larger social settings and contexts.

You can and should have your own reactions to the material. We hope you join us in viewing interactionism as enjoyable, informative, and practical as well. Ultimately, though, that is up to you.

## References

Bloch, C. 2012. *Passion and Paranoia: Emotions and the Culture of Emotion in Academia*. Burlington, VT: Ashgate.

Delaney, K. 2012. *Money at Work: On the Job with Priests, Poker Players, and Hedge Fund Traders*. New York: NYU Press.

Erickson, R. and W. Grove. 2008. "Emotional Labor and Health Care." *Sociology Compass* 2:704–733.

Fine, G. 2015. *Players and Pawns: How Chess Creates Community and Culture*. Chicago, IL: University of Chicago Press.

Fine, G. A. and L. F. Leighton. 1993. "Nocturnal Omissions: Steps Toward a Sociology of Dreams." *Symbolic Interaction* 16(2):95–104.

Harris, S. R. 2015. *An Invitation to the Sociology of Emotions*. New York: Routledge.

Katz, J. 1988. *Seductions of Crime: Moral and Sensual Attractions of Doing Evil*. New York: Basic Books.

Lerum, K. 2001. "'Precarious Situations' in a Strip Club: Exotic Dancers and the Problem of Reality Maintenance." Pp. 279–287 in *The Production of Reality*, 3rd ed., edited by J. O'Brien and P. Kollock. Thousand Oaks, CA: Pine Forge Press.

Martin, P. Y. 2005. *Rape Work: Victims, Gender, and Emotions in Organization and Community Context*. New York: Routledge.

Pierce, J. 1995. *Gender Trials: Emotional Lives in Contemporary Law Firms*. Berkeley, CA: University of California Press.

Prus, R. 1987. "Generic Social Processes: Maximizing Conceptual Development in Ethnographic Research." *Journal of Contemporary Ethnography* 16:250–291.

Prus, R. and S. Grills. 2003. *The Deviant Mystique: Involvements, Subcultural Realities, and Regulation*. Westport, CT: Praeger.

Ruiz-Junco, N. 2017. "Advancing the Sociology of Empathy: A Proposal." *Symbolic Interaction* 40:414–435.

Schweingruber, D. and N. Berns. 2005. "Shaping the Selves of Young Salespeople through Emotion Management." *Journal of Contemporary Ethnography* 34:679–706.

Sharp, S. 2010. "How Does Prayer Help Manage Emotions?" *Social Psychology Quarterly* 73(4):417–437

Shibutani, T. 1955. "Reference Groups as Perspectives." *American Journal of Sociology* 60:562–569.

Smith, A. C. III and S. Kleinman. 1989. "Managing Emotions in Medical School." *Social Psychology Quarterly* 52:56–69.

Turner, R. E. and C. Edgley. 1976. "Death as Theater: A Dramaturgical Analysis of the American Funeral." *Sociology and Social Research* 60(4):377–392.

# Index

*The Social Self and Everyday Life: Understanding the World Through Symbolic Interactionism*,
First Edition. Kathy Charmaz, Scott R. Harris, and Leslie Irvine.
© 2019 John Wiley & Sons, Inc. Published 2019 by John Wiley & Sons, Inc.